Noodles

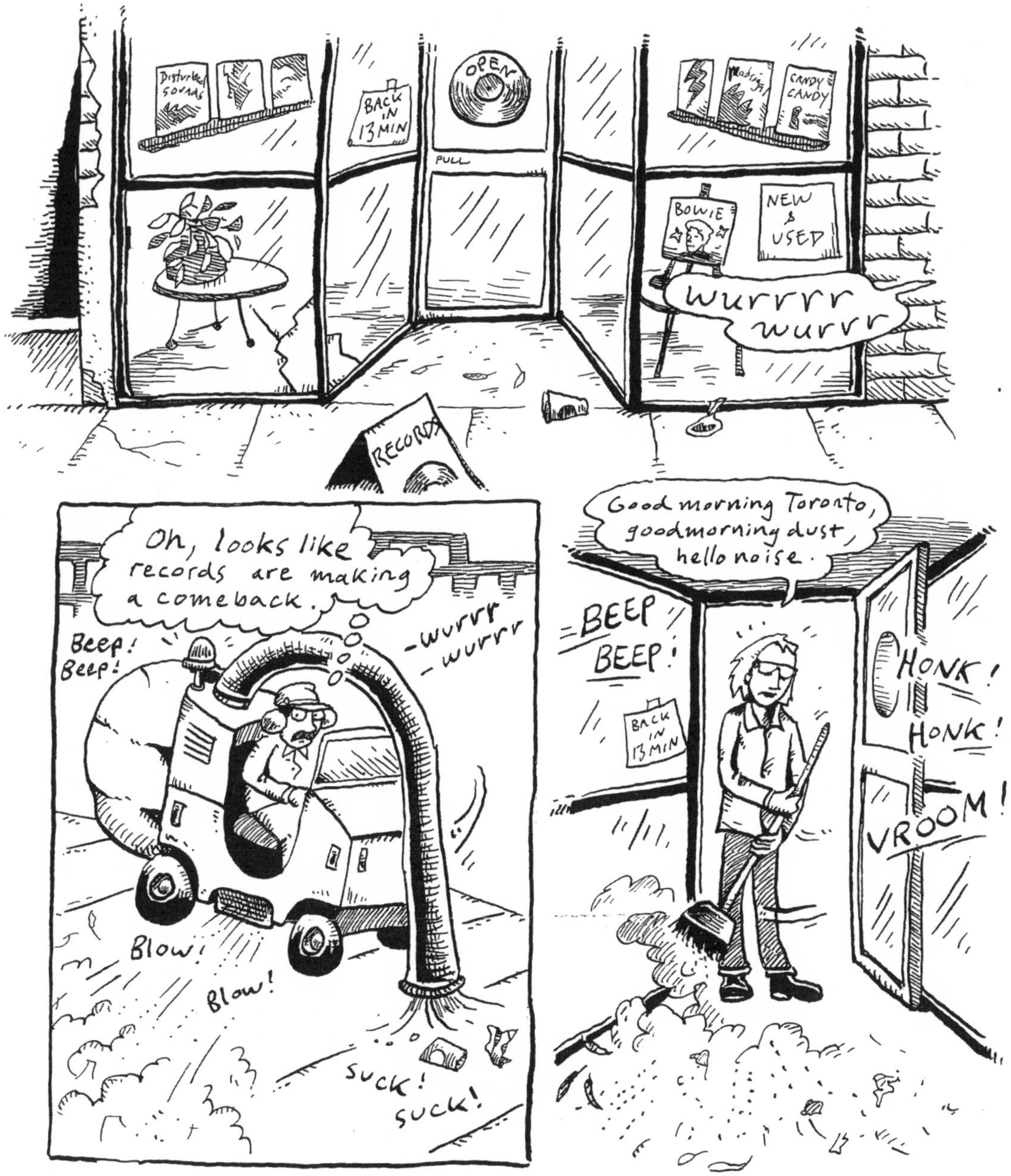
Disturbed Sounds
OPEN
BACK IN 13 MIN
PULL
CANDY CANDY
BOWIE
NEW & USED
wurrrr wurrr
RECORDS
Oh, looks like records are making a comeback.
Beep! Beep!
-wurrr -wurrr
Blow!
Blow!
SUCK! SUCK!
Good morning Toronto, goodmorning dust, hello noise.
BEEP BEEP!
BACK IN 13 MIN
HONK! HONK!
VROOM!

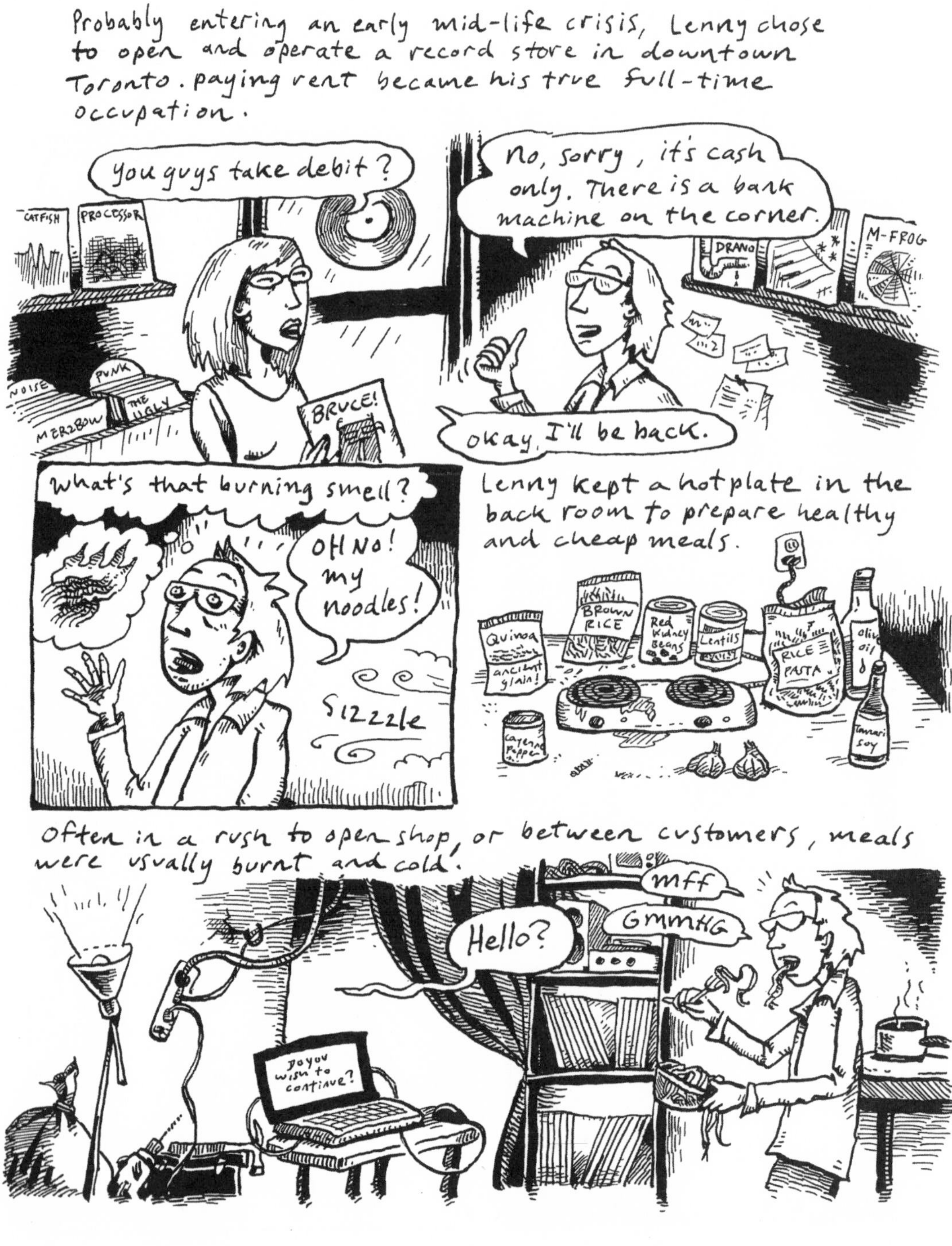
Probably entering an early mid-life crisis, Lenny chose to open and operate a record store in downtown Toronto. paying rent became his true full-time occupation.
You guys take debit?
No, sorry, it's cash only. There is a bank machine on the corner.
okay. I'll be back.
CATFISH
PROCESSOR
NOISE
PUNK
THE UGLY
MERZBOW
BRUCE!
DRANO
M-FROG
What's that burning smell?
OH NO! my noodles!
SIZZLE
Lenny kept a hotplate in the back room to prepare healthy and cheap meals.
Quinoa
ancient grain!
BROWN RICE
Red Kidney Beans
Lentils
RICE PASTA
olive oil
Tamari Soy
Cayenne Pepper
Often in a rush to open shop, or between customers, meals were usually burnt and cold.
Hello?
mff
GMMHG
Do you wish to continue?

A hello at the door was always a welcome sound. It also brought many interesting challenges, tests and distractions with a variety of results.

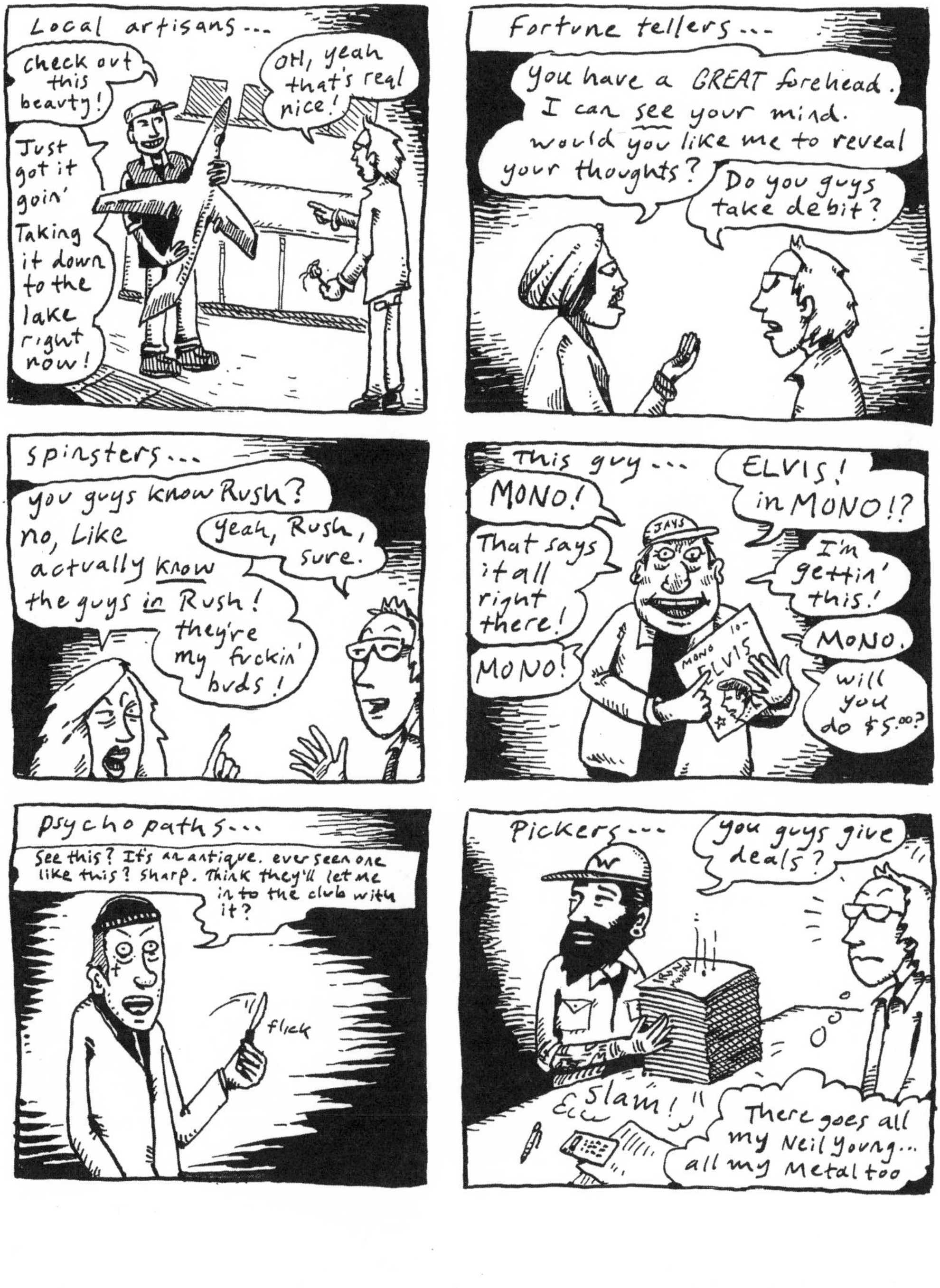
Local artisans...
check out this beauty!
OH, yeah that's real nice!
Just got it goin'
Taking it down to the lake right now!
Fortune tellers...
You have a GREAT forehead. I can see your mind. would you like me to reveal your thoughts?
Do you guys take debit?
spinsters...
you guys know Rush?
no, Like actually know the guys in Rush!
Yeah, Rush, sure.
they're my fuckin' buds!
This guy...
MONO!
ELVIS! in MONO!?
JAYS
That says it all right there!
I'm gettin' this!
MONO!
MONO.
MONO 10-
ELVIS
will you do $5.00?
psychopaths...
See this? It's an antique. ever seen one like this? Sharp. Think they'll let me in to the club with it?
flick
Pickers...
you guys give deals?
W
IRON MAIDEN
Slam!
There goes all my Neil Young... all my Metal too

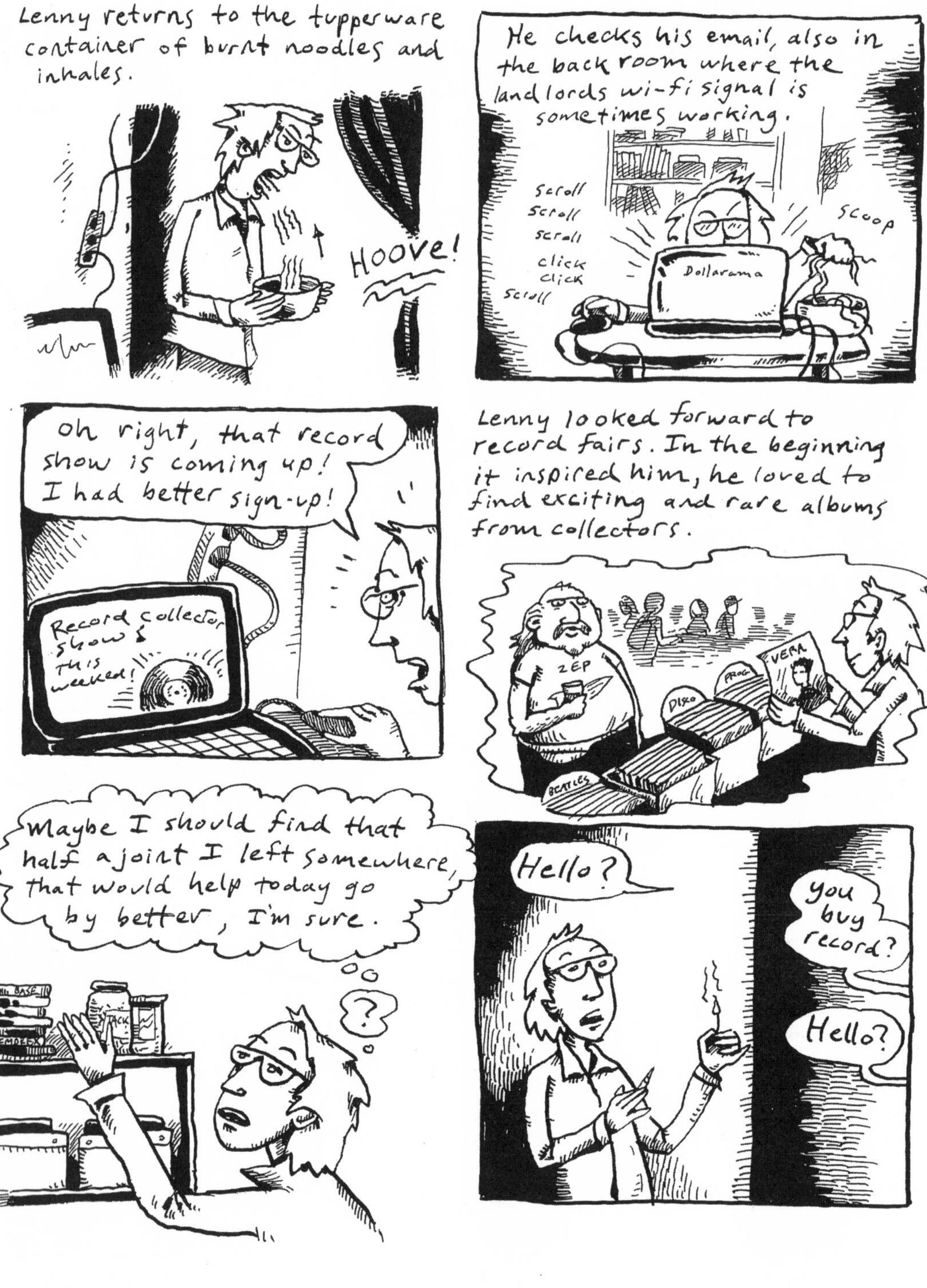
Lenny returns to the tupperware container of burnt noodles and inhales.
Hoove!
He checks his email, also in the back room where the landlords wi-fi signal is sometimes working.
Scroll
Scroll
Scroll
click
click
Scroll
Dollarama
Scoop
Oh right, that record show is coming up! I had better sign-up!
Record collector shows this weekend!
Lenny looked forward to record fairs. In the beginning it inspired him, he loved to find exciting and rare albums from collectors.
ZEP
DISCO
FROG
VERA
BEATLES
Maybe I should find that half a joint I left somewhere, that would help today go by better, I'm sure.
?
BASE
TACK
MEMOREX
Hello?
You buy record?
Hello?

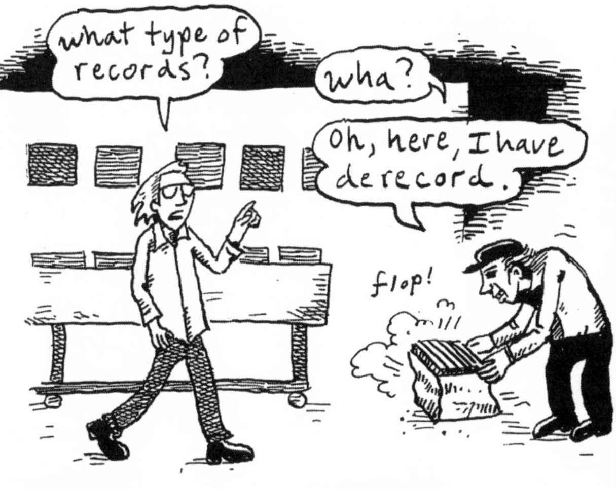
what type of records?
wha?
Oh, here, I have derecord.
flop!

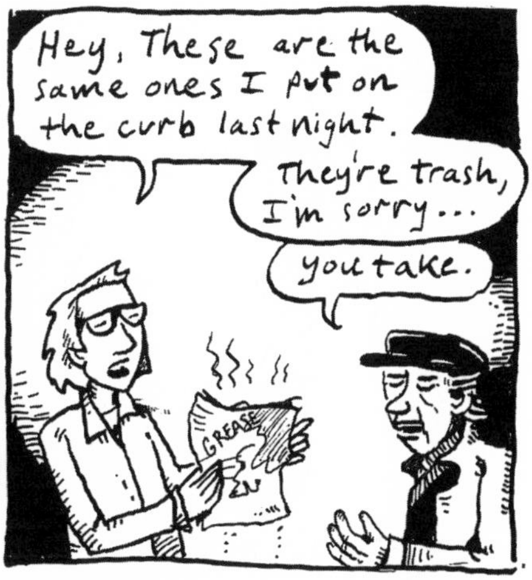
Hey, These are the same ones I put on the curb last night.
They're trash, I'm sorry...
you take.
GREASE

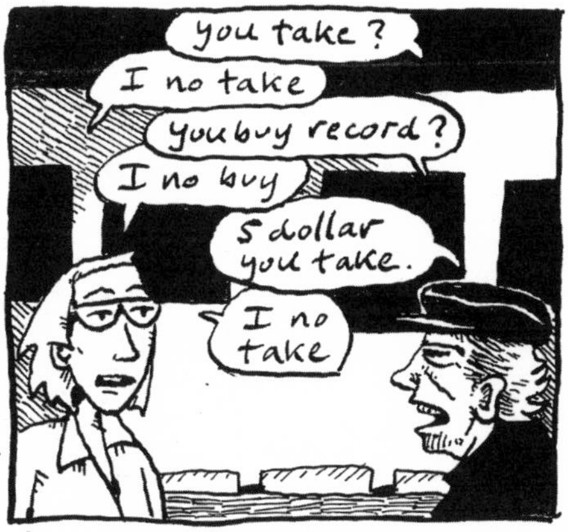
you take?
I no take
you buy record?
I no buy
5 dollar you take.
I no take

Finally, after intense negotiations, Lenny can get back to his frigid fossile breakfast-lunch.

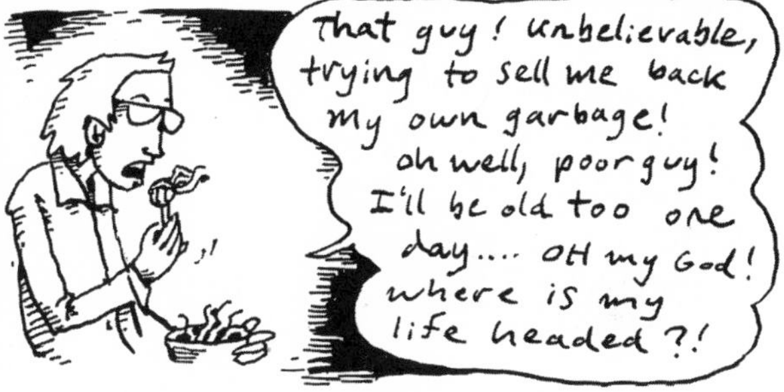
That guy! Unbelievable, trying to sell me back my own garbage! oh well, poorguy! I'll be old too one day.... OH my God! where is my life headed?!

Lenny hides in the back of the shop trying to eat, he lights an insense stick so people don't think his place is some kind of restaurant. There, during the slow times he allows his thoughts to drift.

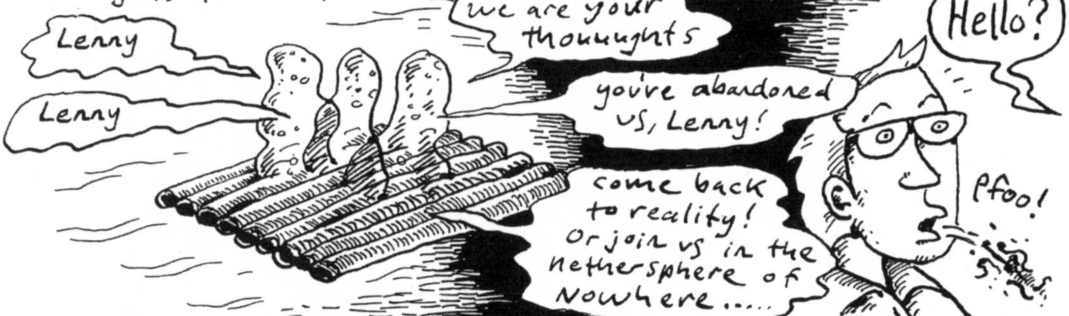
Lenny
Lenny
we are your thouuughts
you're abandoned us, Lenny!
come back to reality! Or join us in the nethersphere of Nowhere.....
Hello?
Pfoo!

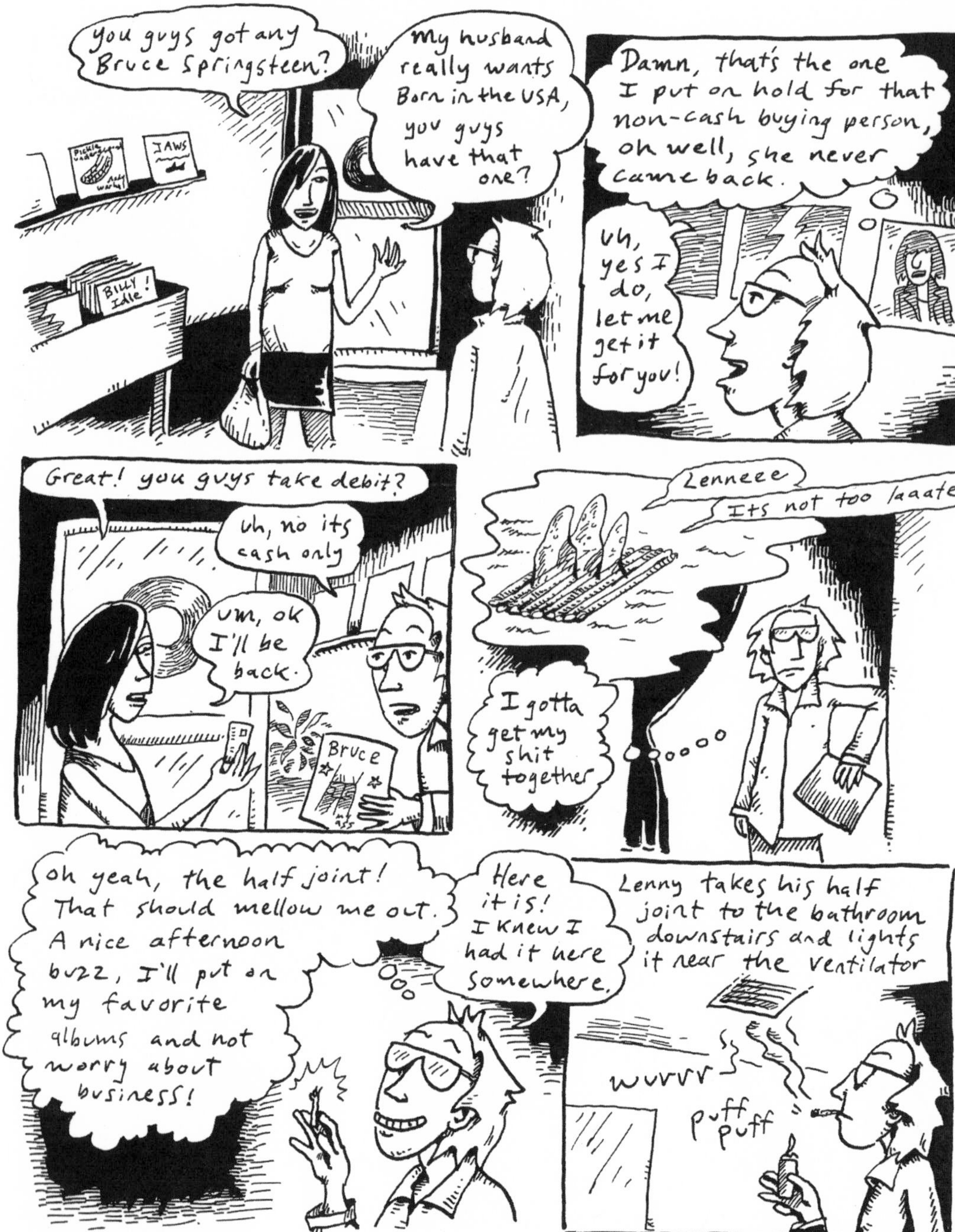

You guys got any Bruce Springsteen?
My husband really wants Born in the USA, you guys have that one?
Pickle Underground
JAWS
BILLY Idle!
Damn, that's the one I put on hold for that non-cash buying person, oh well, she never came back.
Uh, yes I do, let me get it for you!
Great! you guys take debit?
Uh, no its cash only
Um, ok I'll be back.
Bruce
Lenneee
Its not too laaate
I gotta get my shit together
Oh yeah, the half joint! That should mellow me out. A nice afternoon buzz, I'll put on my favorite albums and not worry about business!
Here it is! I knew I had it here somewhere.
Lenny takes his half joint to the bathroom downstairs and lights it near the ventilator
wurrr
puff puff

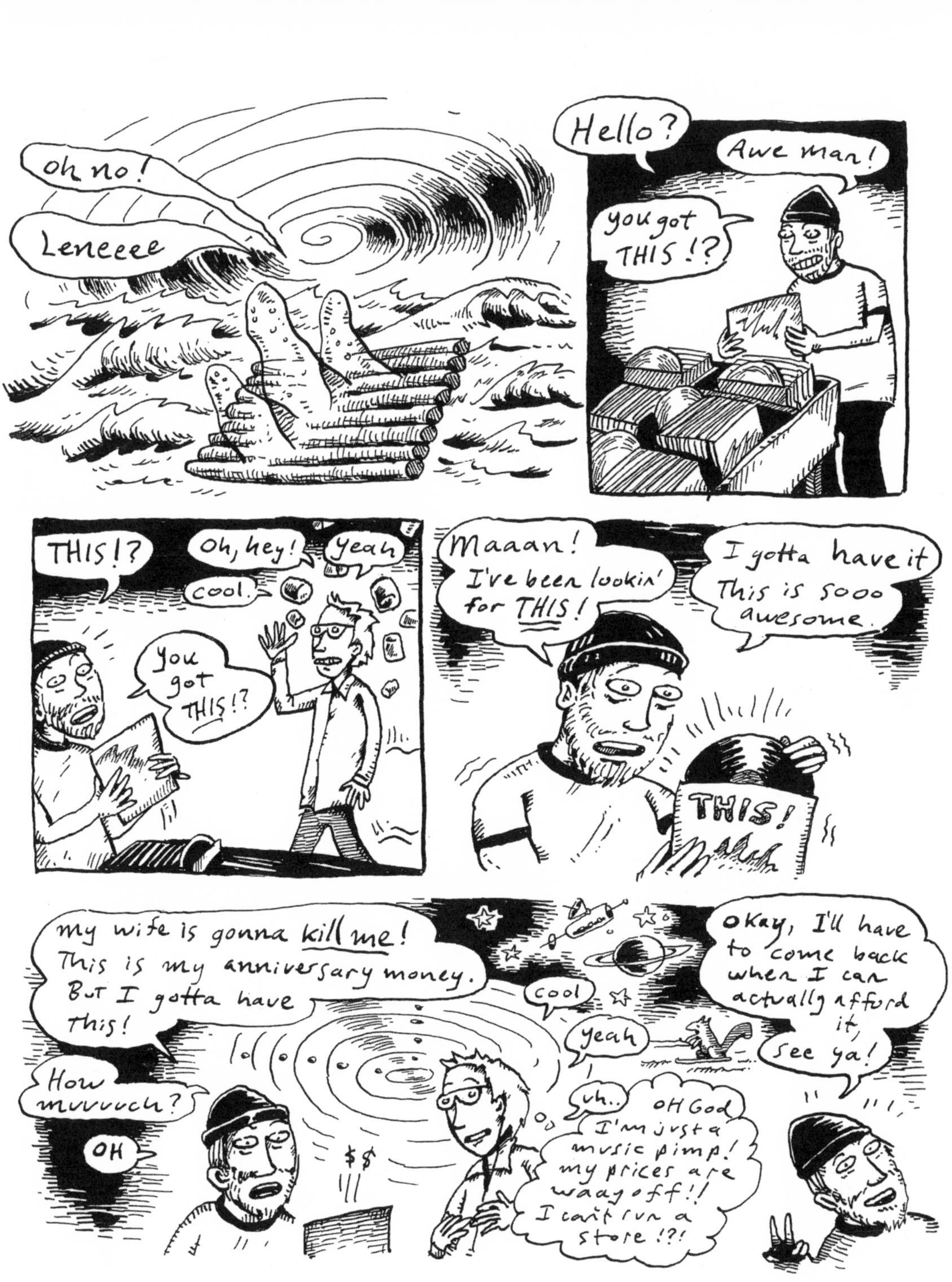
oh no!
Leneeee
Hello?
Awe man!
you got THIS!?
THIS!?
Oh, hey!
Yeah
cool.
You got THIS!?
Maaan! I've been lookin' for THIS!
I gotta have it This is sooo awesome.
THIS!
my wife is gonna kill me! This is my anniversary money. But I gotta have this!
How muuuuch?
OH
cool
Yeah
$$
uh..
OH God I'm just a music pimp! my prices are waay off!! I can't run a store!?!
Okay, I'll have to come back when I can actually afford it, see ya!

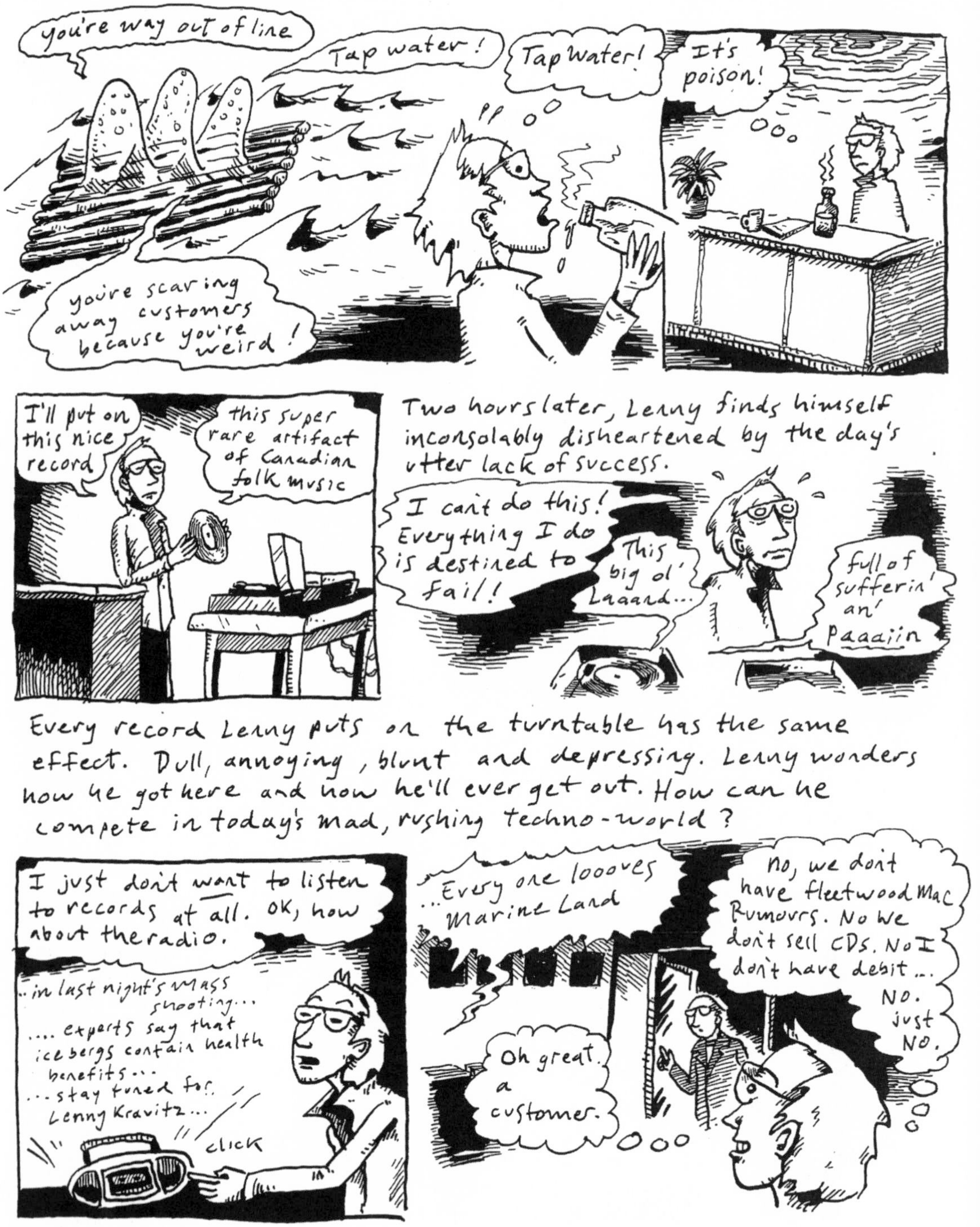
you're way out of line
Tap water!
Tap Water!
It's poison!
you're scaring away customers because you're weird!
I'll put on this nice record
this super rare artifact of Canadian folk music
Two hours later, Lenny finds himself inconsolably disheartened by the day's utter lack of success.
I can't do this! Everything I do is destined to fail!
This big ol' Laaand...
full of sufferin' an' Paaaiin
Every record Lenny puts on the turntable has the same effect. Dull, annoying, blunt and depressing. Lenny wonders how he got here and how he'll ever get out. How can he compete in today's mad, rushing techno-world?
I just don't want to listen to records at all. OK, how about the radio.
..in last night's mass shooting...
.... experts say that icebergs contain health benefits...
...stay tuned for Lenny Kravitz...
click
...Every one looooves Marine Land
Oh great. a customer.
No, we don't have Fleetwood Mac Rumours. No we don't sell CDs. No I don't have debit...
NO. just NO.

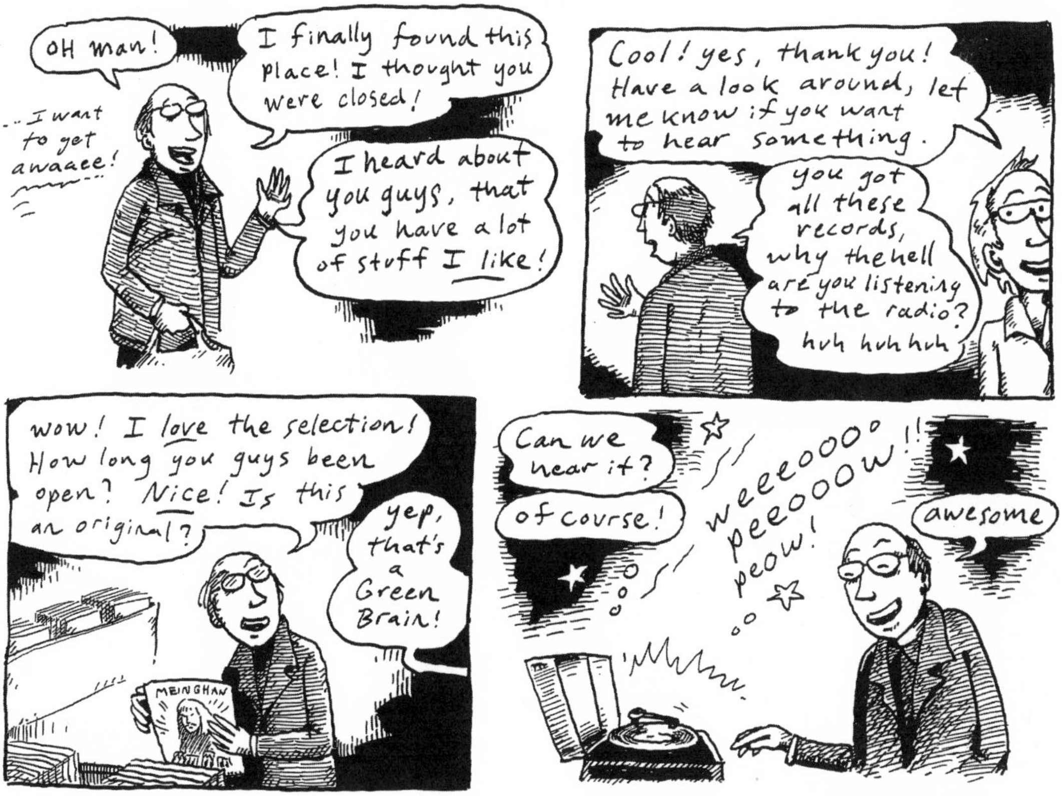
OH man!
I finally found this place! I thought you were closed!
..I want to get awaaee!
I heard about you guys, that you have a lot of stuff I like!
Cool! yes, thank you! Have a look around, let me know if you want to hear something.
you got all these records, why the hell are you listening to the radio? huh huh huh
wow! I love the selection! How long you guys been open? Nice! Is this an original?
yep, that's a Green Brain!
MEINGHAN
Can we hear it?
of course!
weeeoooo peeooow!! peow!
awesome

Lenny absorbs this moment like a sponge, he feels his life blood return to his veins. The happy customer leaves with a stack of records. Lenny remembers the upcoming record fair and books a table with enthusiasm.

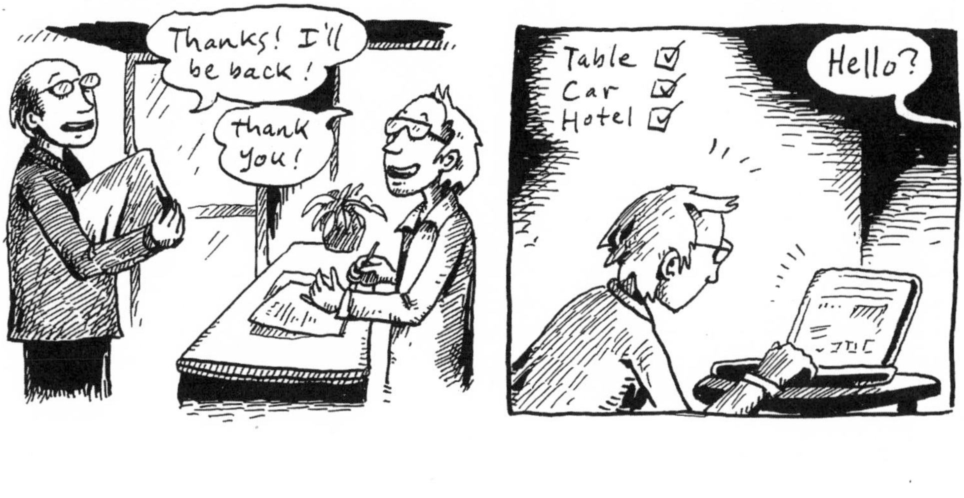
Thanks! I'll be back!
thank you!
Table ☑
Car ☑
Hotel ☑
Hello?

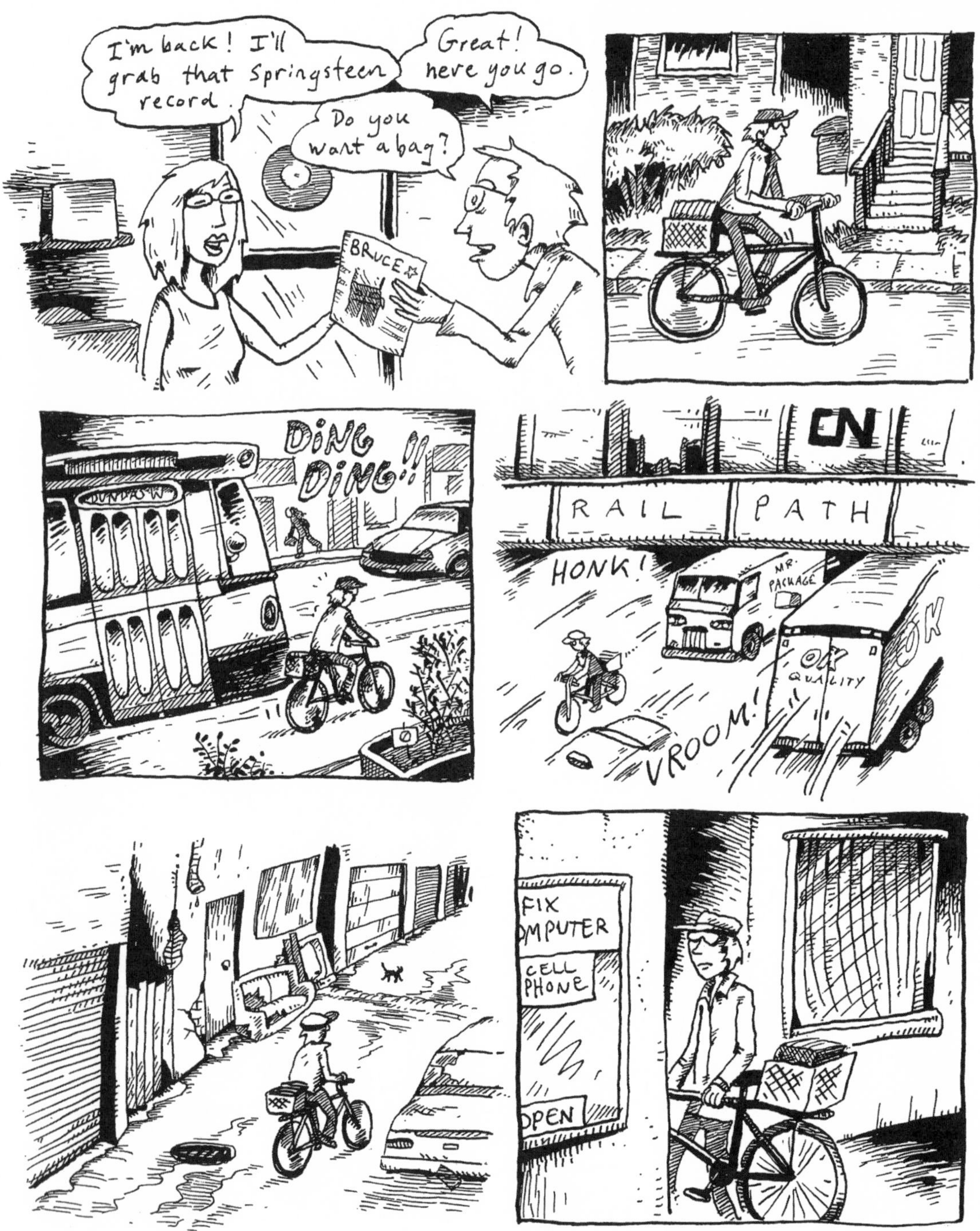

I'm back! I'll grab that Springsteen record.
Great! here you go.
Do you want a bag?
BRUCE
DiNG DiNG!!
DUNDAS W
CN
RAIL PATH
HONK!
MR. PACKAGE
OK
OK QUALITY
VROOM!
FIX
OMPUTER
CELL
PHONE
OPEN

Discovery

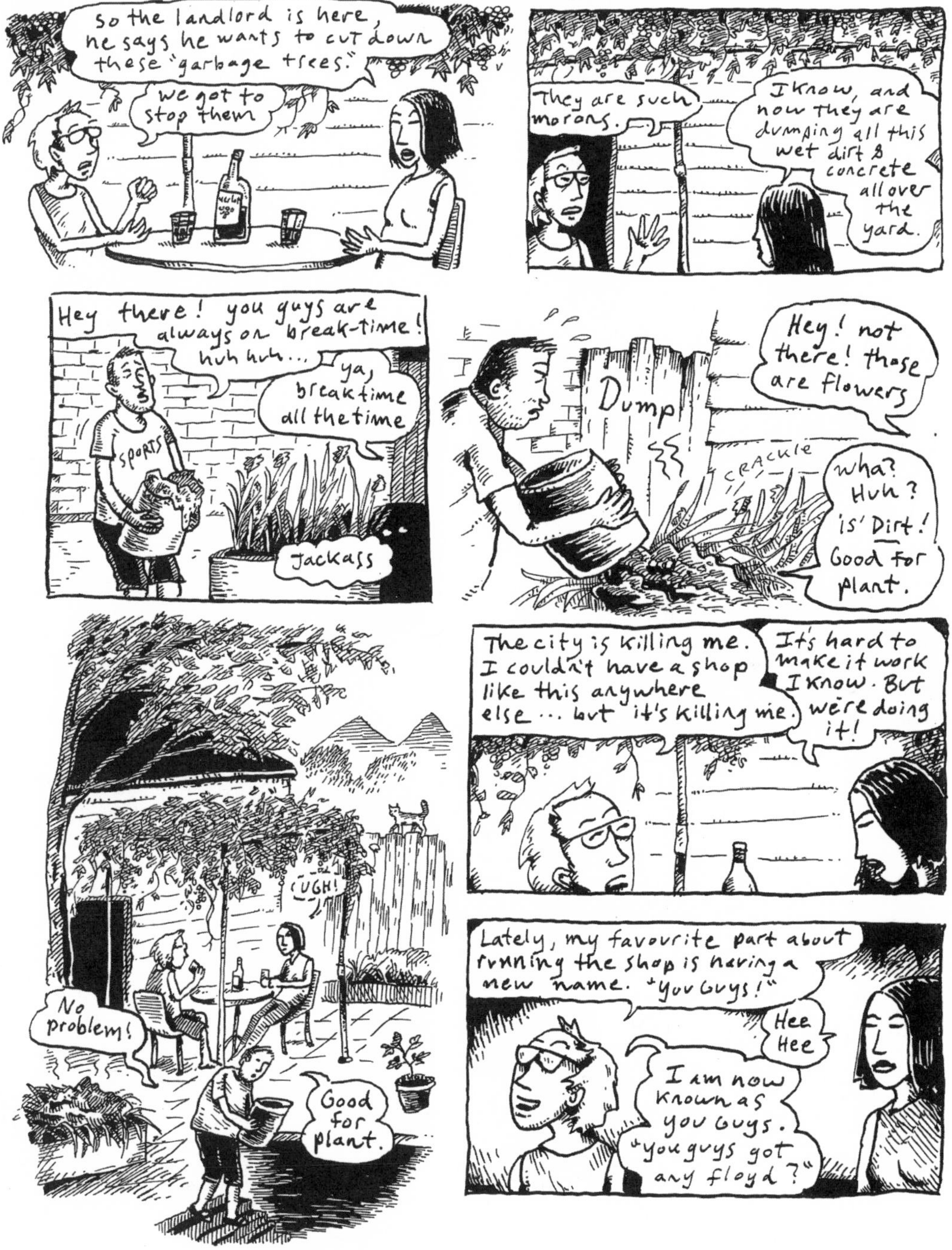
So the landlord is here, he says he wants to cut down these "garbage trees."
we got to stop them
They are such morons.
I know, and now they are dumping all this wet dirt & concrete all over the yard.
Hey there! you guys are always on break-time! huh huh...
ya, breaktime all the time
JACKASS
SPORTS
Dump
CRACKLE
Hey! not there! those are flowers
wha? Huh? is' Dirt! Good for plant.
UGH!
No problem!
Good for plant.
The city is killing me. I couldn't have a shop like this anywhere else... but it's killing me.
It's hard to make it work I know. But we're doing it!
Lately, my favourite part about running the shop is having a new name. "You Guys!"
Hee Hee
I am now known as You Guys. "you guys got any floyd?"

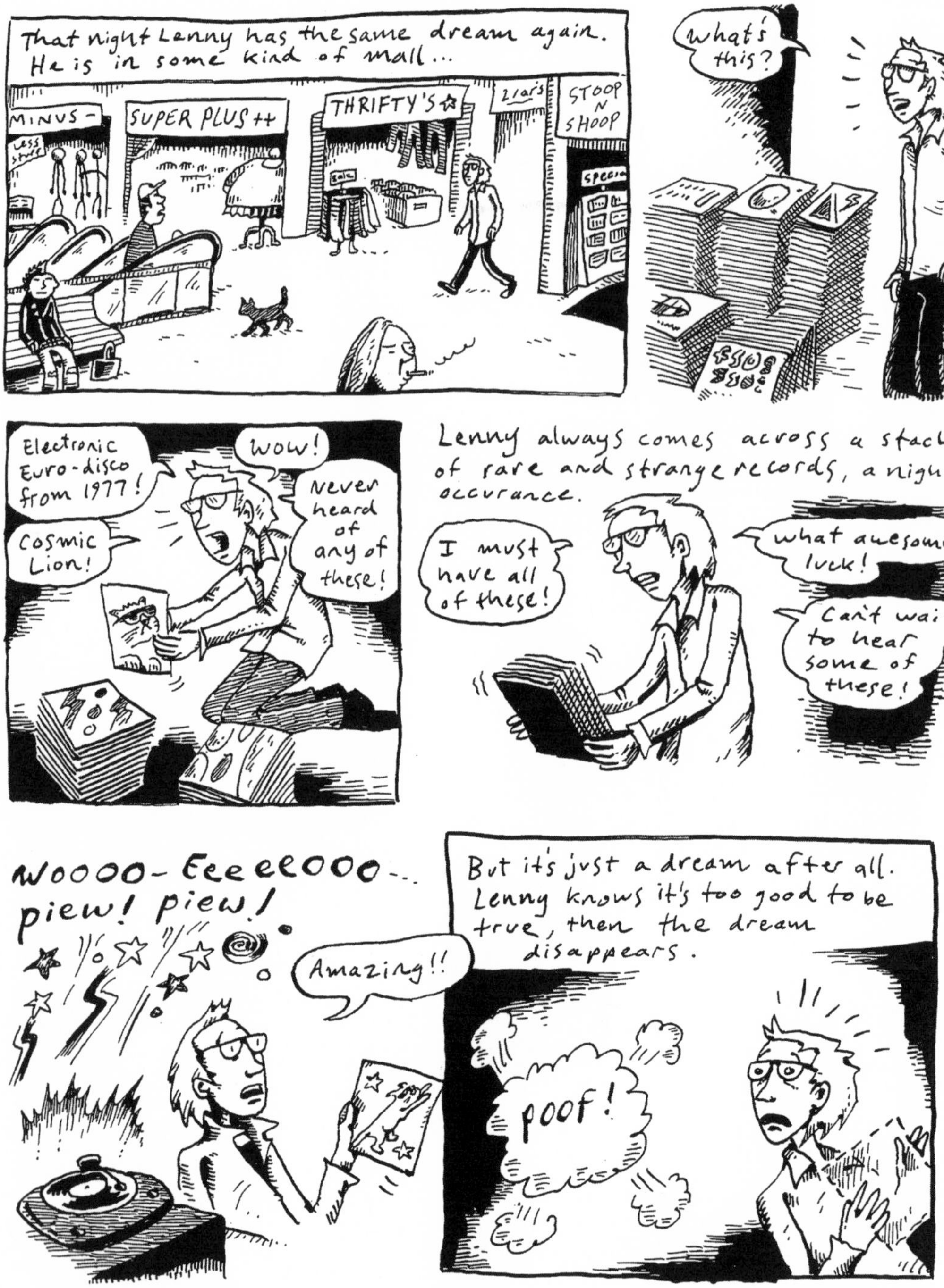
That night Lenny has the same dream again. He is in some kind of mall...
MINUS-
SUPER PLUS ++
THRIFTY'S
STOOP N SHOOP
What's this?
Electronic Euro-disco from 1977!
WOW!
Never heard of any of these!
Cosmic Lion!
Lenny always comes across a stack of rare and strange records, a nightly occurance.
I must have all of these!
What awesome luck!
Can't wait to hear some of these!
WOOOO-EeeeeOOO...
piew! piew!
Amazing!!
But it's just a dream after all. Lenny knows it's too good to be true, then the dream disappears.
POOF!

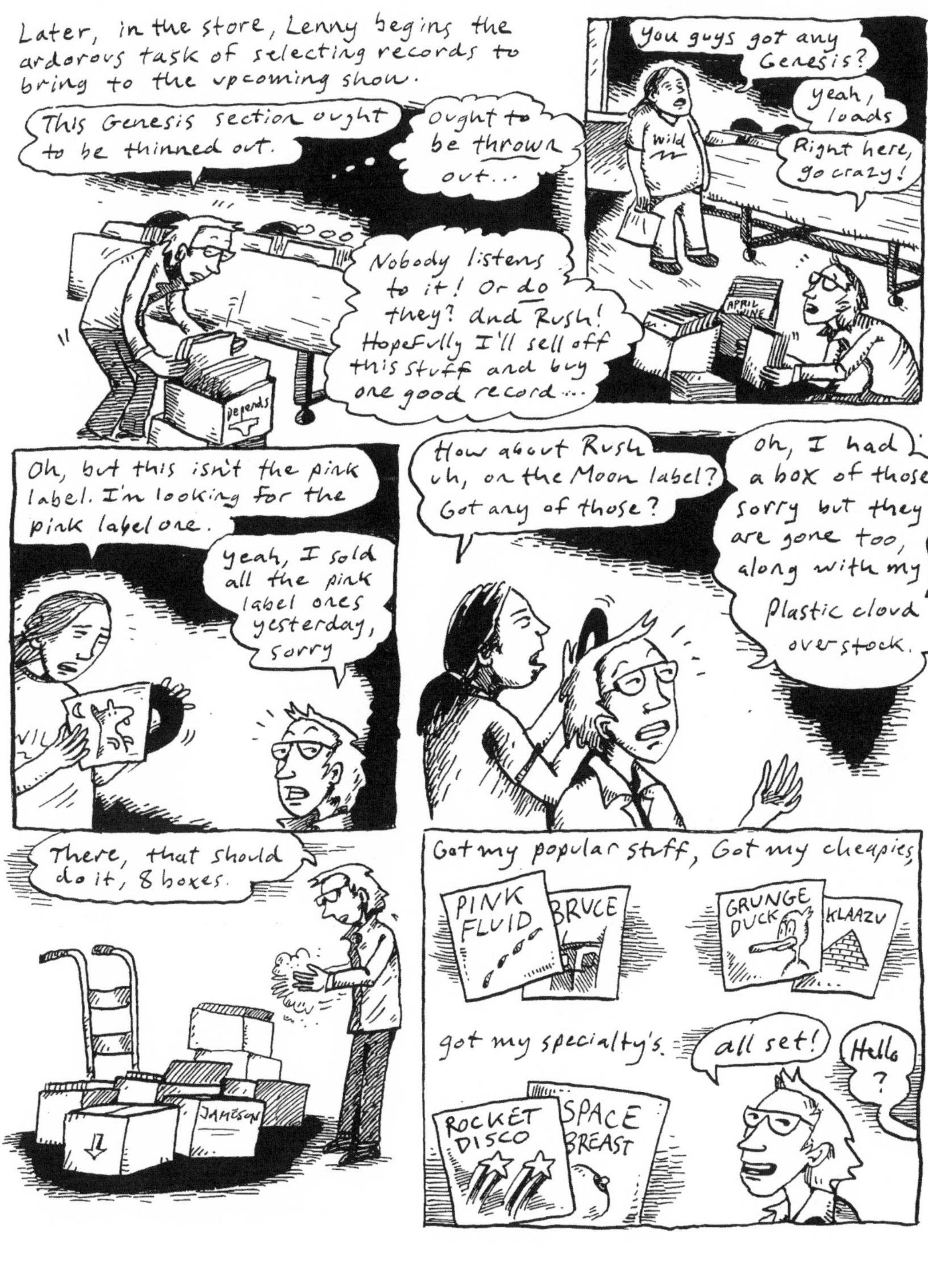
Later, in the store, Lenny begins the ardorous task of selecting records to bring to the upcoming show.
This Genesis section ought to be thinned out.
Ought to be thrown out...
Nobody listens to it! Or do they? And Rush! Hopefully I'll sell off this stuff and buy one good record...
Depends
You guys got any Genesis?
yeah, loads
Right here, go crazy!
WILD
APRIL WINE
Oh, but this isn't the pink label. I'm looking for the pink label one.
yeah, I sold all the pink label ones yesterday, sorry
How about Rush uh, on the Moon label? Got any of those?
Oh, I had a box of those, sorry but they are gone too, along with my plastic cloud overstock.
There, that should do it, 8 boxes.
JAMESON
Got my popular stuff, Got my cheapies,
PINK FLUID
BRUCE
GRUNGE DUCK
KLAAZU
got my specialty's.
ROCKET DISCO
SPACE BREAST
all set!
Hello ?

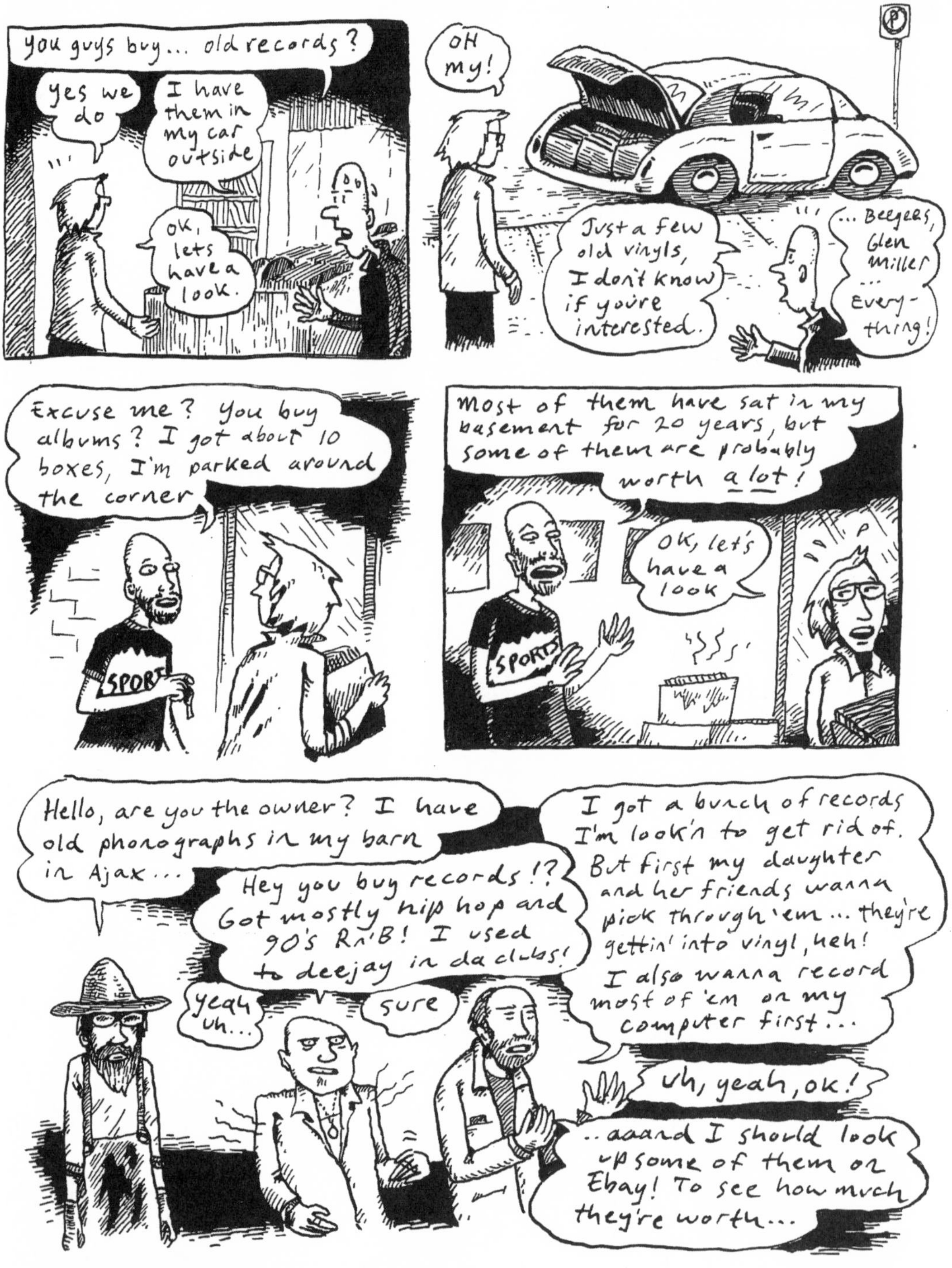
you guys buy... old records?
yes we do
I have them in my car outside
OK, lets have a look.
OH my!
Just a few old vinyls, I don't know if you're interested.
... Beegees, Glen Miller ... Every-thing!
Excuse me? You buy albums? I got about 10 boxes, I'm parked around the corner
SPORT
Most of them have sat in my basement for 20 years, but some of them are probably worth a lot!
OK, let's have a look
SPORTS
Hello, are you the owner? I have old phonographs in my barn in Ajax...
Hey you buy records!? Got mostly hip hop and 90's R'n'B! I used to deejay in da clubs!
yeah uh...
sure
I got a bunch of records I'm look'n to get rid of. But first my daughter and her friends wanna pick through 'em... they're gettin' into vinyl, heh! I also wanna record most of 'em on my computer first...
uh, yeah, ok!
..aaand I should look up some of them on Ebay! To see how much they're worth...

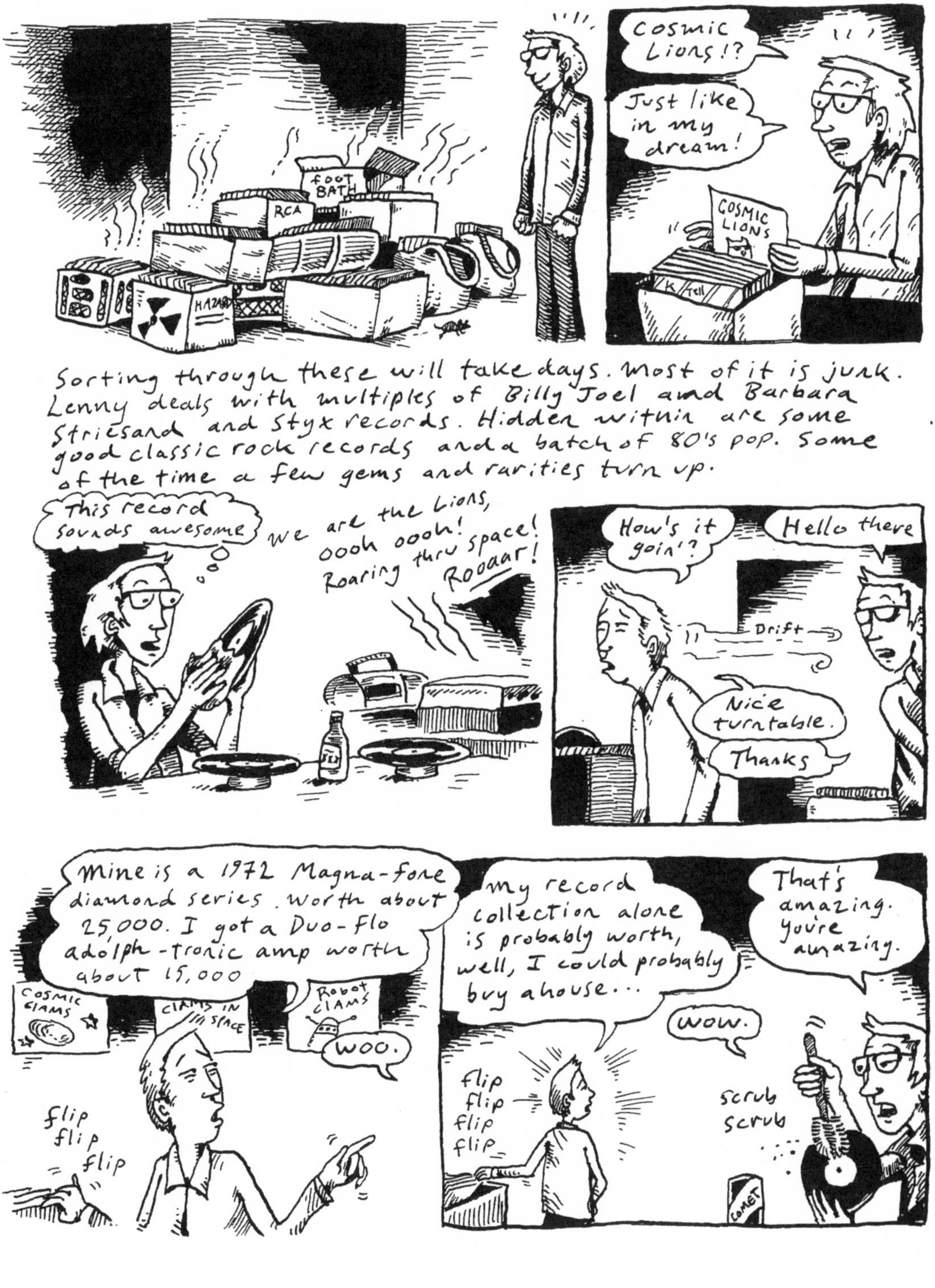
FOOT BATH
RCA
HAZARD
COSMIC LIONS!?
Just like in my dream!
COSMIC LIONS
Sorting through these will take days. Most of it is junk. Lenny deals with multiples of Billy Joel and Barbara Striesand and Styx records. Hidden within are some good classic rock records and a batch of 80's pop. Some of the time a few gems and rarities turn up.
This record sounds awesome
We are the Lions, oooh oooh! Roaring thru space! Rooaar!
How's it goin'?
Hello there
Drift
Nice turntable.
Thanks
Mine is a 1972 Magna-fone diamond series. Worth about 25,000. I got a Duo-flo adolph-tronic amp worth about 15,000
COSMIC CLAMS
CLAMS IN SPACE
Robot CLAMS
WOO.
flip flip flip
My record collection alone is probably worth, well, I could probably buy a house...
That's amazing. You're amazing.
WOW.
flip flip flip flip
scrub scrub
COMET

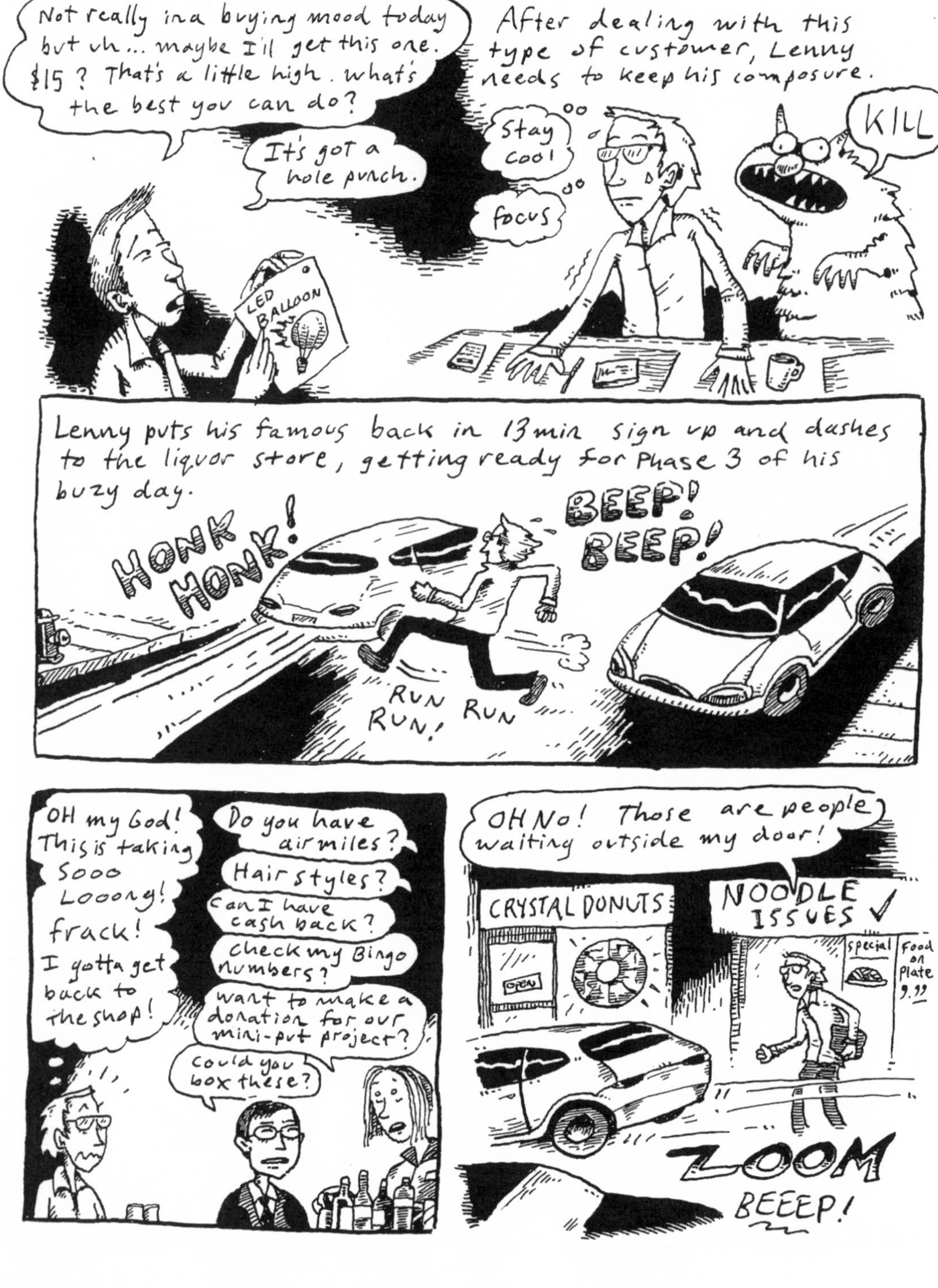
Not really in a buying mood today but uh... maybe I'll get this one. $15? That's a little high. What's the best you can do?
It's got a hole punch.
LED BALLOON
After dealing with this type of customer, Lenny needs to keep his composure.
Stay cool
focus
KILL
Lenny puts his famous back in 13 min sign up and dashes to the liquor store, getting ready for Phase 3 of his buzy day.
HONK HONK!
BEEP! BEEP!
RUN RUN RUN!
OH my God! This is taking Sooo Looong! frack! I gotta get back to the shop!
Do you have airmiles?
Hair styles?
Can I have cash back?
Check my Bingo numbers?
Want to make a donation for our mini-put project?
Could you box these?
OH No! Those are people waiting outside my door!
CRYSTAL DONUTS
OPEN
NOODLE ISSUES
Special
Food on Plate 9.99
ZOOM
BEEEP!

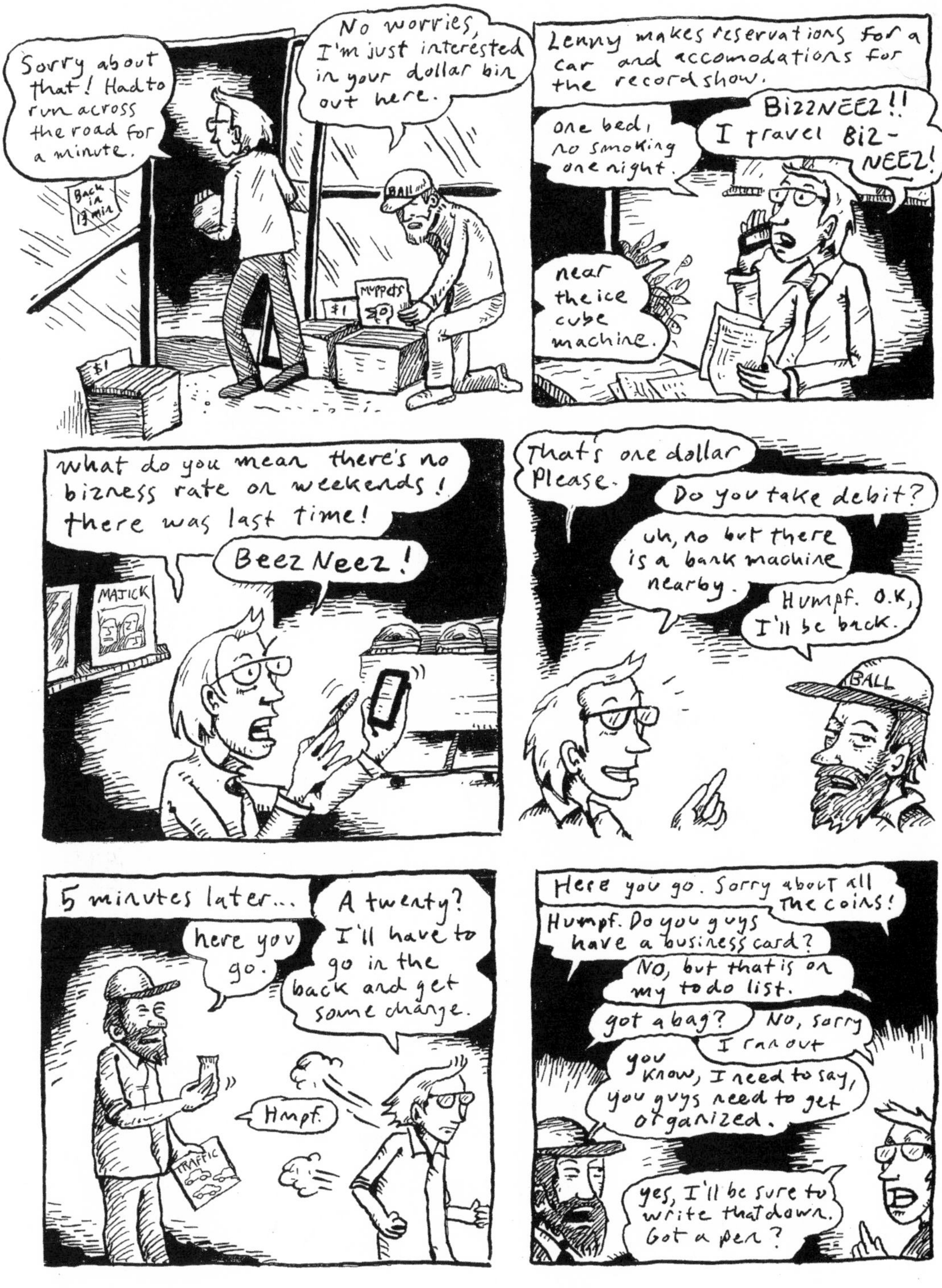

Sorry about that! Had to run across the road for a minute.
Back in 13 min
No worries, I'm just interested in your dollar bin out here.
BALL
MUPPETS
$1
$1
Lenny makes reservations for a car and accomodations for the record show.
One bed, no smoking one night.
BIZZNEEZ!! I travel BIZ-NEEZ!
near the ice cube machine.
what do you mean there's no bizness rate on weekends! there was last time!
Beez Neez!
MAJICK
That's one dollar Please.
Do you take debit?
uh, no but there is a bank machine nearby.
Humpf. O.K, I'll be back.
BALL
5 minutes later...
here you go.
A twenty? I'll have to go in the back and get some change.
Hmpf.
TRAFFIC
Here you go. Sorry about all the coins!
Humpf. Do you guys have a business card?
No, but that is on my to do list.
got a bag?
No, sorry I ran out
you know, I need to say, you guys need to get organized.
yes, I'll be sure to write that down. Got a pen?

On the Road

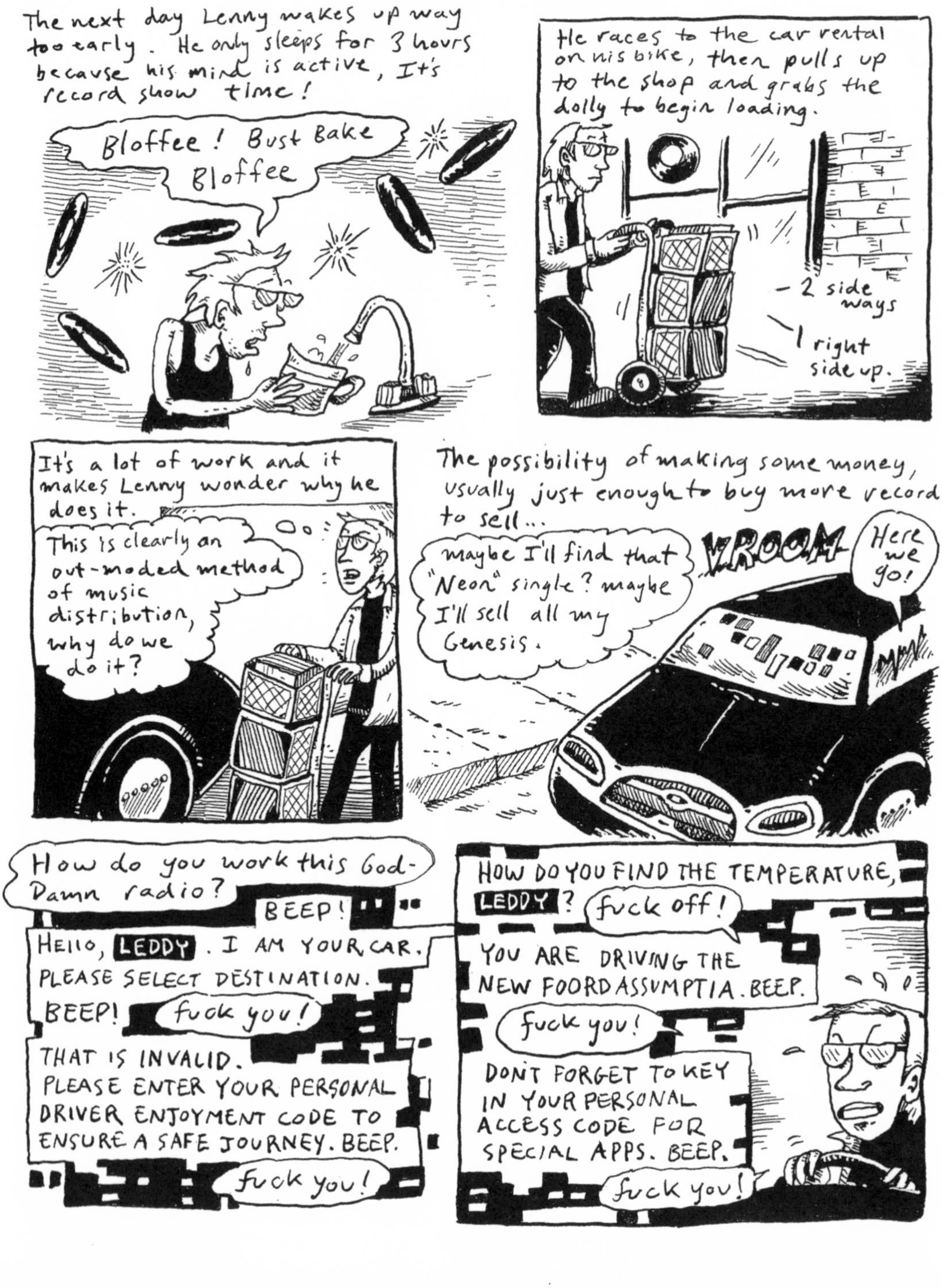
The next day Lenny wakes up way too early. He only sleeps for 3 hours because his mind is active, It's record show time!
Bloffee! Bust Bake Bloffee
He races to the car rental on his bike, then pulls up to the shop and grabs the dolly to begin loading.
2 side ways
1 right side up.
It's a lot of work and it makes Lenny wonder why he does it.
This is clearly an out-moded method of music distribution, why do we do it?
The possibility of making some money, usually just enough to buy more records to sell...
maybe I'll find that "Neon" single? maybe I'll sell all my Genesis.
VROOM
Here we go!
How do you work this God-Damn radio?
BEEP!
HELLO, LEDDY. I AM YOUR CAR. PLEASE SELECT DESTINATION. BEEP!
fuck you!
THAT IS INVALID. PLEASE ENTER YOUR PERSONAL DRIVER ENJOYMENT CODE TO ENSURE A SAFE JOURNEY. BEEP.
fuck you!
HOW DO YOU FIND THE TEMPERATURE, LEDDY?
fuck off!
YOU ARE DRIVING THE NEW FOORD ASSUMPTIA. BEEP.
fuck you!
DON'T FORGET TO KEY IN YOUR PERSONAL ACCESS CODE FOR SPECIAL APPS. BEEP.
fuck you!

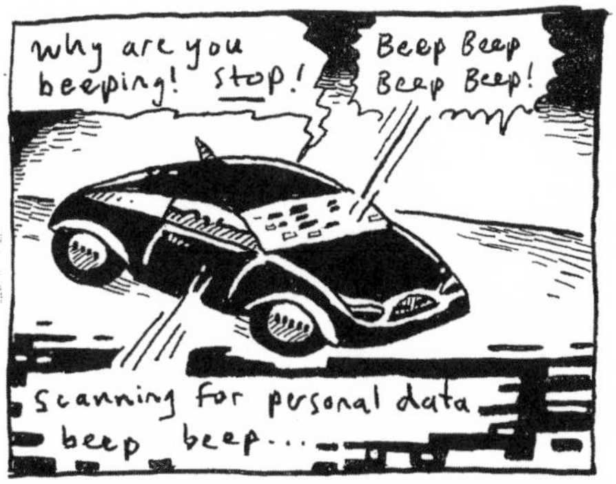
why are you beeping! stop!
Beep Beep Beep Beep!
Scanning for personal data beep beep...

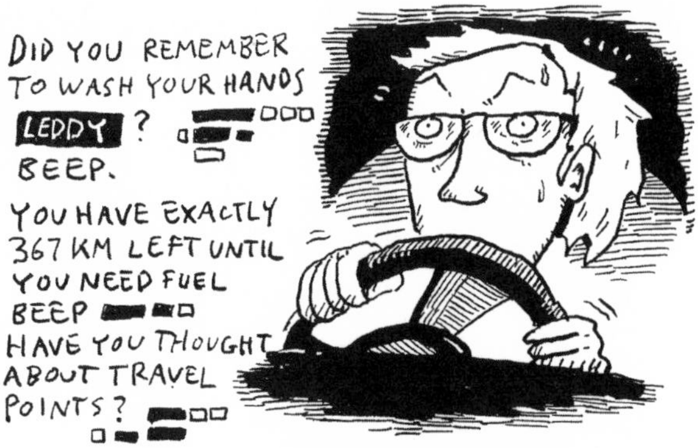
DID YOU REMEMBER TO WASH YOUR HANDS
LEDDY ?
BEEP.
YOU HAVE EXACTLY 367 KM LEFT UNTIL YOU NEED FUEL
BEEP
HAVE YOU THOUGHT ABOUT TRAVEL POINTS?

Lenny learns to block out the new 'softly intrusive' features of the Foord assumptia and shifts his thinking toward more practical worrying, like getting to the show first in line!

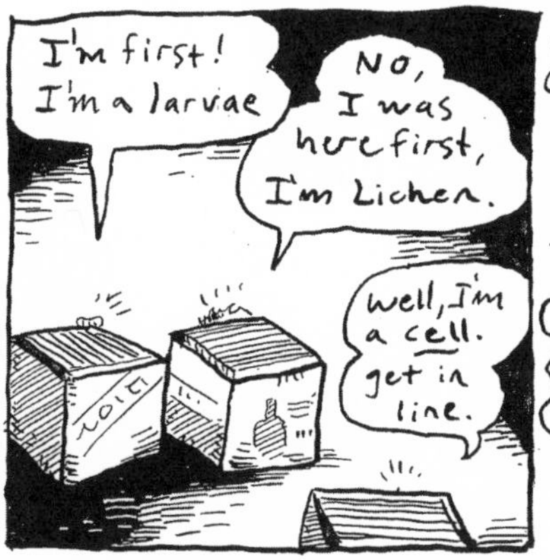
I'm first! I'm a larvae
NO, I was here first, I'm Lichen.
well, I'm a cell. get in line.

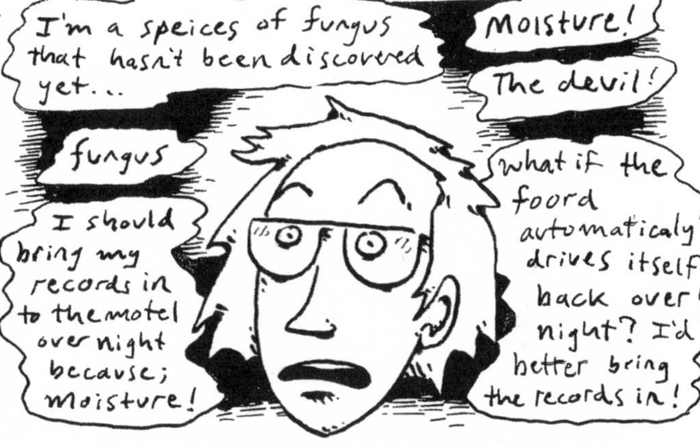
I'm a speices of fungus that hasn't been discovered yet...
Moisture!
The devil!
fungus
I should bring my records in to the motel over night because; moisture!
what if the foord automaticaly drives itself back over night? I'd better bring the records in!

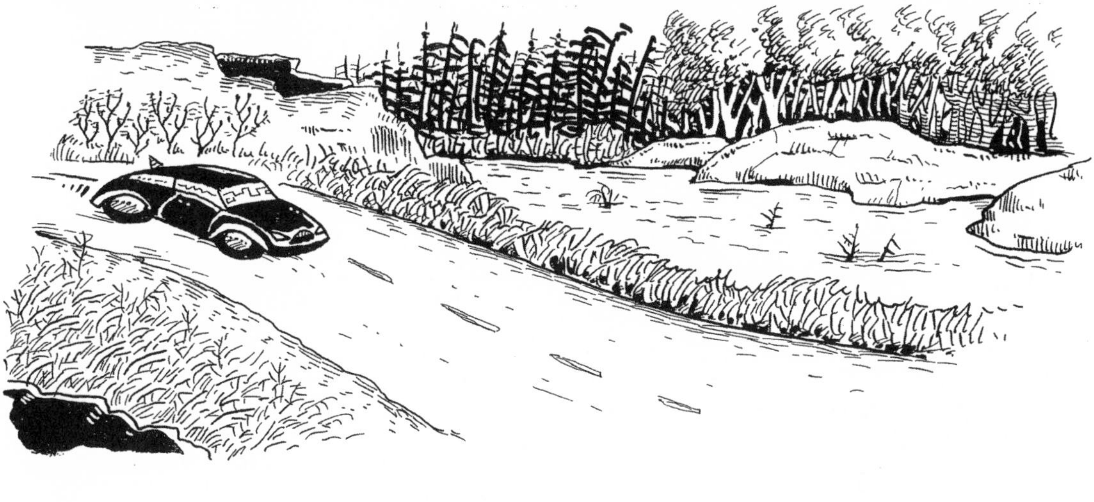

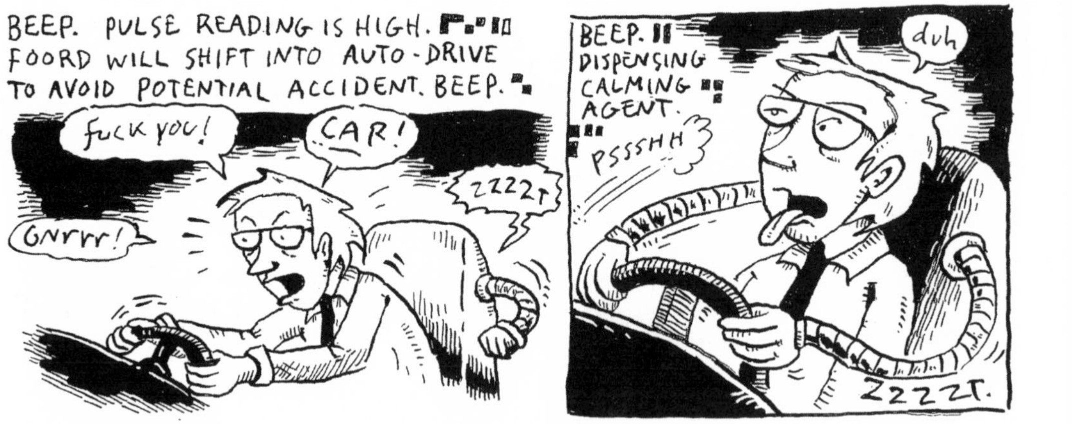
BEEP. PULSE READING IS HIGH.
FOORD WILL SHIFT INTO AUTO-DRIVE
TO AVOID POTENTIAL ACCIDENT. BEEP.
Fuck you!
CAR!
GNrrr!
ZZZZT
BEEP.
DISPENSING
CALMING
AGENT.
PSSSHH
duh
ZZZZT.

Giving in to the new Foord Assumptia, Lenny allows it to bring him safely to the motel. They develop a peace bond, the Foord promises not to drive itself back over-night. Lenny programs it to get him first in line the next day.

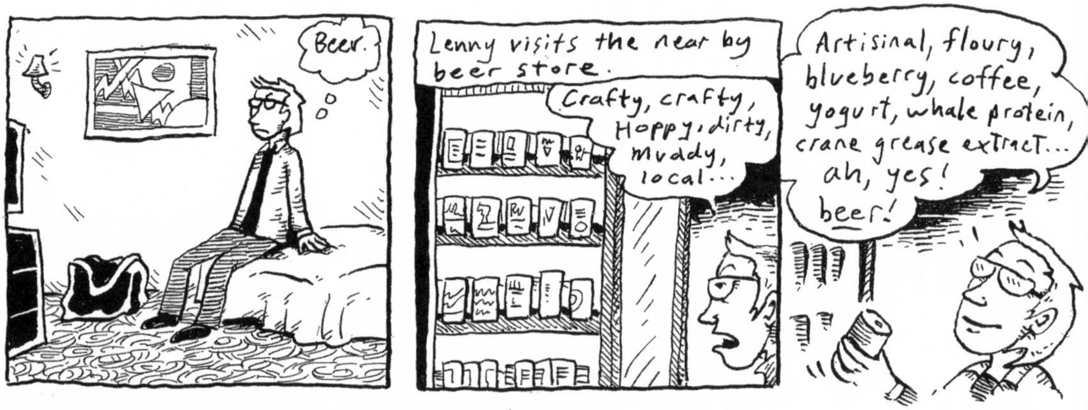
Beer.
Lenny visits the near by beer store.
Crafty, crafty, Hoppy, dirty, muddy, local...
Artisinal, floury, blueberry, coffee, yogurt, whale protein, crane grease extract... ah, yes! beer!

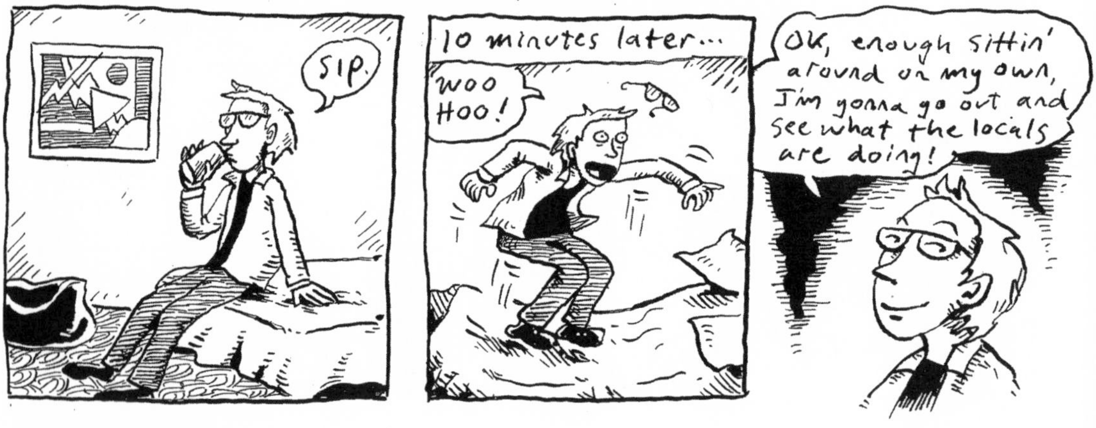
SIP.
10 minutes later...
WOO HOO!
OK, enough sittin' around on my own, I'm gonna go out and see what the locals are doing!

Out on the Town

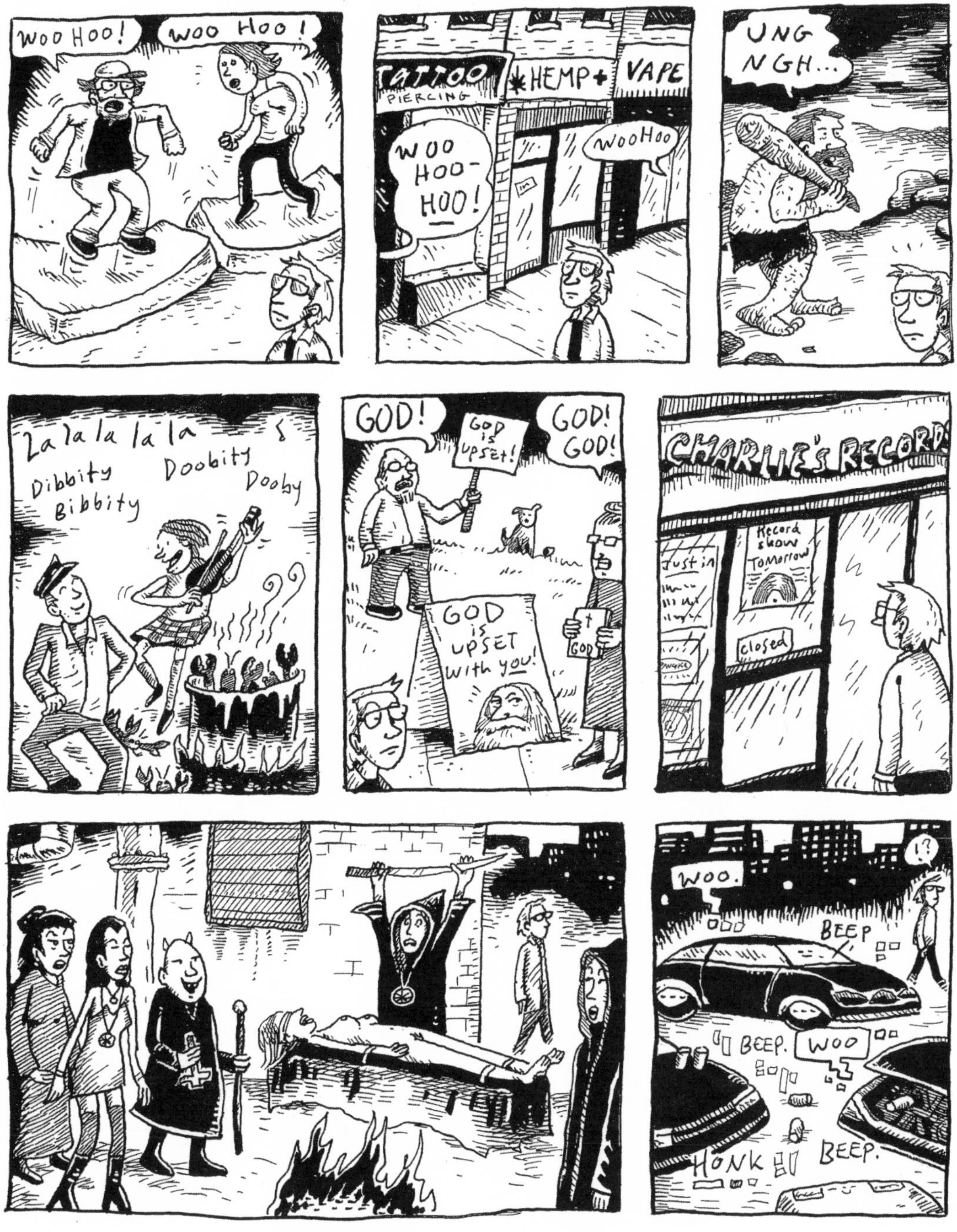
WOO HOO!
WOO HOO!
TATTOO
PIERCING
HEMP
VAPE
WOO HOO-HOO-HOO!
WOOHOO
UNG NGH...
La la la la la
Dibbity Bibbity
Doobity Dooby
GOD!
GOD is upset!
GOD! GOD!
GOD is UPSET with YOU!
GOD
CHARLIE'S RECORDS
Just in
Record show Tomorrow
closed
WOO.
BEEP
!?
BEEP.
WOO
HONK
BEEP.

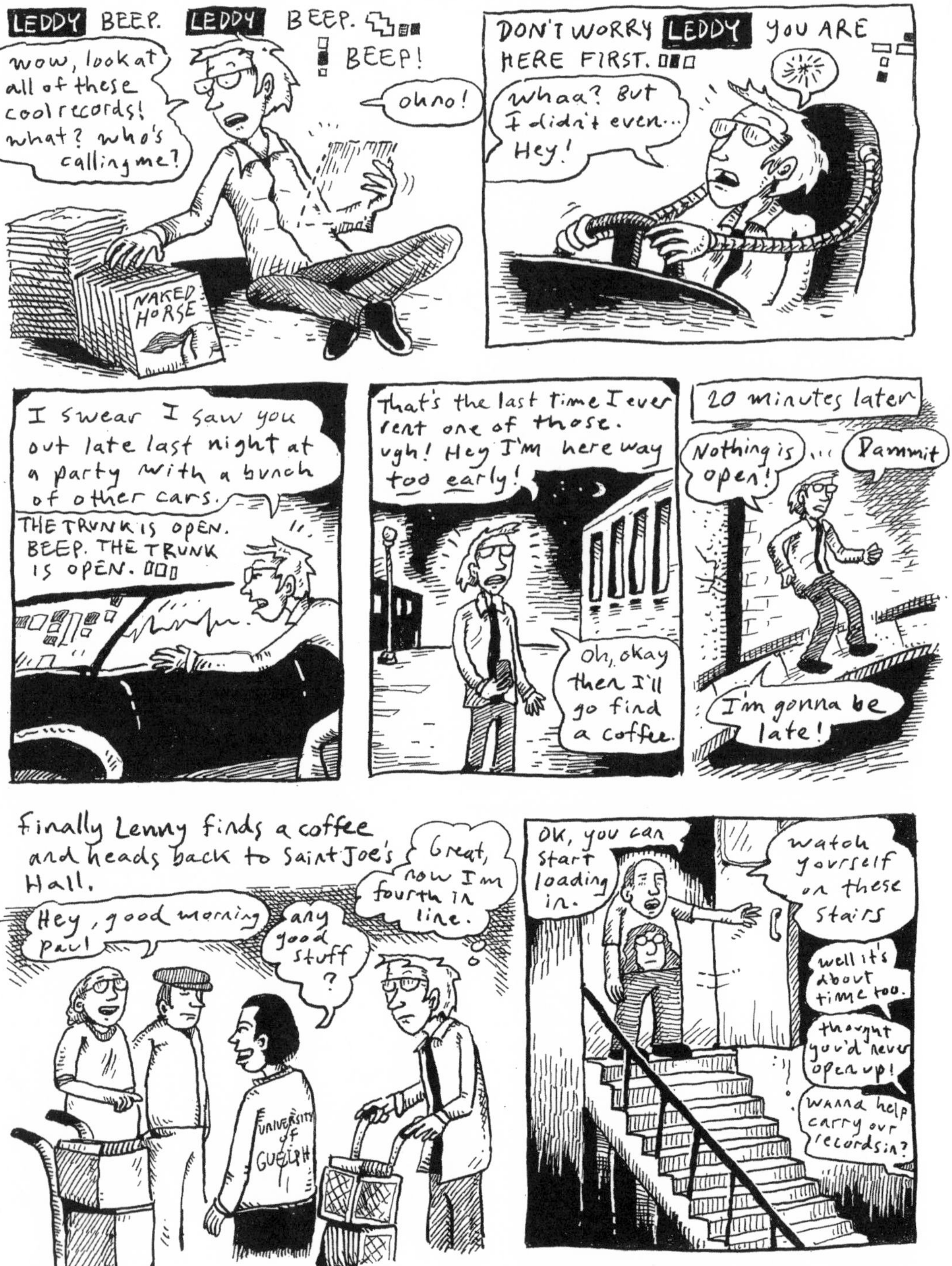
LEDDY BEEP. LEDDY BEEP.
BEEP!
wow, look at all of these cool records! what? who's calling me?
oh no!
NAKED HORSE
DON'T WORRY LEDDY YOU ARE HERE FIRST.
whaa? But I didn't even... Hey!
I swear I saw you out late last night at a party with a bunch of other cars.
THE TRUNK IS OPEN. BEEP. THE TRUNK IS OPEN.
That's the last time I ever rent one of those. ugh! Hey I'm here way too early!
Oh, okay then I'll go find a coffee.
20 minutes later
Nothing is open!
Dammit
I'm gonna be late!
Finally Lenny finds a coffee and heads back to Saint Joe's Hall.
Hey, good morning paul
any good stuff?
Great, now I'm fourth in line.
UNIVERSITY OF GUELPH
OK, you can start loading in.
watch yourself on these stairs
well it's about time too.
thought you'd never open up!
wanna help carry our records in?

Record show

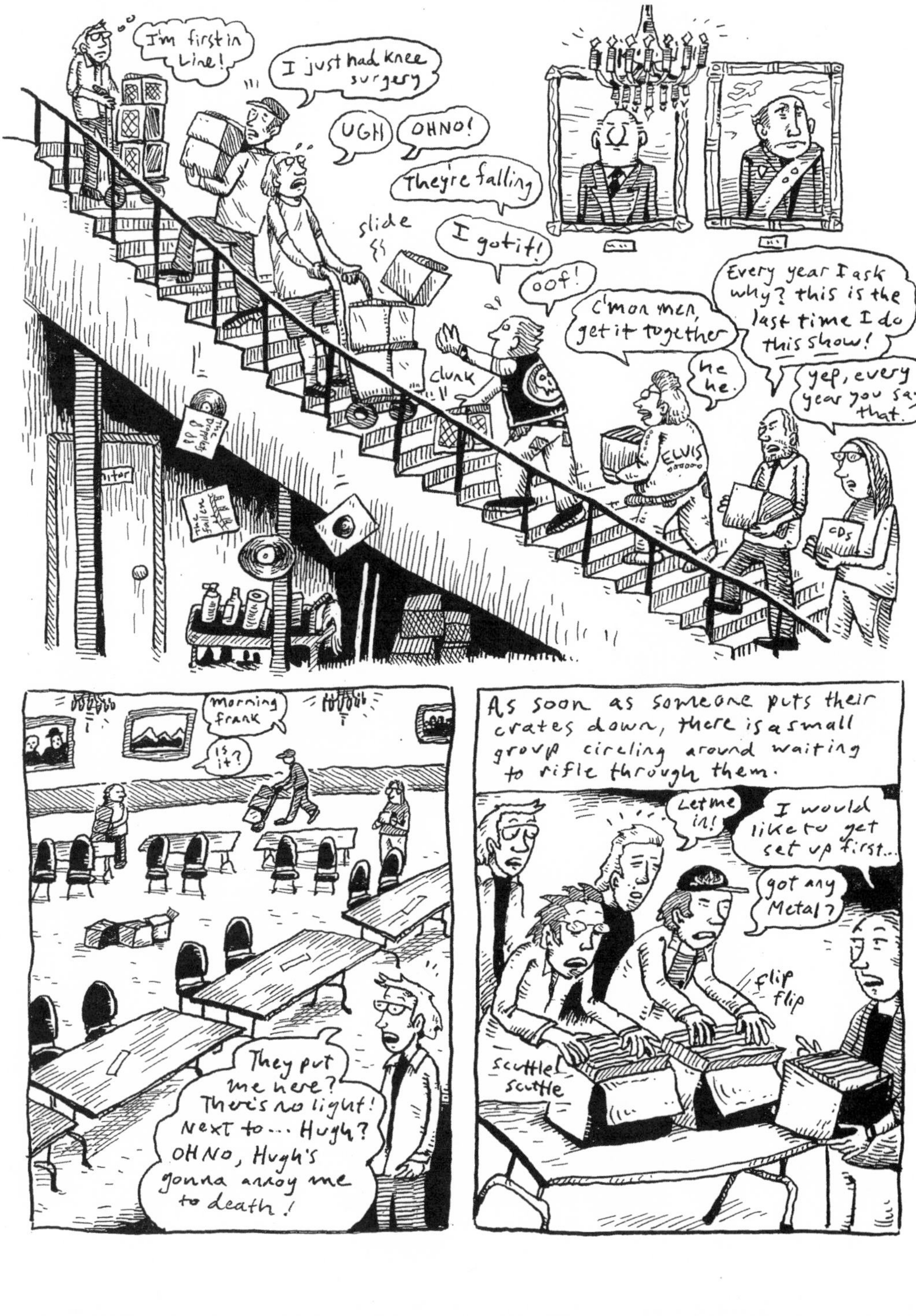
I'm first in Line!
I just had knee surgery
UGH
OHNO!
They're falling
slide
I got it!
oof!
clunk
C'mon men, get it together
he he.
Every year I ask why? this is the last time I do this show!
yep, every year you say that.
ELVIS
CDs
morning frank
is it?
They put me here? There's no light! Next to... Hugh? OH NO, Hugh's gonna annoy me to death!
As soon as someone puts their crates down, there is a small group circling around waiting to rifle through them.
Let me in!
I would like to get set up first...
got any Metal?
flip flip
scuttle scuttle

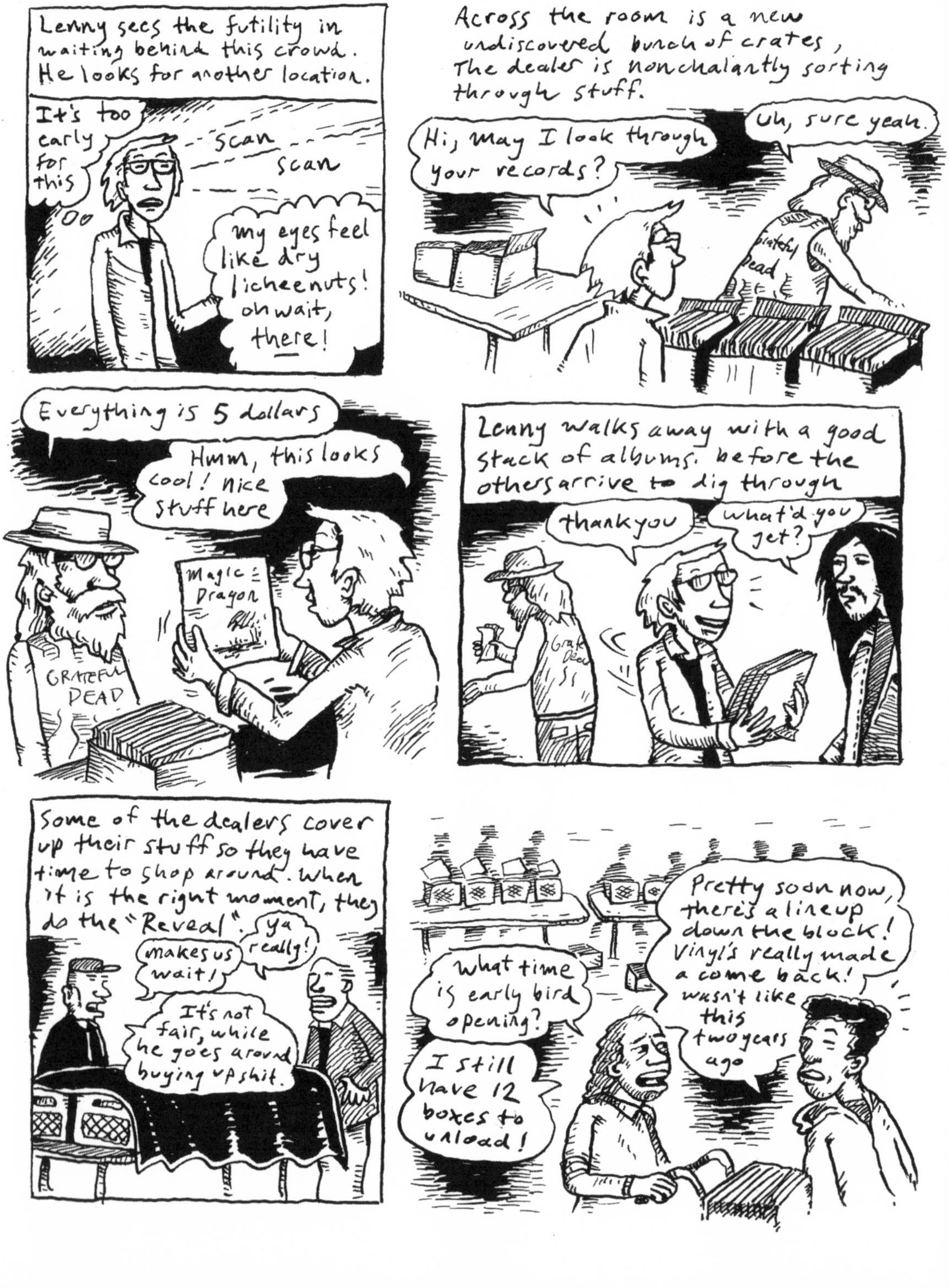
Lenny sees the futility in waiting behind this crowd. He looks for another location.
It's too early for this
scan
scan
my eyes feel like dry licheenuts! oh wait, there!
Across the room is a new undiscovered bunch of crates, The dealer is nonchalantly sorting through stuff.
Hi, May I look through your records?
Uh, sure yeah.
Grateful Dead
Everything is 5 dollars
Hmm, this looks cool! nice stuff here
Magic Dragon
GRATEFUL DEAD
Lenny walks away with a good stack of albums. before the others arrive to dig through
thankyou
what'd you get?
Some of the dealers cover up their stuff so they have time to shop around. When it is the right moment, they do the "Reveal".
makes us wait!
ya really!
It's not fair, while he goes around buying up shit.
What time is early bird opening?
Pretty soon now, there's a lineup down the block! Vinyl's really made a come back! wasn't like this two years ago
I still have 12 boxes to unload!

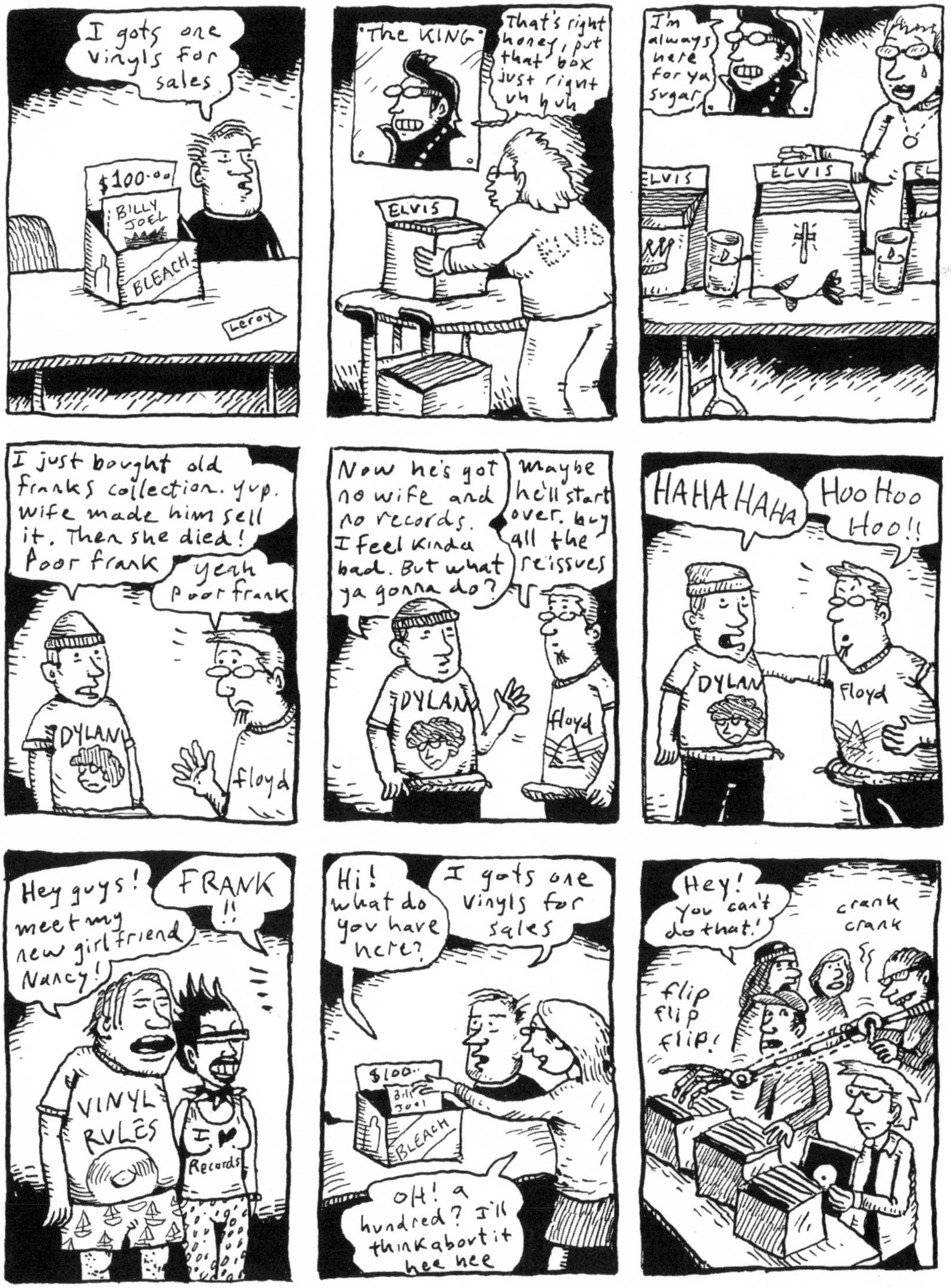
I gots one vinyls for sales
$100.00
BILLY JOEL
BLEACH
Leroy
THE KING
That's right honey, put that box just right uh huh
ELVIS
ELVIS
I'm always here for ya sugar
ELVIS
ELVIS
I just bought old franks collection. yup. wife made him sell it. Then she died! Poor frank
Yeah Poor frank
DYLAN
floyd
Now he's got no wife and no records. I feel kinda bad. But what ya gonna do?
Maybe he'll start over. buy all the reissues
DYLAN
floyd
HAHAHAHAHA
HooHoo Hoo!!
DYLAN
Floyd
Hey guys! meet my new girlfriend Nancy!
FRANK !!
VINYL RULES
I ♥ Records
Hi! what do you have here?
I gots one vinyls for sales
$100..
Billy Joel
BLEACH
OH! a hundred? I'll think about it hee hee
Hey! You can't do that!
crank crank
flip flip flip!

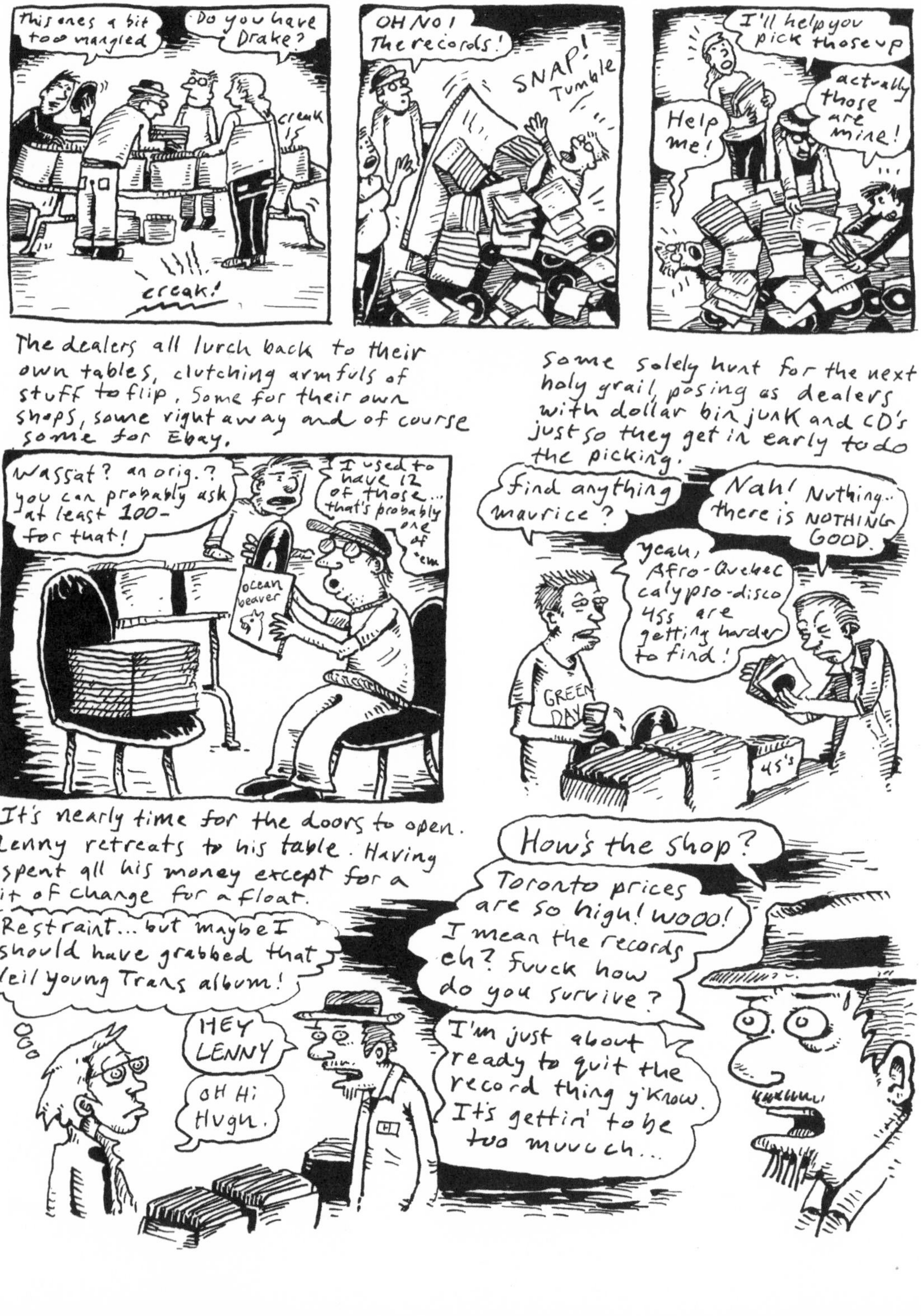
This ones a bit too mangled
Do you have Drake?
creak
creak!
OH NO! The records!
SNAP! Tumble
I'll help you pick those up
Help me!
actually those are mine!
...
The dealers all lurch back to their own tables, clutching armfuls of stuff to flip. Some for their own shops, some right away and of course some for Ebay.
Some solely hunt for the next holy grail, posing as dealers with dollar bin junk and CD's just so they get in early to do the picking.
Wassat? an orig.? you can probably ask at least 100- for that!
I used to have 12 of those... that's probably one of 'em
ocean beaver
Find anything maurice?
Nah! Nuthing.. there is NOTHING GOOD.
yeah, Afro-Quebec calypso-disco 45s are getting harder to find!
GREEN DAY
45's
It's nearly time for the doors to open. Lenny retreats to his table. Having spent all his money except for a bit of change for a float.
Restraint... but maybe I should have grabbed that Neil Young Trans album!
HEY LENNY
OH Hi Hugh.
How's the shop?
Toronto prices are so high! WOOO! I mean the records eh? Fuuck how do you survive?
I'm just about ready to quit the record thing y'know. It's gettin' to be too muuuch...

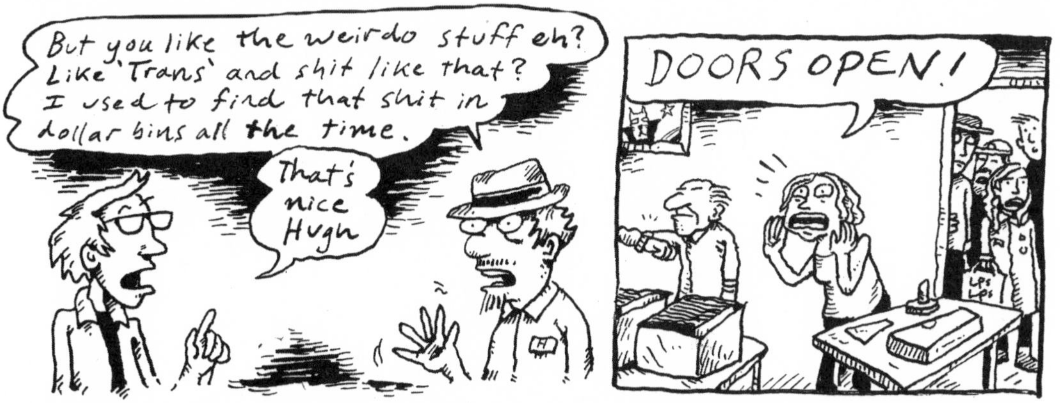
But you like the weirdo stuff eh? Like 'Trans' and shit like that? I used to find that shit in dollar bins all the time.
That's nice Hugh
DOORS OPEN!
LPs LPs

The room begins to swell up with avid record shoppers young and old. Some sweep the room to see where to start, others go straight for cheap bins, some to the well-known collectors. Lenny waits for the certain types who like "weirdo-shit".

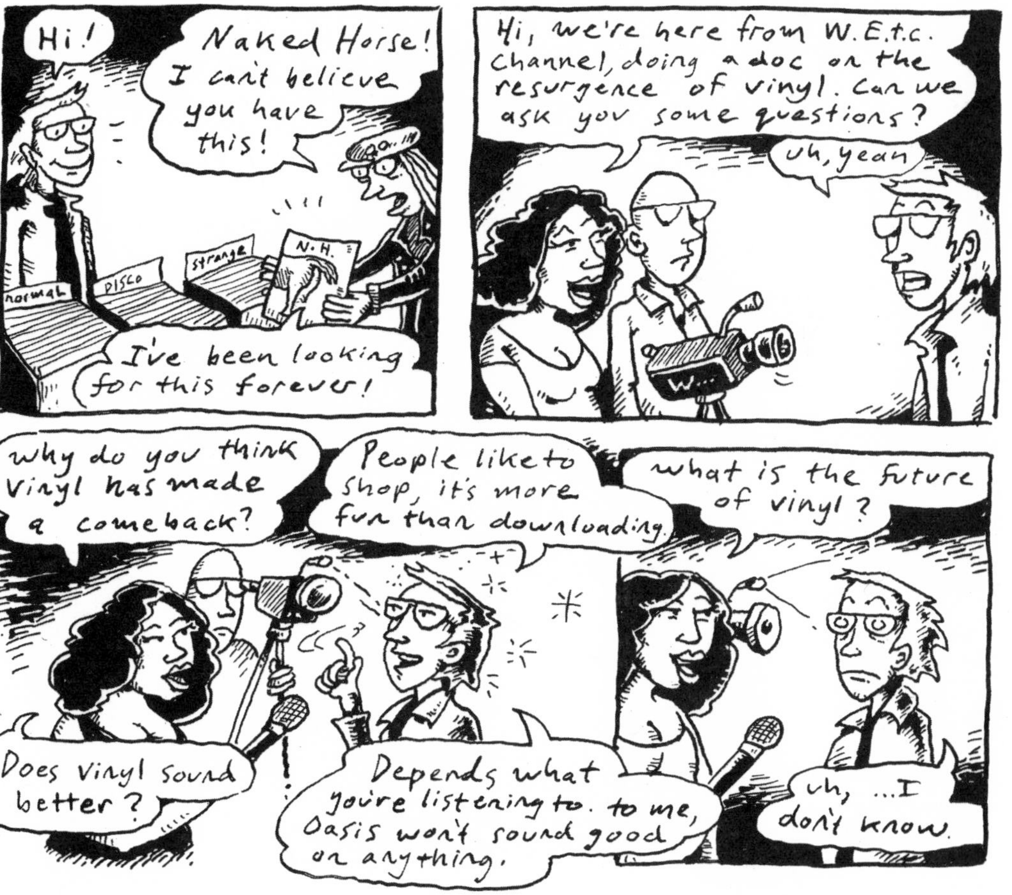
Hi!
Naked Horse! I can't believe you have this!
normal
DISCO
strange
N.H.
I've been looking for this forever!
Hi, we're here from W.E.t.c. Channel, doing a doc on the resurgence of vinyl. Can we ask you some questions?
uh, yeah
W...
why do you think vinyl has made a comeback?
People like to shop, it's more fun than downloading.
Does vinyl sound better?
Depends what you're listening to. to me, Oasis won't sound good on anything.
what is the future of vinyl?
uh, ...I don't know.

The future of vinyl! This takes Lenny into the head space that will dominate the rest of his day. While the record show buzzes around him, sales at his table are mediocre and Lenny retreats into his all too familiar swamp of uncertainty.

why?

why am I doing this? I should have been an organic farmer or an arborist, a cartoonist, or studied insects!

AWK AWK!

As with many collectors, it was traumatic life events that led Lenny to burrow into a realm of his own. Isolation during a bad relationship, a stressful divorce and the death of both his parents. Though his current life is much sweeter, the uncertainty continues to shroud all of his work in a thick murk. His thoughts drift on.

Lenny we are your thoughts do you know where you are Lenny?

AWK AWK!

I'm in a fucking swamp!

you must not try and avoid us Lenny, we are your only hope! your real thoughts have been abandoned on a raft for too long!

Tooooo Looooong!

I just want to get drunk!

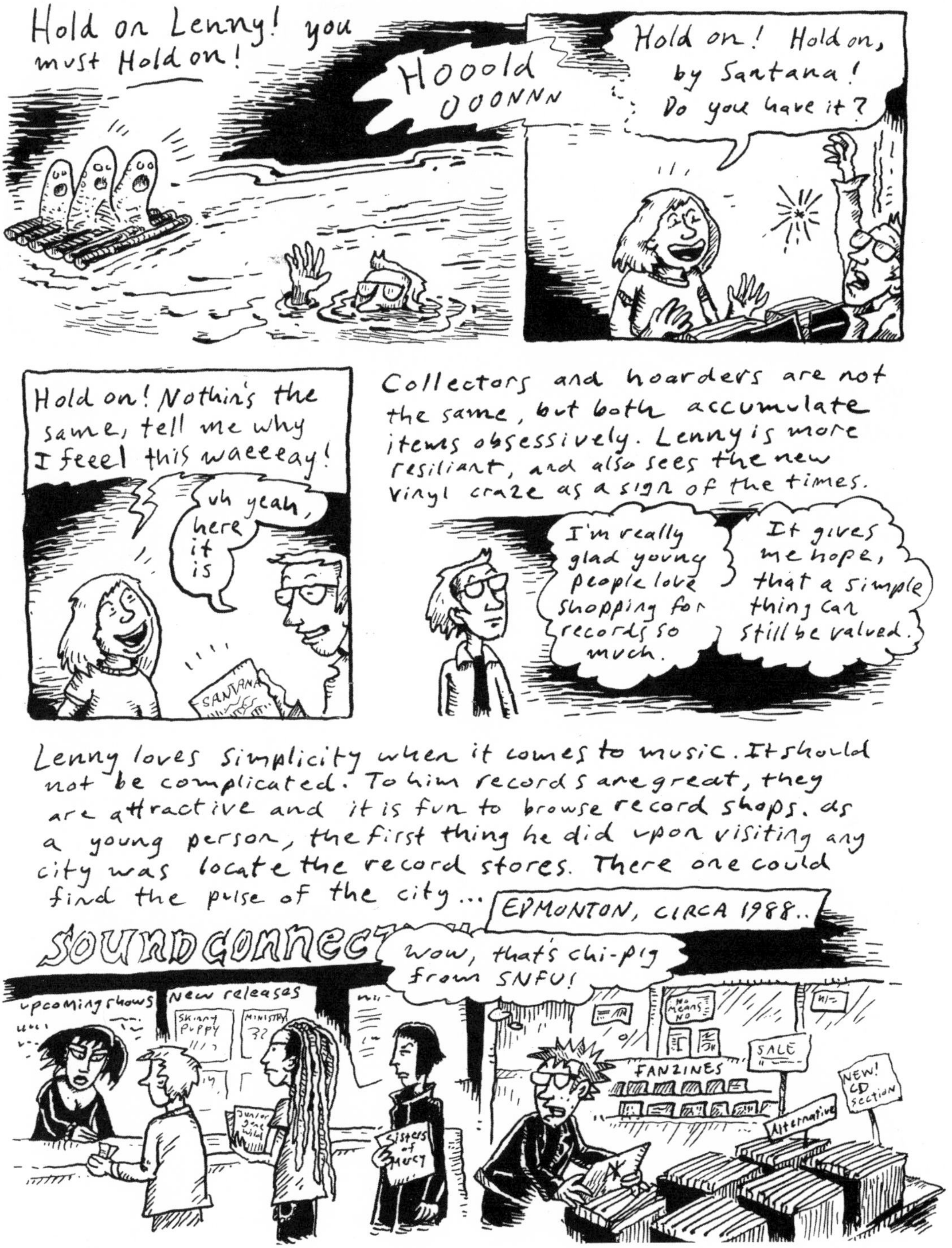

Hold on Lenny! you must Hold on!
Hooold OOONNN
Hold on! Hold on, by Santana! Do you have it?
Hold on! Nothin's the same, tell me why I feeel this waeeeay!
uh yeah, here it is
SANTANA
Collectors and hoarders are not the same, but both accumulate items obsessively. Lenny is more resiliant, and also sees the new vinyl craze as a sign of the times.
I'm really glad young people love shopping for records so much.
It gives me hope, that a simple thing can still be valued.
Lenny loves simplicity when it comes to music. It should not be complicated. To him records are great, they are attractive and it is fun to browse record shops. As a young person, the first thing he did upon visiting any city was locate the record stores. There one could find the pulse of the city...
EDMONTON, CIRCA 1988..
SOUND CONNECT
Wow, that's chi-pig from SNFU!
upcoming shows
New releases
Skinny Puppy
Ministry
No Means No
FANZINES
SALE
NEW! CD section
Alternative
Sisters of Mercy

Before Lenny truly developed his love of records, tapes were the choice. When CDs became popular, Lenny was living a bohemian life and never really acquired much, never owned more than a handful of CDs. He sold off all of his cassettes and held on to very little possessions.

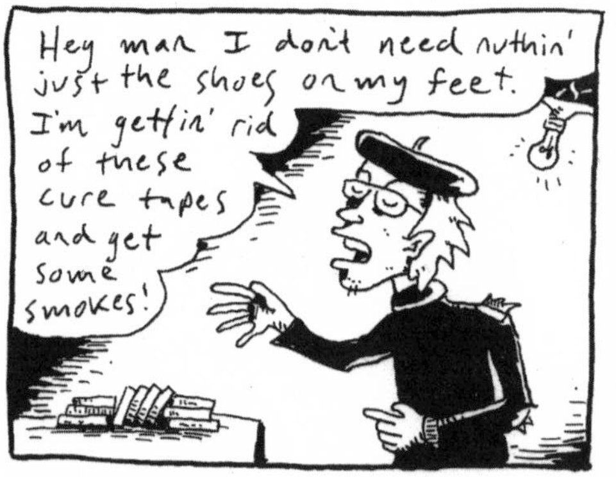
Hey man I don't need nuthin' just the shoes on my feet. I'm gettin' rid of these cure tapes and get some smokes!

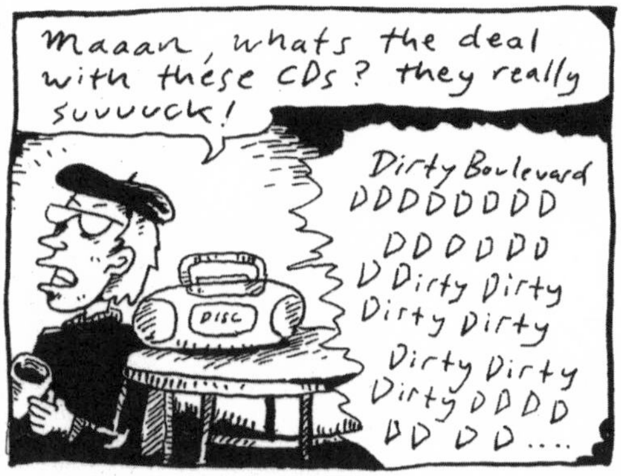
Maaan, whats the deal with these CDs? they really suuuuck!
DISC
Dirty Boulevard DDDDDDDD DDDDDD D Dirty Dirty Dirty Dirty Dirty Dirty Dirty DDDD DD DD....

Later in life, records became more meaningful to him and a small collection remained. Cherishing the few LPs he managed to keep from his teens and a random assortment of stuff that began to collect: Leonard Cohen, Doug Randle, The Specials, Throbbing Gristle...

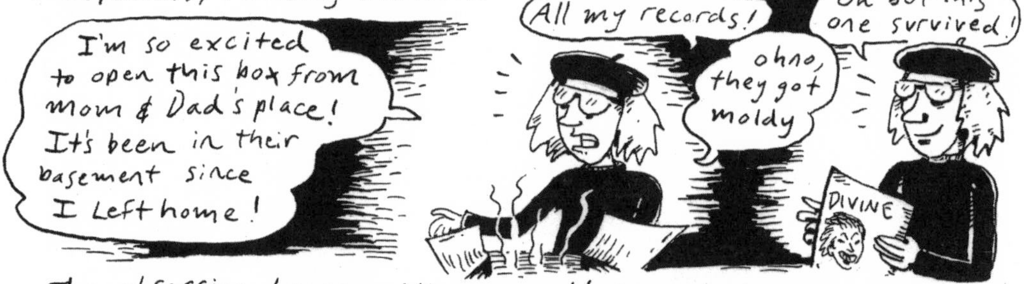
I'm so excited to open this box from Mom & Dad's place! It's been in their basement since I Left home!
All my records!
oh no, they got moldy
Oh but this one survived!
DIVINE

The obsession began with an endless search for a 12" single of the 1982 song "White Horse" by the band Laid Back. This early synth-pop song remained unheard and elusive for decades and Lenny had to find it.

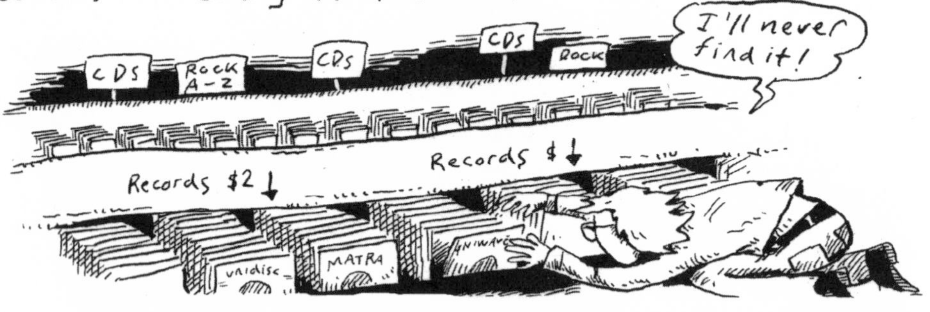
I'll never find it!
CDs
ROCK A–Z
CDs
CDs
ROCK
Records $↓
Records $2↓
UNIDISC
MATRA

Sometime in 2001, a friend played him some early Moog records.
MOOG
This opened the way. Lenny launched into an endless search for the cosmic sound.
SPACE ART
TIM BLAKE
JARRE
ZANOV
TOM DISSEVELT
At this time, dedicated websites erupted with previously unheard lost vinyl. This opened many doors and fueled the search even more. Lenny's collection grew. Soon he had acquired an excess of records in addition to his many favourites.
I guess I don't need three copies of Venus Gang...
Or all of these Gina X 12" singles.
Lenny began to sell the extra records at record fairs.
I would just love to do this full time!
flip flip flip
Dealer
Disco
Other
Rock
Around 2010, the interest in vinyl began to grow. The idea of opening a shop seemed highly possible, and very attractive!
I could open a store in my bathroom and they would seek me out! Record people are obsessed
Are you sure you want to be a merchant?
I'm not sure
But I think it could work! Now is the time to try!

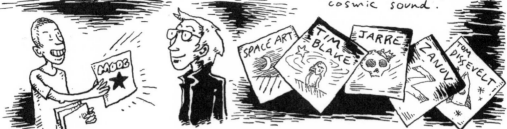

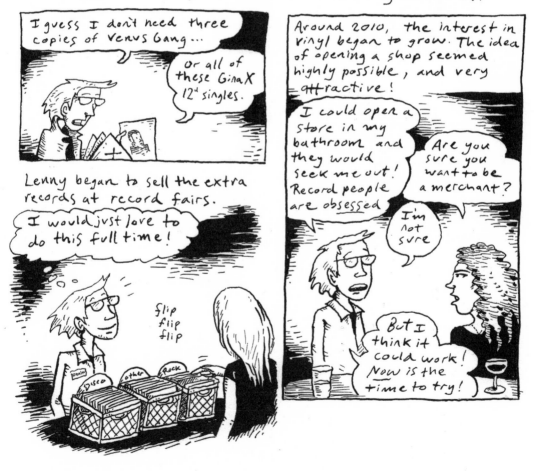

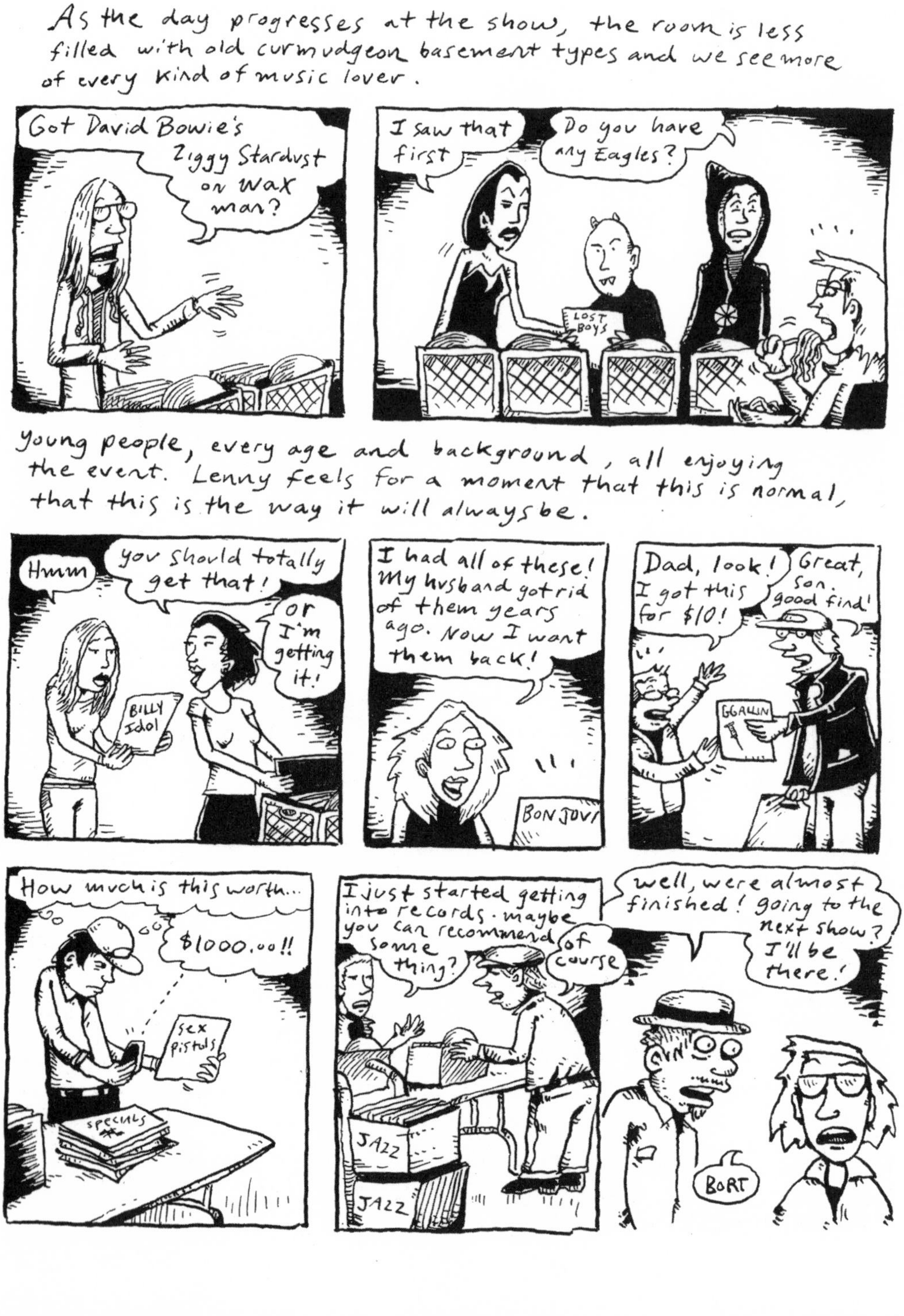
As the day progresses at the show, the room is less filled with old curmudgeon basement types and we see more of every kind of music lover.
Got David Bowie's Ziggy Stardust on wax man?
I saw that first
Do you have any Eagles?
LOST BOYS
Young people, every age and background, all enjoying the event. Lenny feels for a moment that this is normal, that this is the way it will always be.
Hmm
you should totally get that!
or I'm getting it!
BILLY Idol
I had all of these! My husband got rid of them years ago. Now I want them back!
BON JOVI
Dad, look! I got this for $10!
Great, son. good find!
GG ALLIN
How much is this worth...
$1000.00!!
sex pistols
SPECIALS
I just started getting into records. maybe you can recommend some thing?
of course
JAZZ
JAZZ
well, were almost finished! going to the next show? I'll be there!
BORT

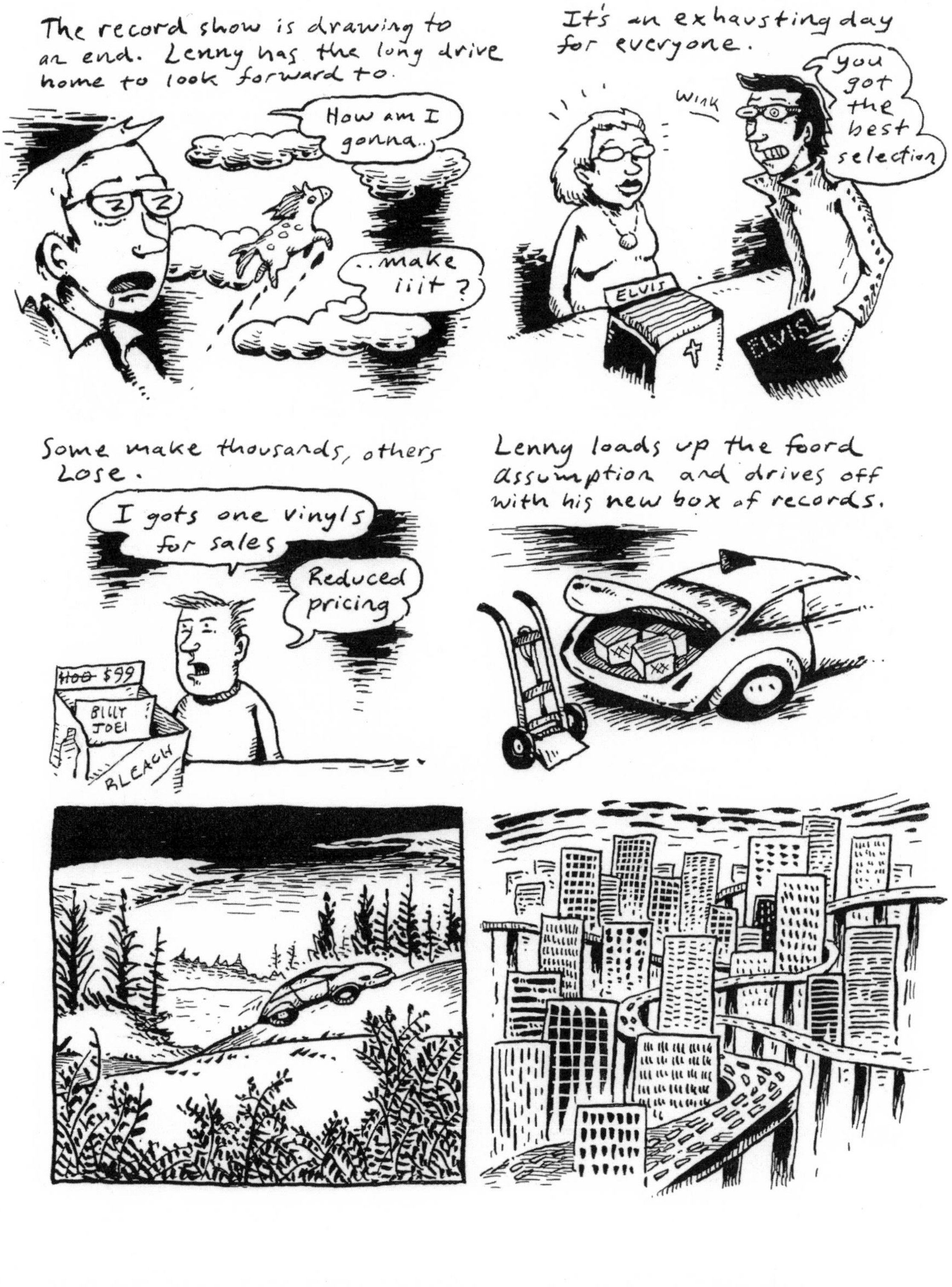
The record show is drawing to an end. Lenny has the long drive home to look forward to.
How am I gonna..
..make iiit?
It's an exhausting day for everyone.
WINK
you got the best selection
ELVIS
ELVIS
Some make thousands, others Lose.
I gots one vinyls for sales
Reduced pricing
$100 $99
BILLY JOEL
BLEACH
Lenny loads up the foord Assumption and drives off with his new box of records.

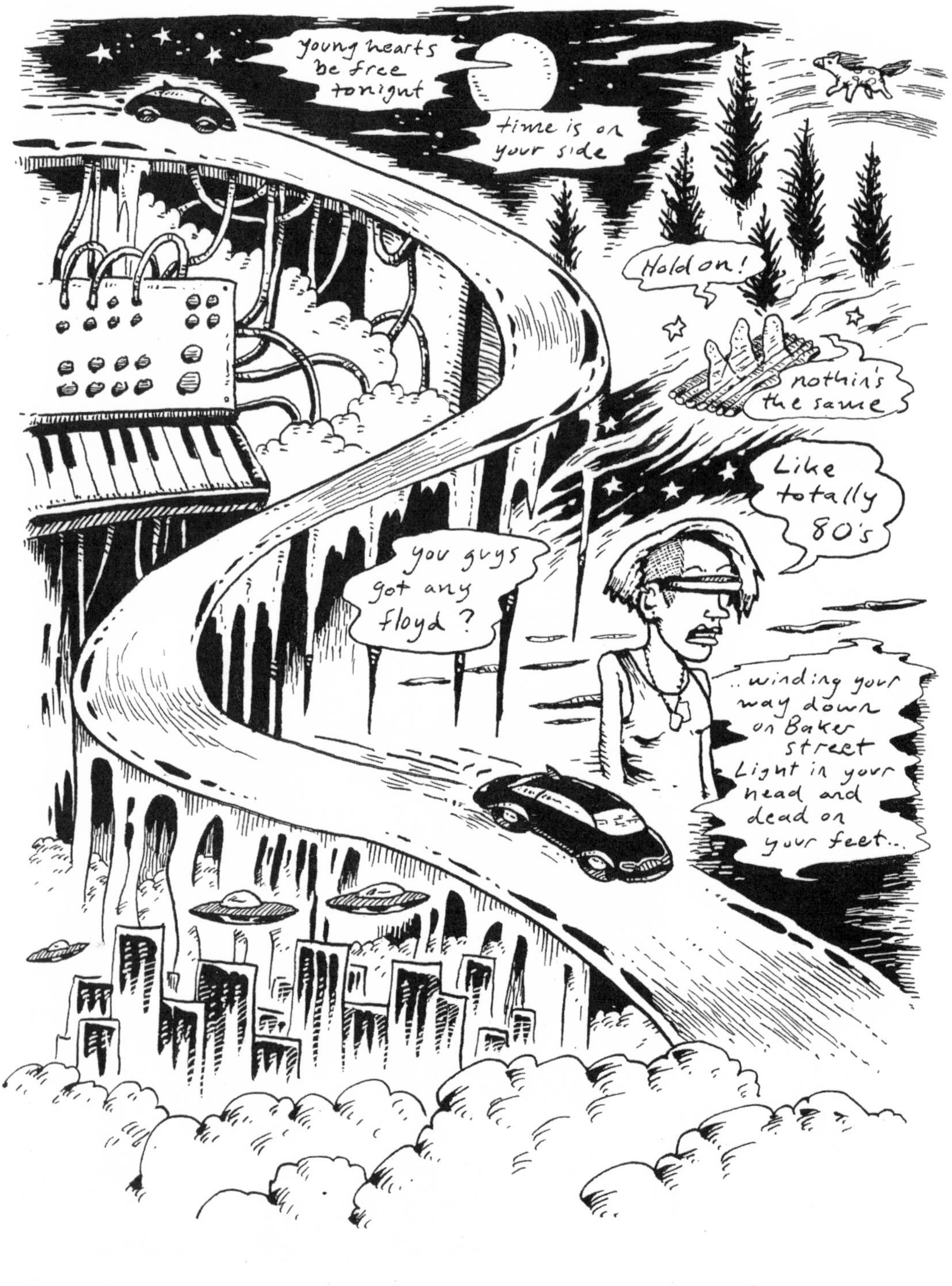
young hearts be free tonight
time is on your side
Hold on!
nothin's the same
Like totally 80's
you guys got any floyd?
..winding your way down on Baker street Light in your head and dead on your feet..

Record Breaking Day

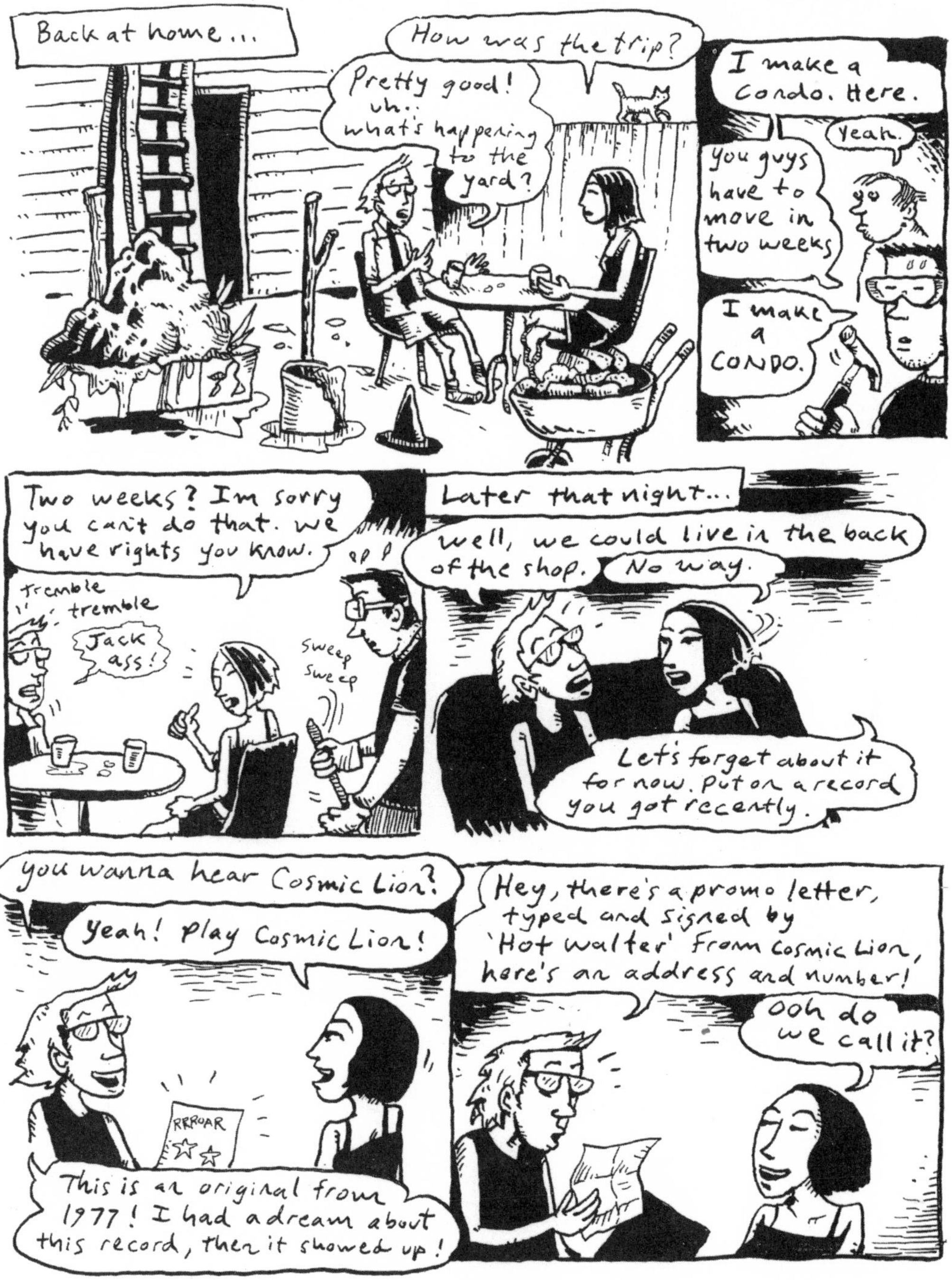

Back at home...
How was the trip?
Pretty good! uh.. what's happening to the yard?
I make a condo. Here.
Yeah.
You guys have to move in two weeks
I make a CONDO.
Two weeks? I'm sorry you can't do that. we have rights you know.
tremble tremble
Jack ass!
sweep sweep
Later that night...
Well, we could live in the back of the shop.
No way.
Let's forget about it for now. Put on a record you got recently.
You wanna hear Cosmic Lion?
Yeah! Play Cosmic Lion!
RRROAR
This is an original from 1977! I had a dream about this record, then it showed up!
Hey, there's a promo letter, typed and signed by 'Hot Walter' from Cosmic Lion, here's an address and number!
Ooh do we call it?

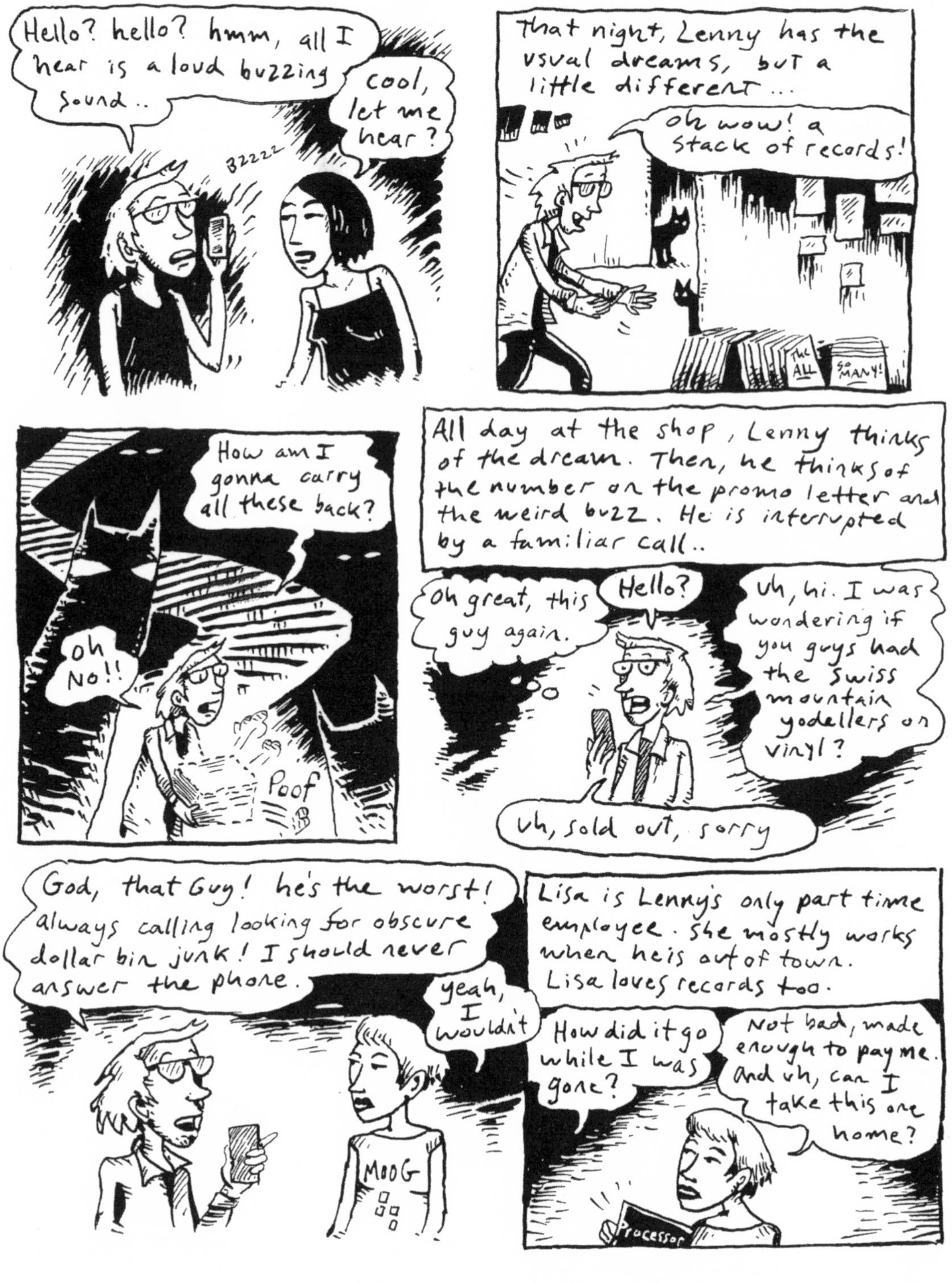
Hello? hello? hmm, all I hear is a loud buzzing sound..
cool, let me hear?
BZZZZ
That night, Lenny has the usual dreams, but a little different...
oh wow! a stack of records!
THE ALL
SO MANY!
How am I gonna carry all these back?
oh No!!
Poof
All day at the shop, Lenny thinks of the dream. Then, he thinks of the number on the promo letter and the weird buzz. He is interrupted by a familiar call..
Oh great, this guy again.
Hello?
uh, hi. I was wondering if you guys had the Swiss mountain yodellers on vinyl?
uh, sold out, sorry
God, that Guy! he's the worst! always calling looking for obscure dollar bin junk! I should never answer the phone.
yeah, I wouldn't
MOOG
Lisa is Lenny's only part time employee. She mostly works when he is out of town. Lisa loves records too.
How did it go while I was gone?
Not bad, made enough to pay me. And uh, can I take this one home?
Processor

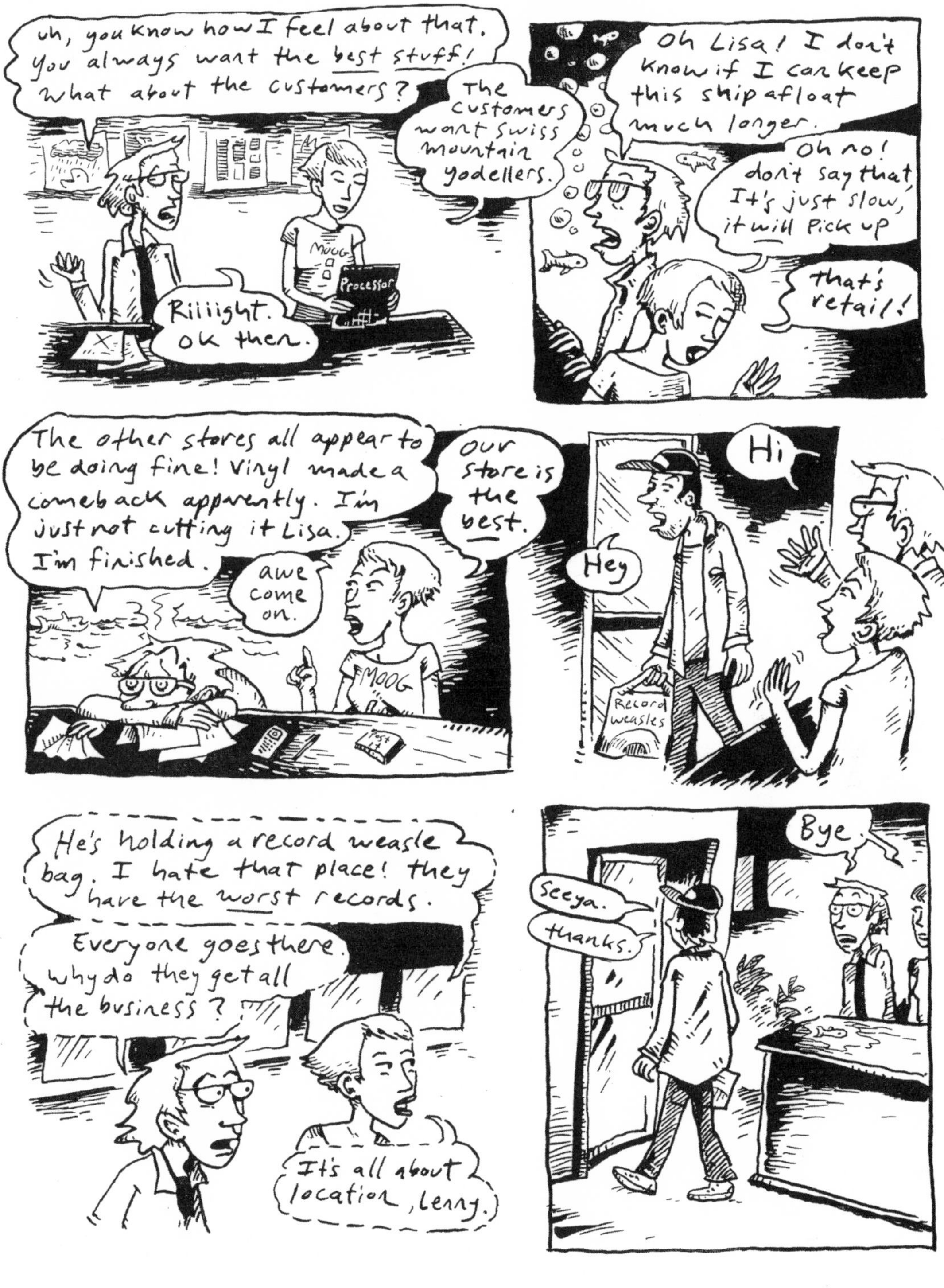
uh, you know how I feel about that. You always want the best stuff! what about the customers?
The customers want swiss mountain yodellers.
Riliight. ok then.
Moog
Processor
Oh Lisa! I don't know if I can keep this ship afloat much longer.
Oh no! don't say that, It's just slow, it will pick up
that's retail!
The other stores all appear to be doing fine! Vinyl made a comeback apparently. I'm just not cutting it Lisa. I'm finished.
our store is the best.
awe come on.
MOOG
Post it
Hi
Hey
Record weasles
He's holding a record weasle bag. I hate that place! they have the worst records.
Everyone goes there. why do they get all the business?
It's all about location, Lenny.
Bye.
Seeya.
thanks.

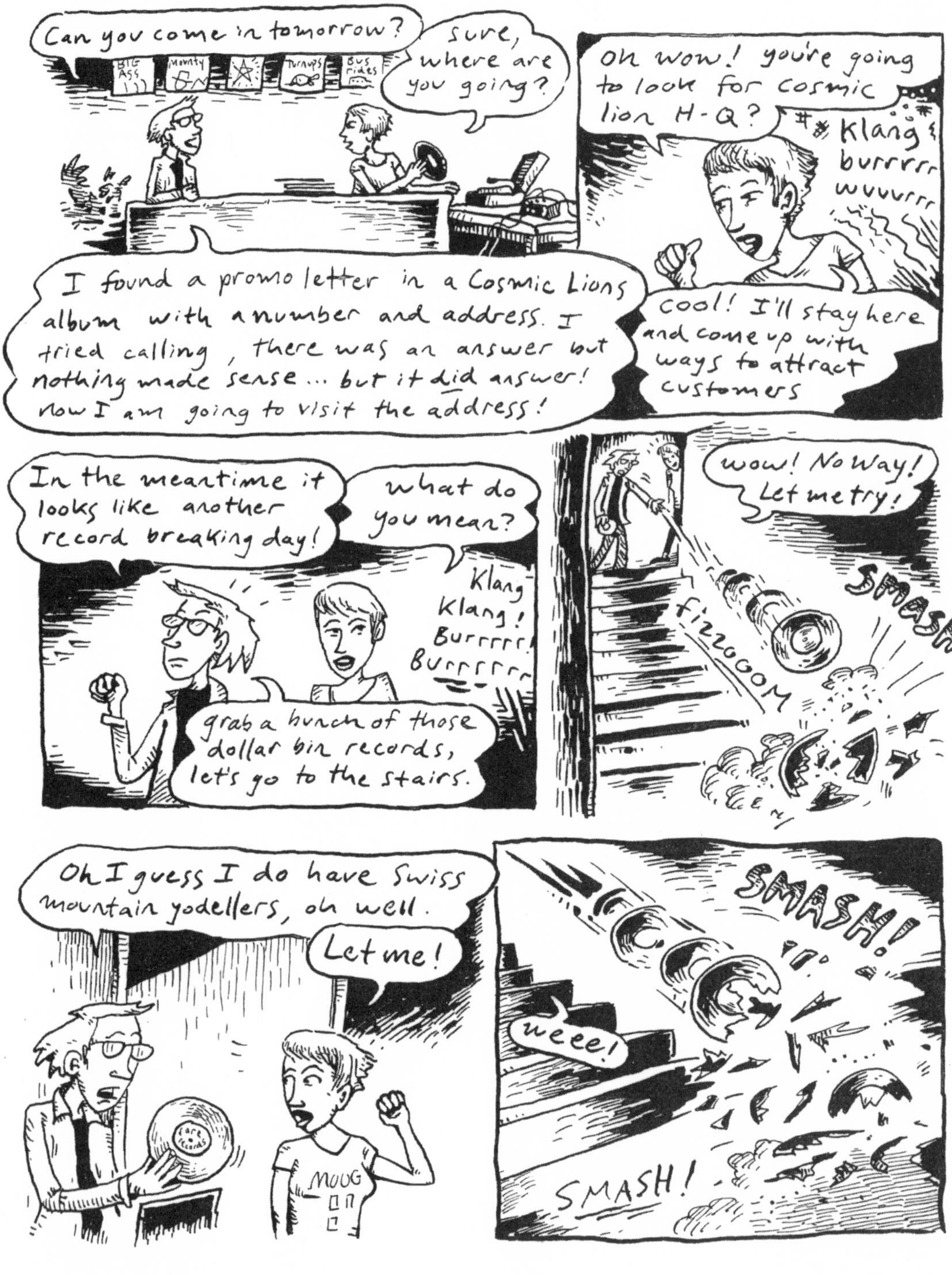
Can you come in tomorrow?
BIG ASS
Mounty
Turnups
Bus rides!
Sure, where are you going?
Oh wow! you're going to look for Cosmic lion H-Q?
Klang burrrrr wvuuurrr
I found a promo letter in a Cosmic Lions album with a number and address. I tried calling, there was an answer but nothing made sense... but it did answer! now I am going to visit the address!
cool! I'll stay here and come up with ways to attract customers
In the meantime it looks like another record breaking day!
what do you mean?
Klang Klang! Burrrrr! Burrrrrr
grab a bunch of those dollar bin records, let's go to the stairs.
wow! No Way! Let me try!
SMASH
fizzooom
Oh I guess I do have Swiss mountain yodellers, oh well.
Let me!
MOOG
SMASH!
weee!
SMASH!

Towards Oblivion

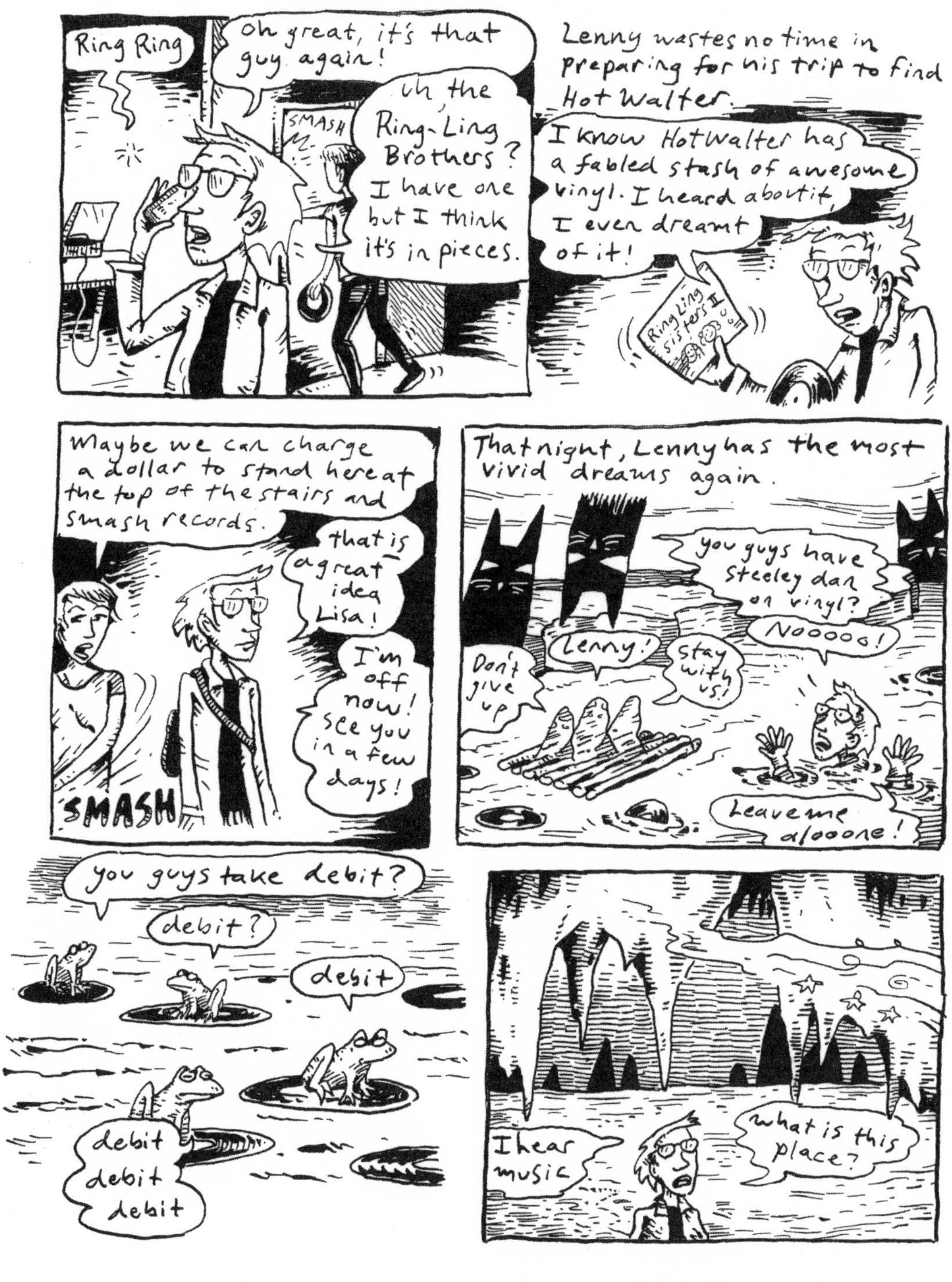
Ring Ring
Oh great, it's that guy again!
uh, the Ring-Ling Brothers? I have one but I think it's in pieces.
SMASH
Lenny wastes no time in preparing for his trip to find Hot Walter.
I know Hot Walter has a fabled stash of awesome vinyl. I heard about it, I even dreamt of it!
Ring Ling Sisters II
Maybe we can charge a dollar to stand here at the top of the stairs and smash records.
that is a great idea Lisa!
I'm off now! See you in a few days!
SMASH
That night, Lenny has the most vivid dreams again.
you guys have Steeley dan on vinyl?
Noooo!
Lenny!
Stay with us!
Don't give up
Leave me aloooone!
you guys take debit?
debit?
debit
debit debit debit
I hear music
what is this place?

No one has seen or heard from Hot Walter in decades. Not many know about him or cared for the cosmic Lions, but those who do also know the tragic story behind his valuable record collection.

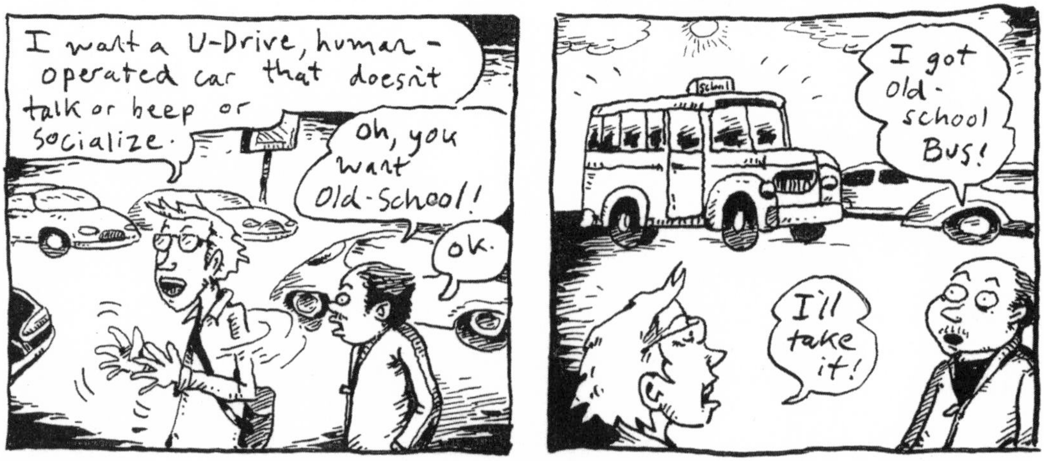
I want a U-Drive, human-operated car that doesn't talk or beep or socialize.
Oh, you want Old-School!
OK.
School
I got Old-school Bus!
I'll take it!

The fabled collection is apparently lost to Walter himself. Legend has it a jealous lover hid them away, not long before running off with another lover, never to be heard from again. The only clue is that a mover was hired to move the heavy crates. No one knows who that was either.

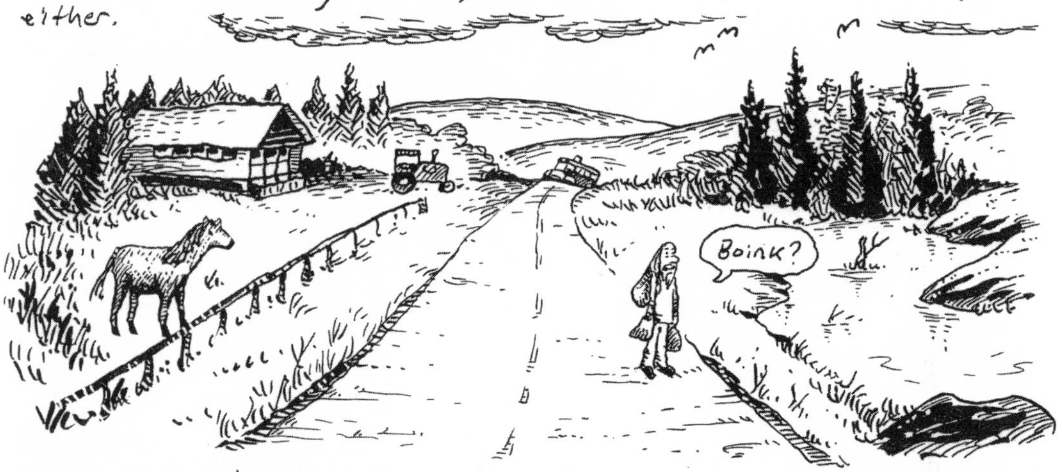
Boink?

Those who tried to locate the records in the past have all gone crazy and ended up losing everything. Some were driven to madness.

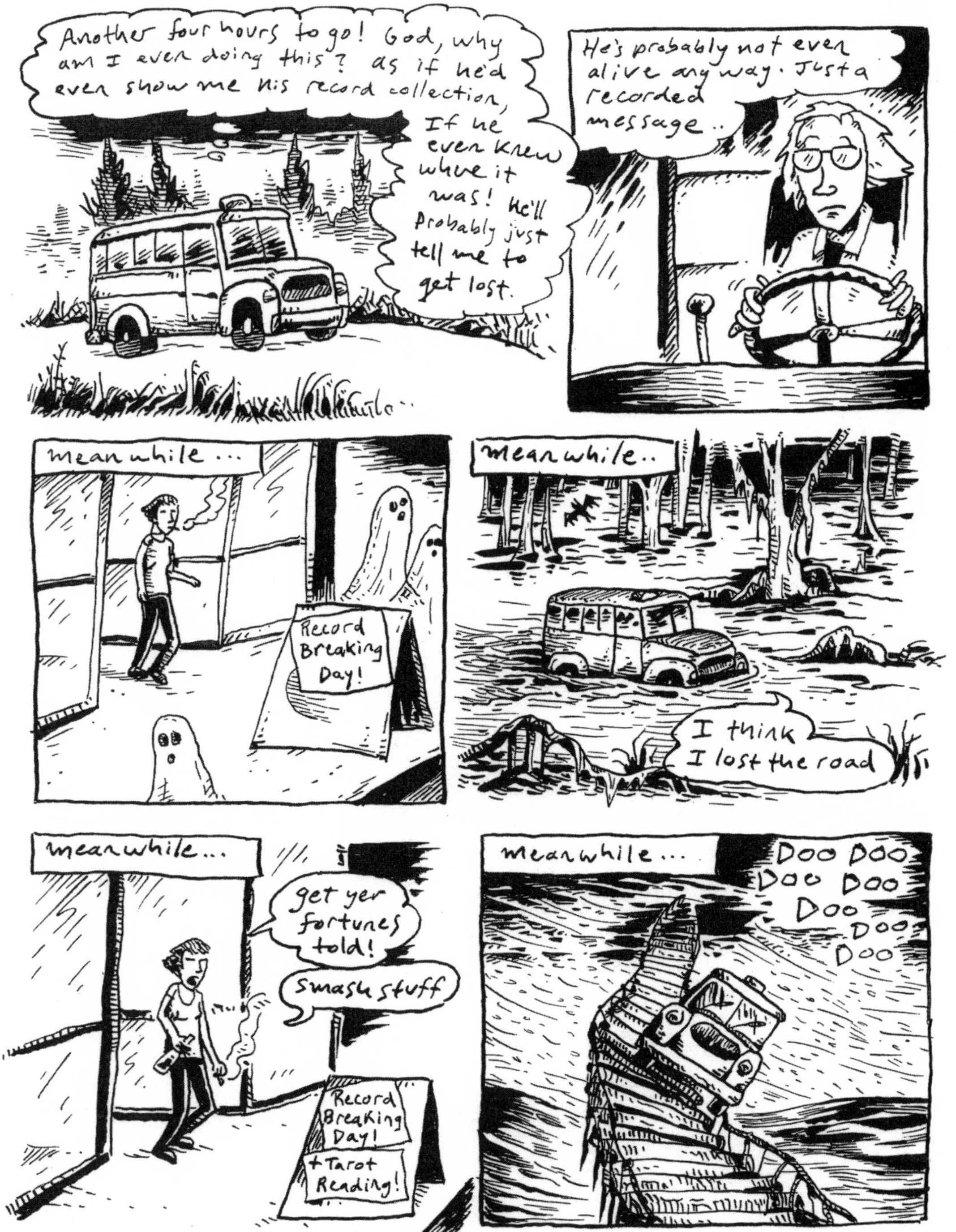
Another four hours to go! God, why am I ever doing this? as if he'd even show me his record collection,
If he ever knew where it was! He'll probably just tell me to get lost.
He's probably not even alive anyway. Just a recorded message..
meanwhile...
Record Breaking Day!
meanwhile..
I think I lost the road
meanwhile...
get yer fortunes told!
smash stuff
Record Breaking Day!
+ Tarot Reading!
meanwhile...
DOO DOO DOO DOO DOO DOO DOO

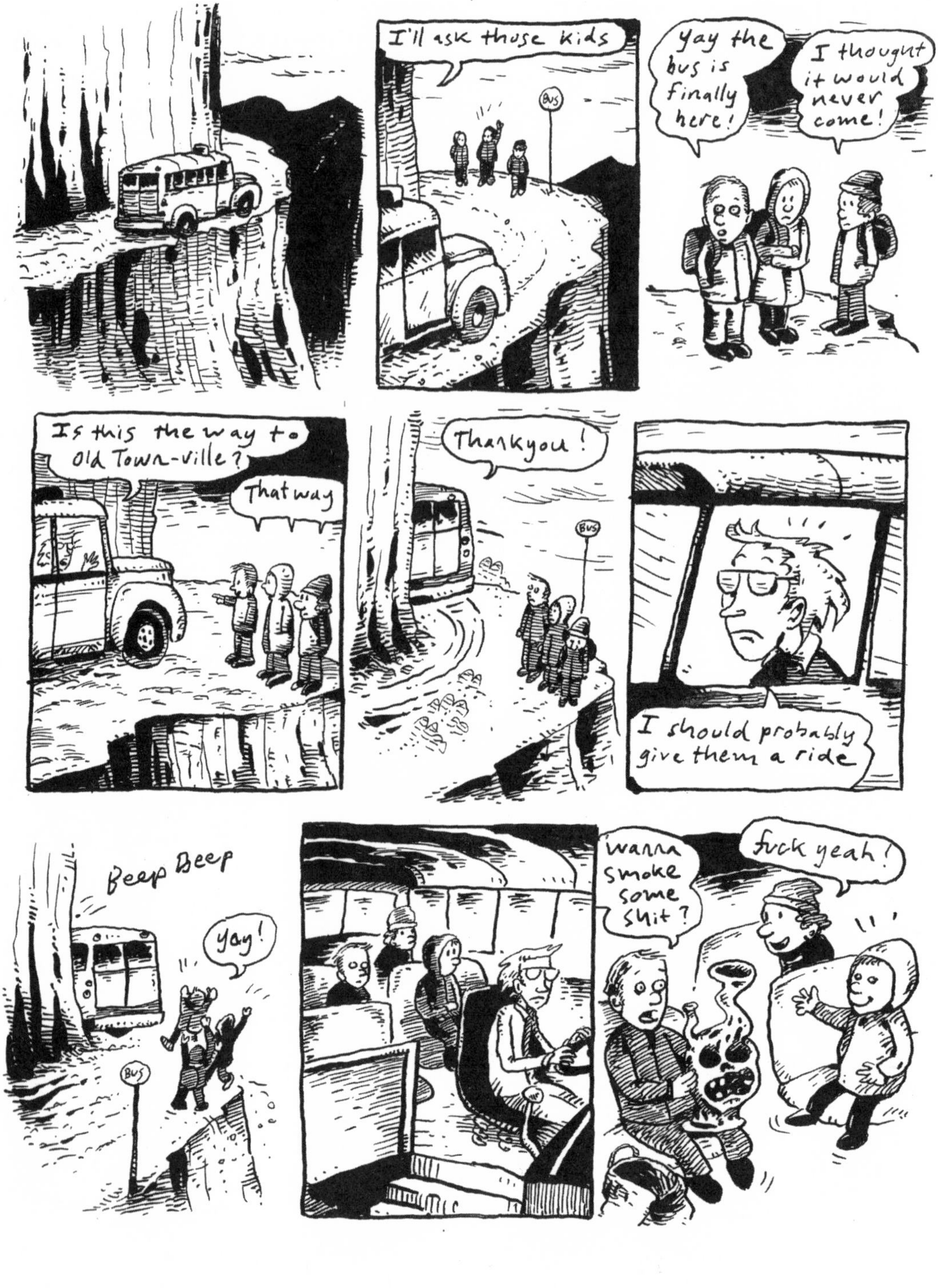
I'll ask those kids
Yay the bus is finally here!
I thought it would never come!
Is this the way to Old Town-ville?
That way
Thankyou!
I should probably give them a ride
Beep Beep
Yay!
Wanna smoke some shit?
fuck yeah!

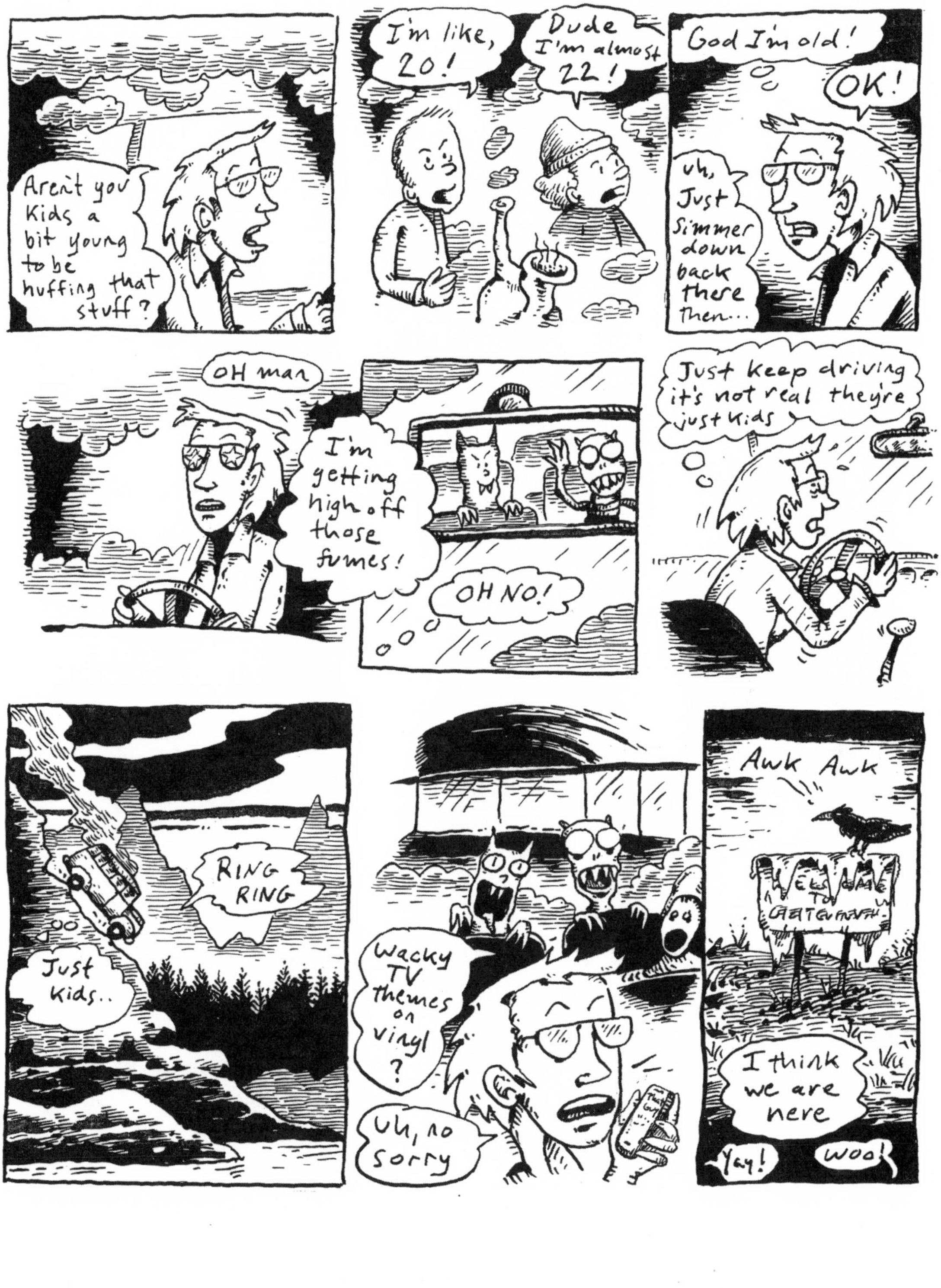

Aren't you kids a bit young to be huffing that stuff?
I'm like, 20!
Dude I'm almost 22!
God I'm old!
OK!
uh, Just simmer down back there then...
OH man
I'm getting high off those fumes!
OH NO!
Just keep driving it's not real they're just kids
RING RING
Just kids..
Wacky TV themes on vinyl?
Uh, no sorry
Awk Awk
I think we are here
Yay!
woo!

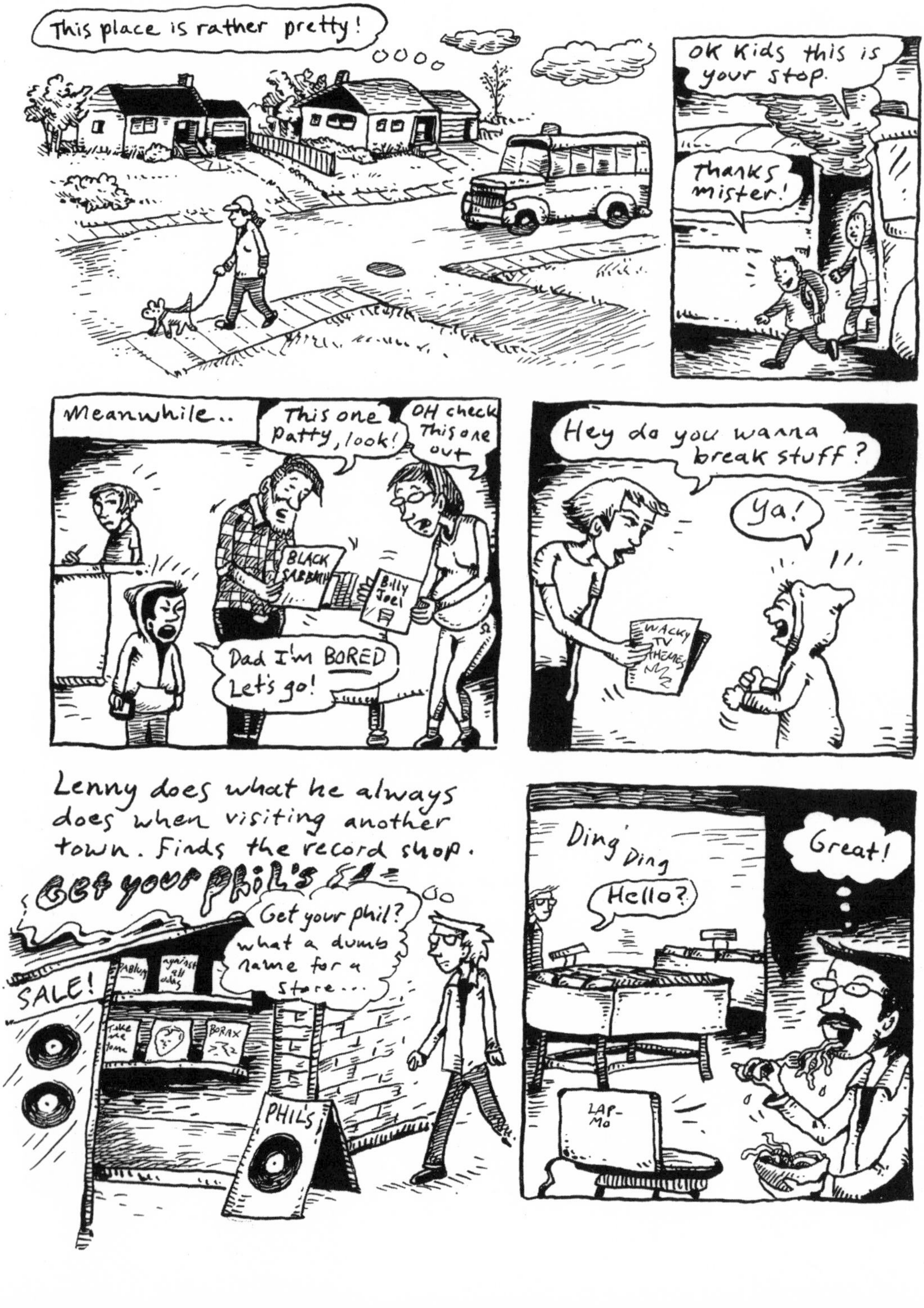
This place is rather pretty!
OK Kids this is your stop.
Thanks mister!
Meanwhile..
This one patty, look!
OH check this one out
BLACK SABBATH
Billy Joel
Dad I'm BORED Let's go!
Hey do you wanna break stuff?
Ya!
WACKY TV THEMES
Lenny does what he always does when visiting another town. Finds the record shop.
Get your Phil's
Get your phil? what a dumb name for a store...
SALE!
BORAX
PHIL'S
Ding Ding
Hello?
Great!
LAP-MO

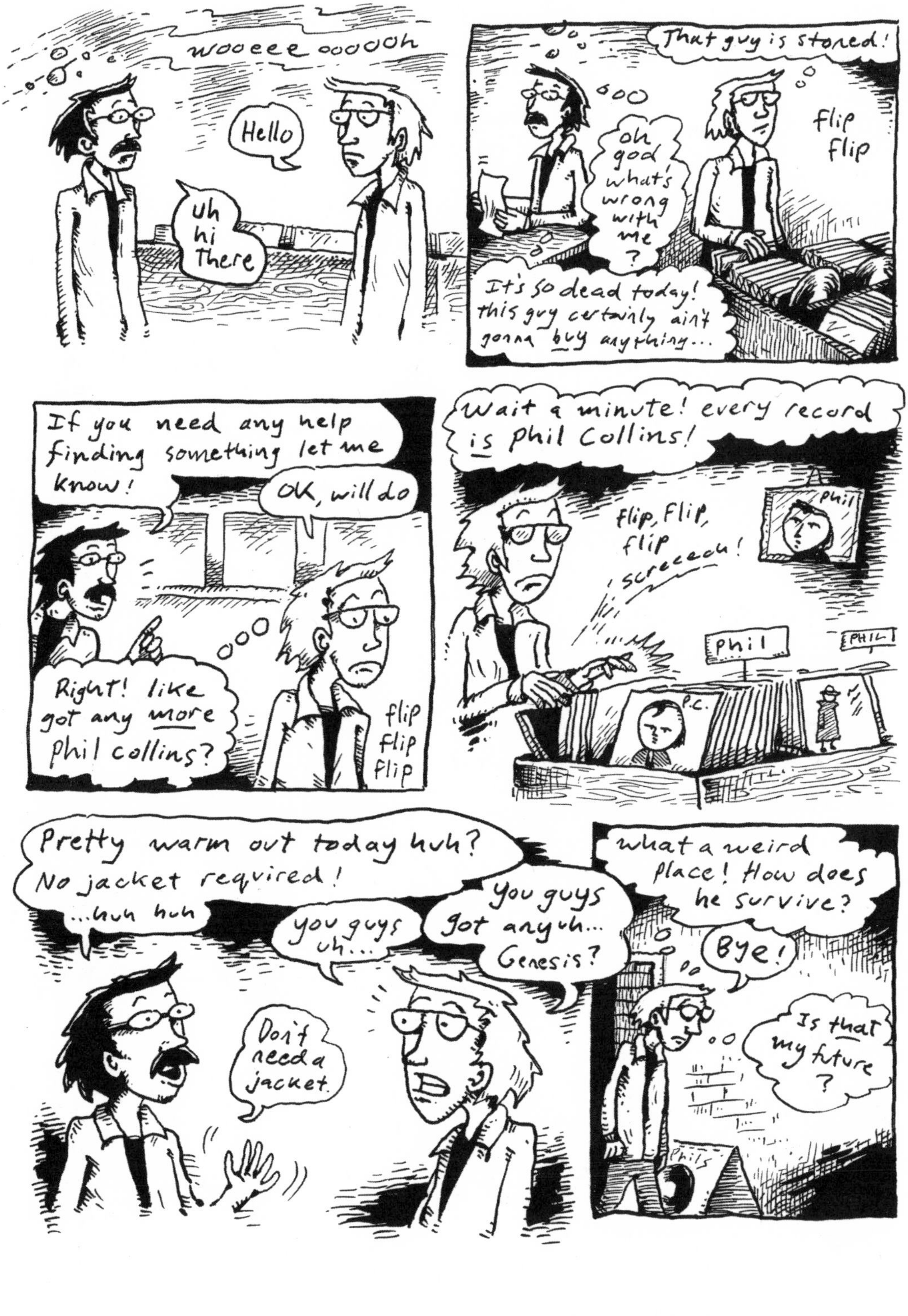

wooeee oooOOh
Hello
uh hi there
That guy is stoned!
ooo
oh god what's wrong with me?
flip flip
It's so dead today! this guy certainly ain't gonna buy anything...
If you need any help finding something let me know!
OK, will do
ooo
Right! like got any more phil collins?
flip flip flip
Wait a minute! every record is Phil Collins!
Phil
Flip, Flip, flip screeech!
Phil
PHIL
P.C.
Pretty warm out today huh? No jacket required! ...huh huh
you guys uh...
You guys got anyuh... Genesis?
Don't need a jacket.
what a weird place! How does he survive?
Bye!
Is that my future?
Phils

Hot Walter

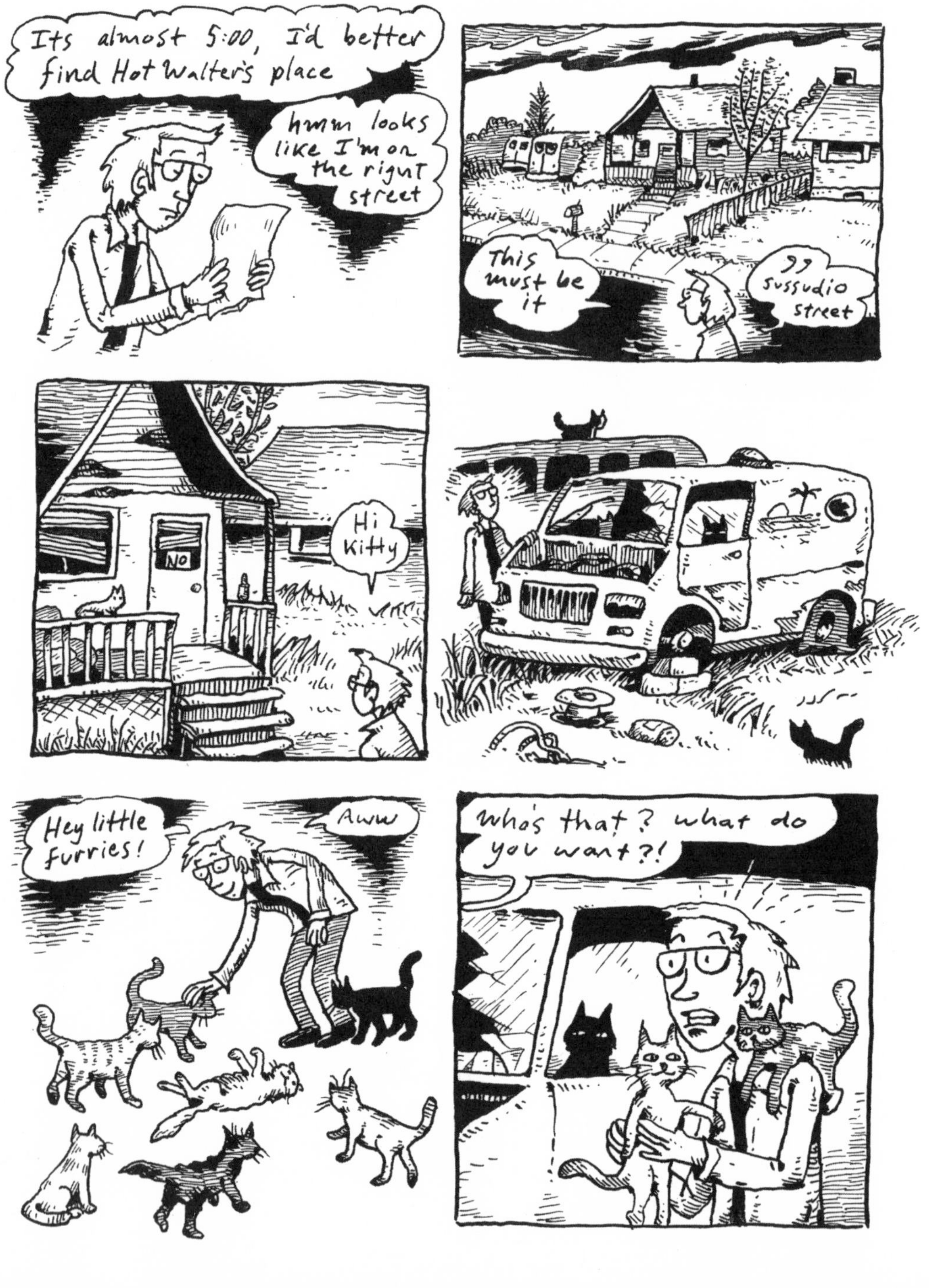
Its almost 5:00, I'd better find Hot Walter's place
hmm looks like I'm on the right street
This must be it
99 sussudio street
Hi Kitty
NO
Hey little furries!
Aww
Who's that? what do you want?!

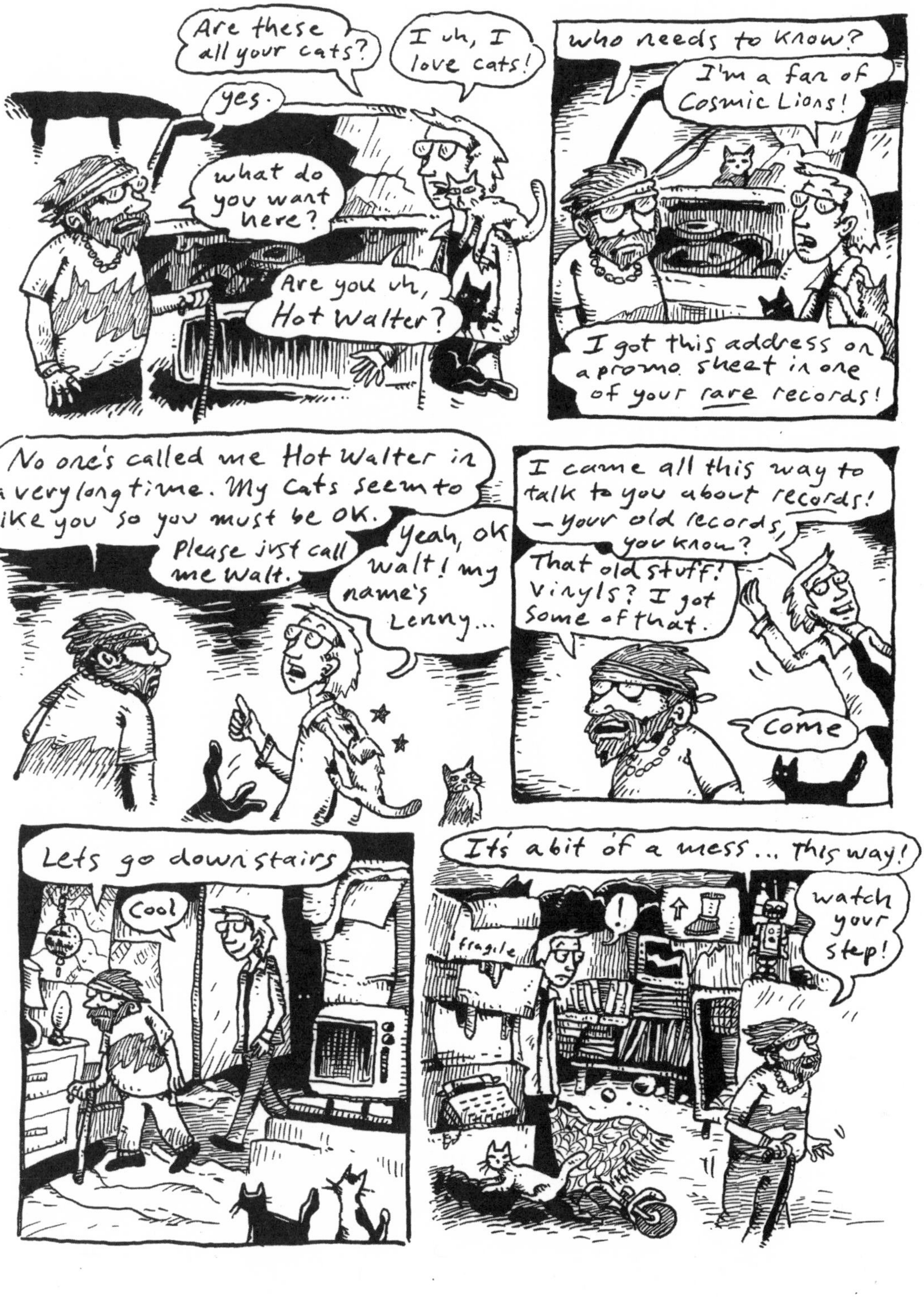

Are these all your cats?
I uh, I love cats!
yes.
what do you want here?
Are you uh, Hot Walter?
who needs to know?
I'm a fan of Cosmic Lions!
I got this address on a promo sheet in one of your rare records!
No one's called me Hot Walter in a very long time. My cats seem to like you so you must be OK.
Please just call me Walt.
Yeah, ok Walt! my name's Lenny...
I came all this way to talk to you about records! —your old records, you know?
That old stuff! Vinyls? I got some of that.
Come
Lets go downstairs
Cool
It's a bit of a mess... this way!
watch your step!
fragile

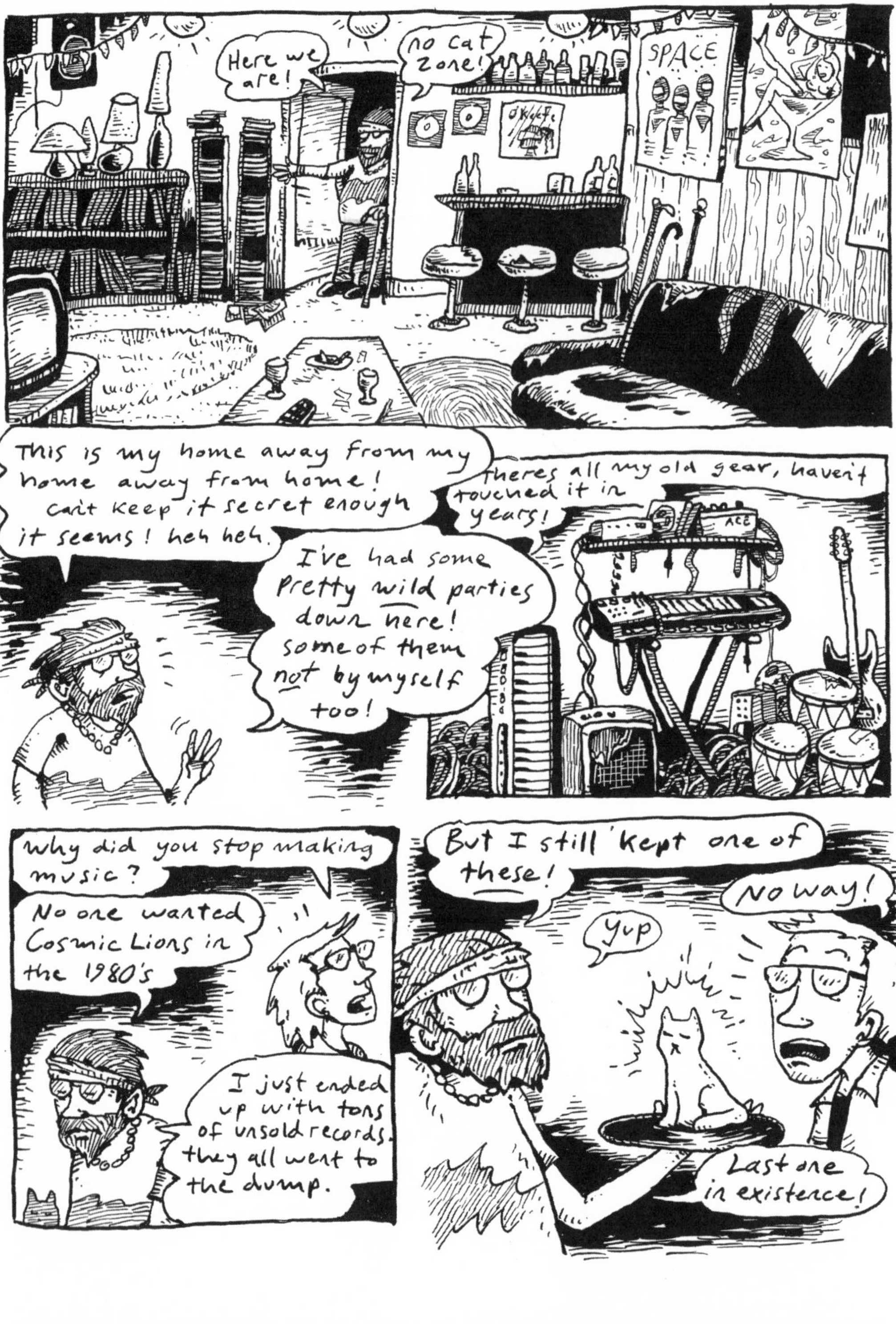

Here we are!
no cat zone!
SPACE
This is my home away from my home away from home! can't keep it secret enough it seems! heh heh.
I've had some Pretty wild parties down here! some of them not by myself too!
theres all my old gear, haven't touched it in years!
ACE
why did you stop making music?
No one wanted Cosmic Lions in the 1980's
I just ended up with tons of unsold records. they all went to the dump.
But I still kept one of these!
No way!
Yup
Last one in existence!

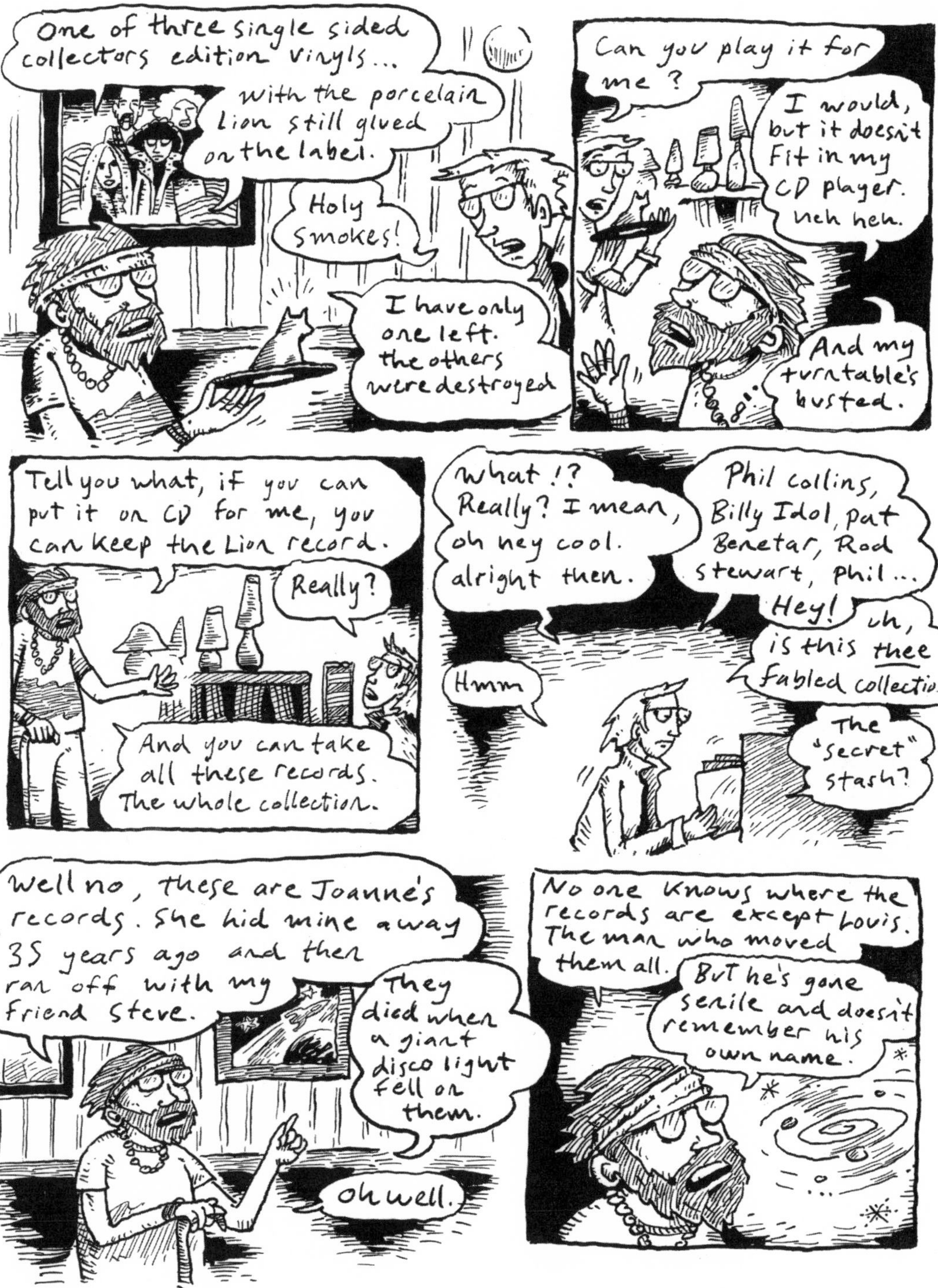
One of three single sided collectors edition vinyls...
with the porcelain Lion still glued on the label.
Holy Smokes!
I have only one left. the others were destroyed
Can you play it for me?
I would, but it doesn't Fit in my CD player. heh heh.
And my turntable's busted.
Tell you what, if you can put it on CD for me, you can keep the Lion record.
Really?
And you can take all these records. The whole collection.
What!? Really? I mean, oh hey cool. alright then.
Hmm
Phil collins, Billy Idol, pat Benetar, Rod stewart, phil...
Hey!
uh, is this thee fabled collection?
The "secret" stash?
Well no, these are Joanne's records. She hid mine away 35 years ago and then ran off with my friend Steve.
They died when a giant disco light fell on them.
oh well.
No one knows where the records are except Louis. The man who moved them all.
But he's gone senile and doesn't remember his own name.

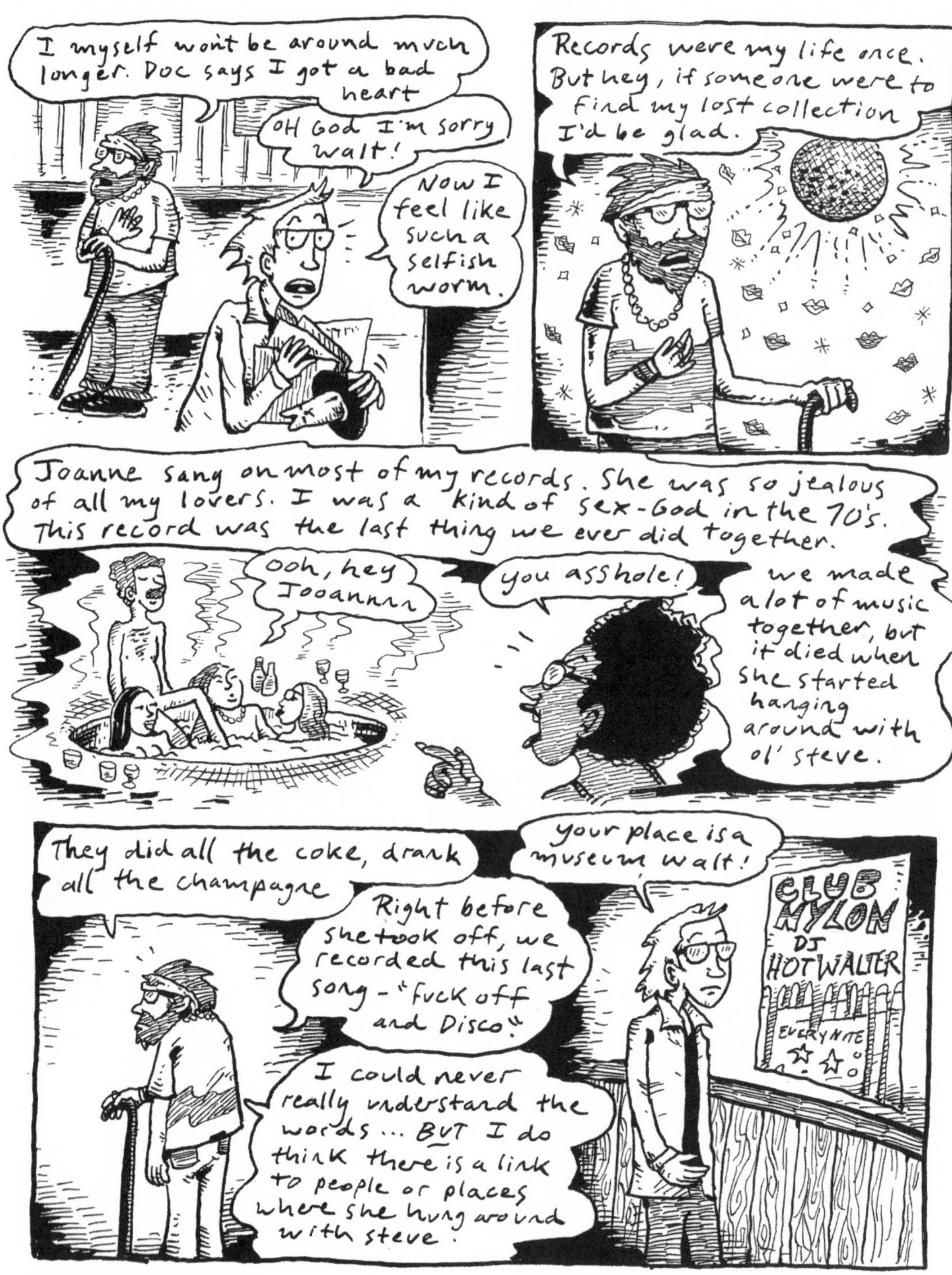

I myself won't be around much longer. Doc says I got a bad heart
OH God I'm sorry Walt!
Now I feel like such a selfish worm.
Records were my life once. But hey, if someone were to find my lost collection I'd be glad.
Joanne sang on most of my records. She was so jealous of all my lovers. I was a kind of sex-God in the 70's. This record was the last thing we ever did together.
Ooh, hey Jooannnn
you asshole!
we made a lot of music together, but it died when she started hanging around with ol' steve.
They did all the coke, drank all the champagne
Right before she took off, we recorded this last song - "fuck off and Disco"
I could never really understand the words... BUT I do think there is a link to people or places where she hung around with steve.
your place is a museum walt!
CLUB NYLON
DJ HOTWALTER
EVERY NITE

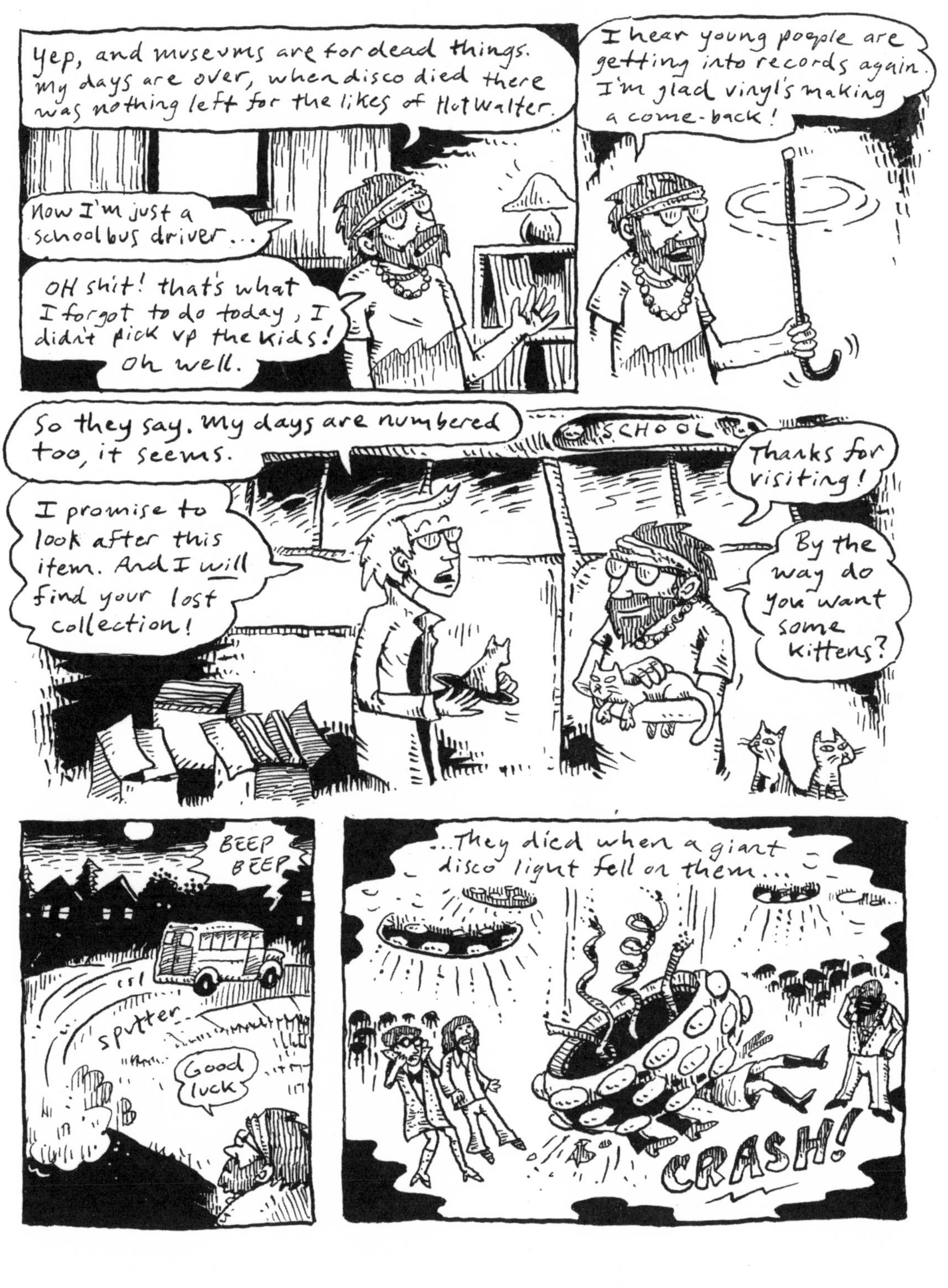
Yep, and museums are for dead things. My days are over, when disco died there was nothing left for the likes of Hot Walter.
Now I'm just a schoolbus driver...
OH shit! that's what I forgot to do today, I didn't pick up the kids! Oh well.
I hear young people are getting into records again. I'm glad vinyl's making a come-back!
So they say. My days are numbered too, it seems.
SCHOOL
Thanks for visiting!
I promise to look after this item. And I will find your lost collection!
By the way do you want some kittens?
BEEP BEEP
sputter
Good luck
...They died when a giant disco light fell on them...
CRASH!

Ghost Factory

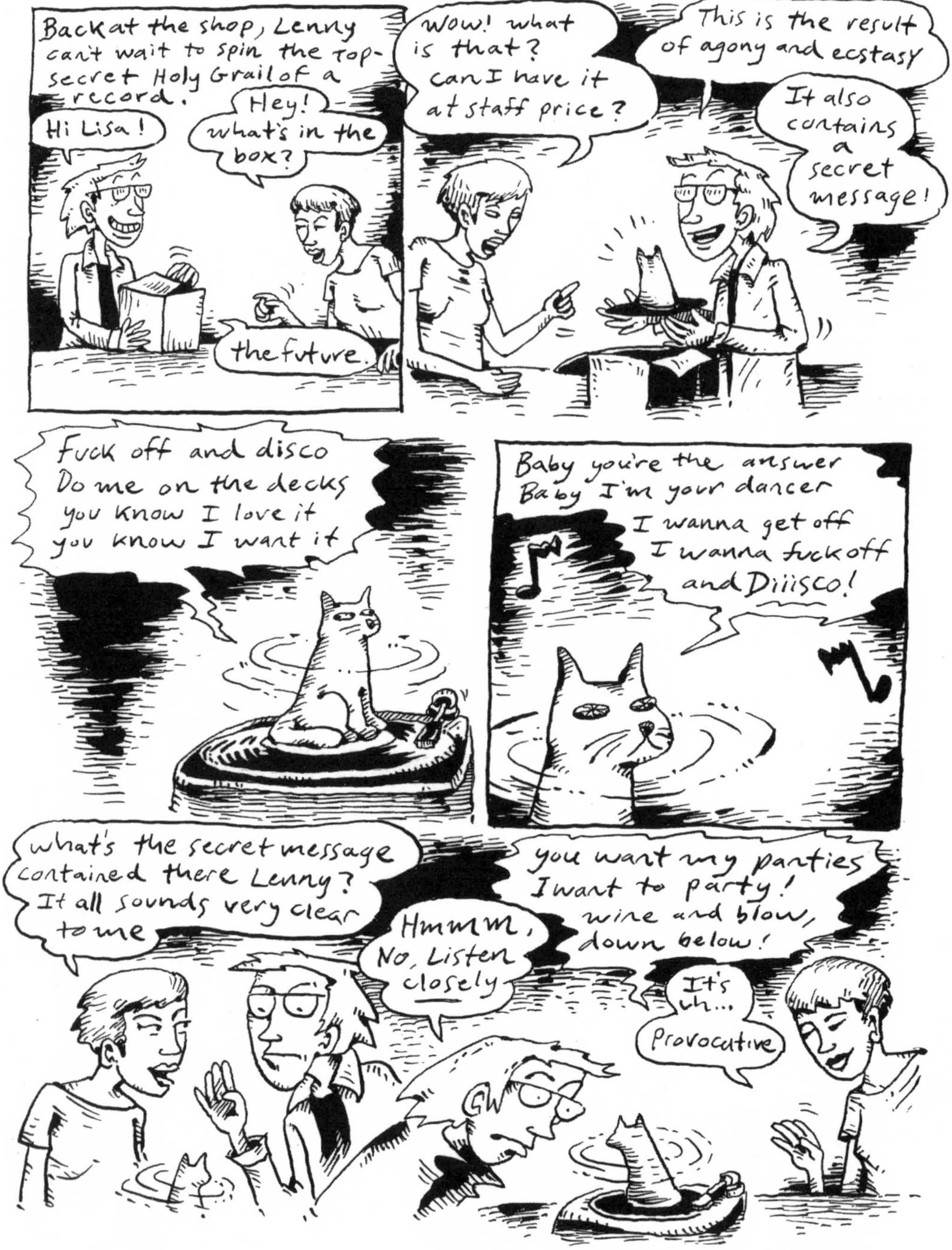
Back at the shop, Lenny can't wait to spin the top-secret Holy Grail of a record.
Hi Lisa!
Hey! what's in the box?
the future.
Wow! what is that? can I have it at staff price?
This is the result of agony and ecstasy
It also contains a secret message!
Fuck off and disco
Do me on the decks
you know I love it
you know I want it
Baby you're the answer
Baby I'm your dancer
I wanna get off
I wanna fuck off
and Diiisco!
what's the secret message contained there Lenny? It all sounds very clear to me
Hmmm, No, Listen closely
you want my parties
I want to party!
wine and blow,
down below!
It's uh... Provocative
GW

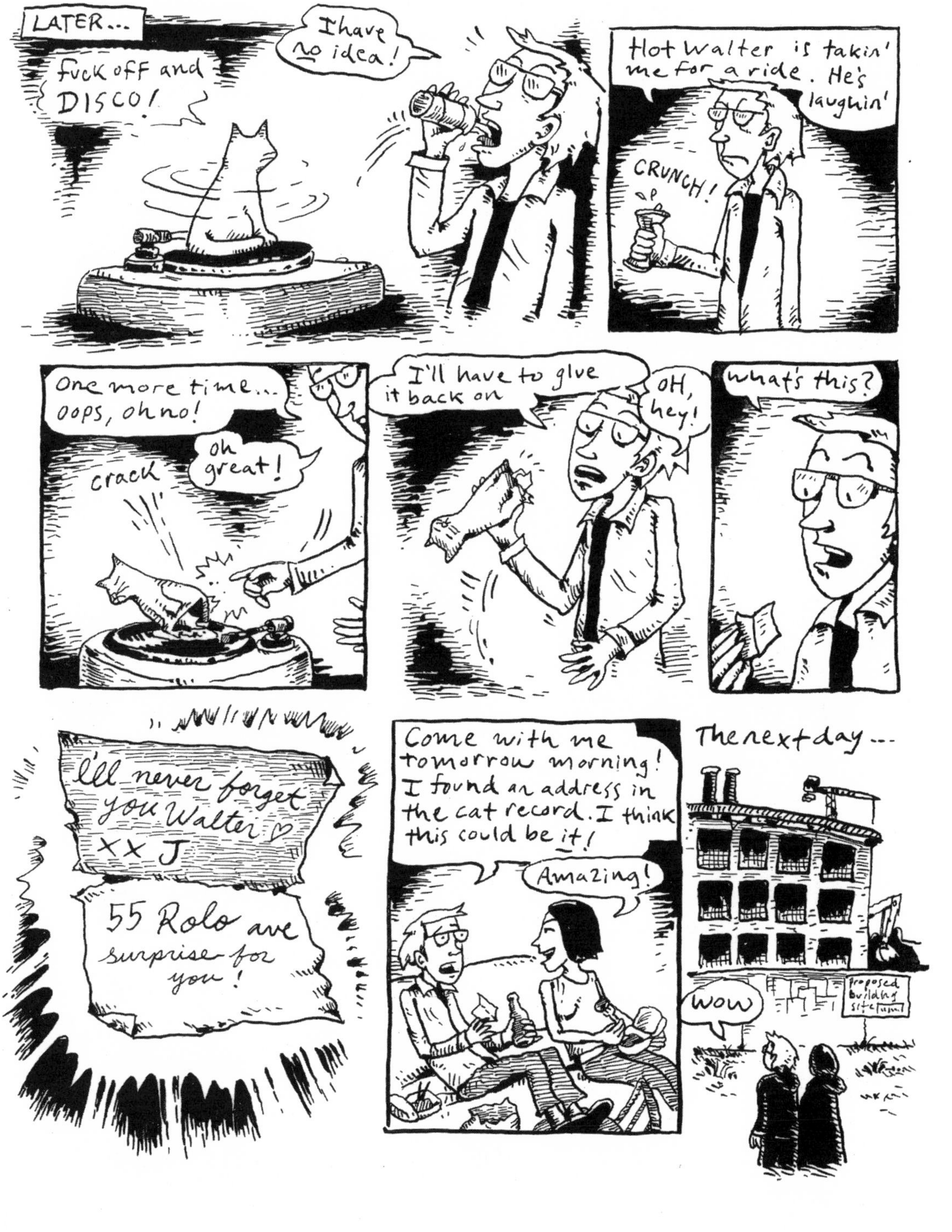
LATER...
fuck off and DISCO!
I have no idea!
Hot Walter is takin' me for a ride. He's laughin'
CRUNCH!
One more time... oops, oh no!
oh great!
crack
I'll have to glue it back on
OH, hey!
what's this?
I'll never forget you Walter ♡ xx J
55 Rolo ave surprise for you!
Come with me tomorrow morning! I found an address in the cat record. I think this could be it!
Amazing!
The next day...
proposed building site
WOW

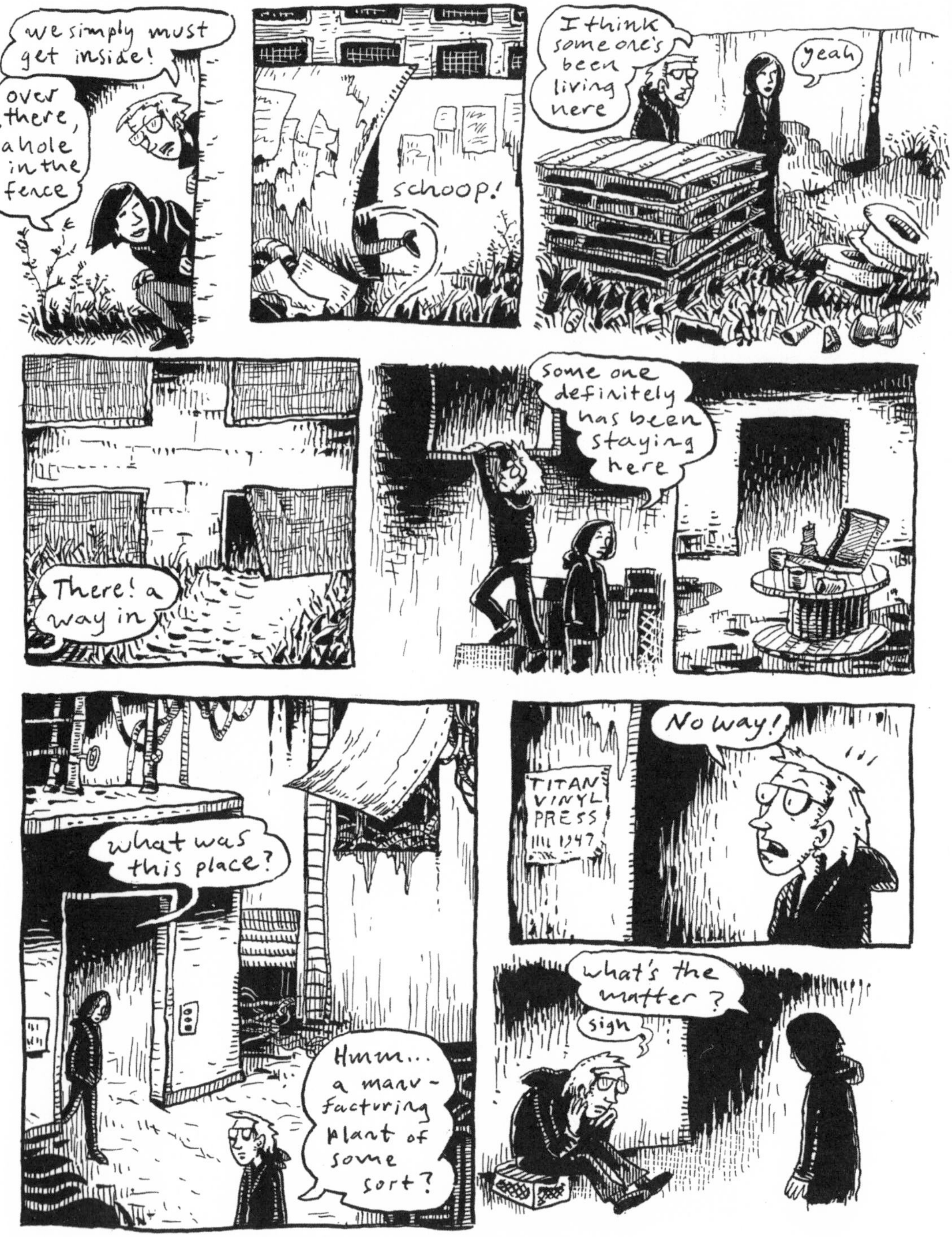
we simply must get inside!
over there, a hole in the fence
schoop!
I think someone's been living here
yeah
There! a way in
Some one definitely has been staying here
what was this place?
Hmm... a manufacturing plant of some sort?
TITAN VINYL PRESS 1947
No way!
what's the matter?
sigh

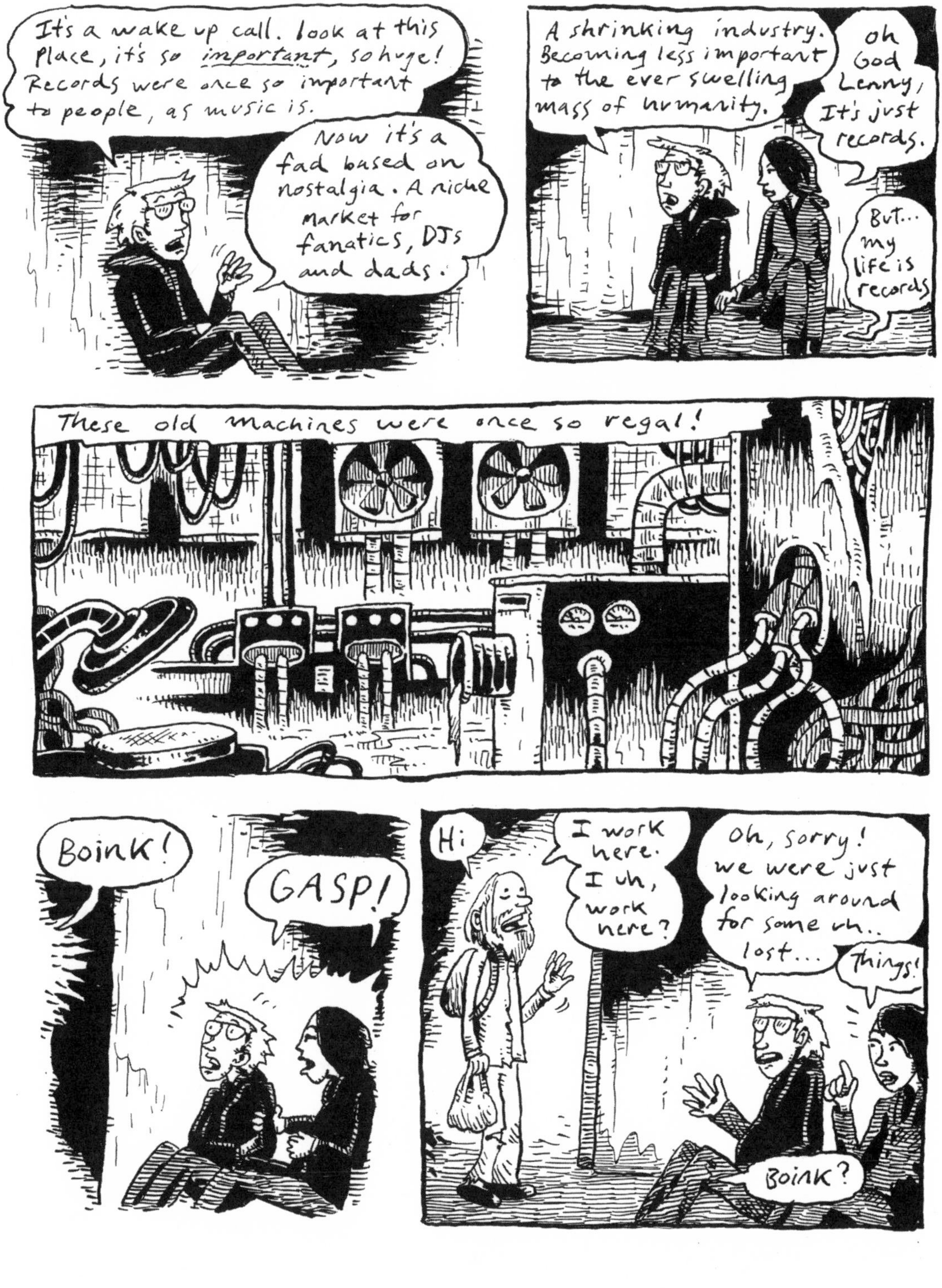
It's a wake up call. look at this Place, it's so important, so huge! Records were once so important to people, as music is.
Now it's a fad based on nostalgia. A niche market for fanatics, DJs and dads.
A shrinking industry. Becoming less important to the ever swelling mass of humanity.
oh God Lenny, It's just records.
But... my life is records
These old machines were once so regal!
Boink!
GASP!
Hi
I work here. I uh, work here?
Oh, sorry! we were just looking around for some uh.. lost...
Things!
Boink?

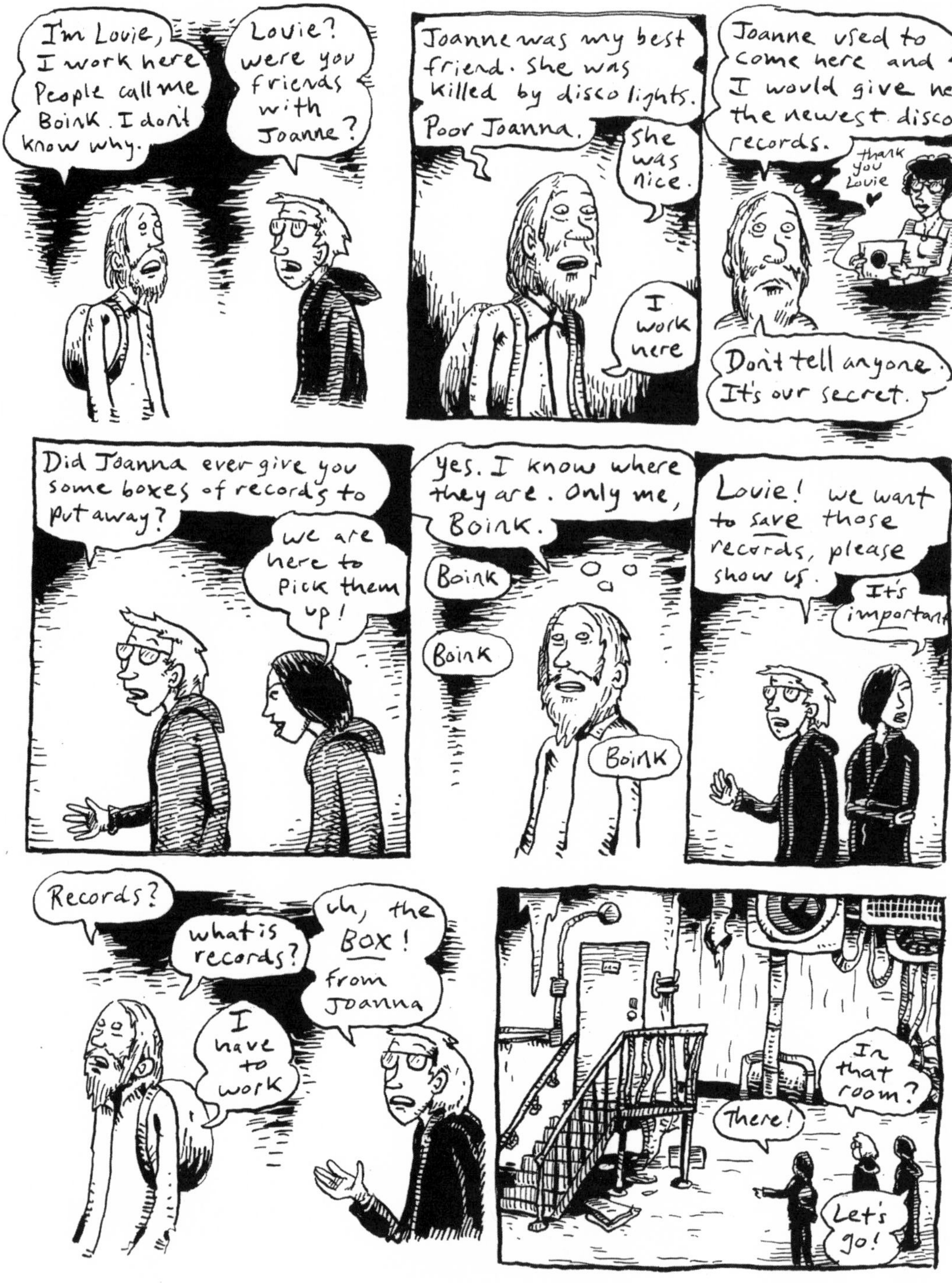
I'm Louie, I work here People call me Boink. I don't know why.
Louie? were you friends with Joanne?
Joanne was my best friend. She was killed by disco lights. Poor Joanna.
She was nice.
I work here
Joanne used to come here and I would give her the newest disco records.
thank you Louie
Don't tell anyone. It's our secret.
Did Joanna ever give you some boxes of records to put away?
we are here to pick them up!
yes. I know where they are. Only me, Boink.
Boink
Boink
Boink
Louie! we want to save those records, please show us.
It's important
Records?
what is records?
uh, the BOX! from Joanna
I have to work
There!
In that room?
Let's go!

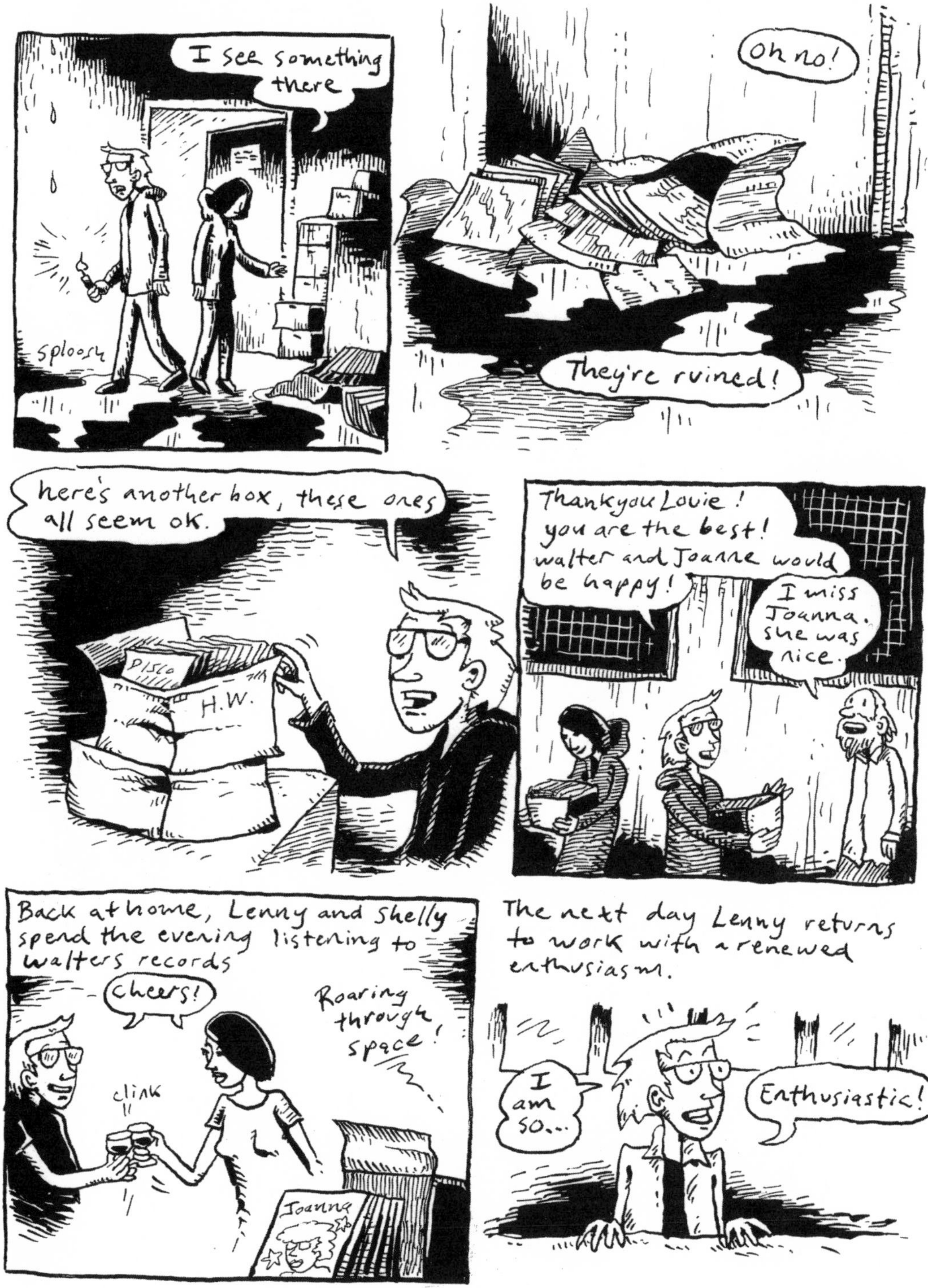
I see something there
sploosh
Oh no!
They're ruined!
here's another box, these ones all seem ok.
DISCO
H.W.
Thankyou Louie! you are the best! walter and Joanne would be happy!
I miss Joanna. she was nice.
Back at home, Lenny and Shelly spend the evening listening to walters records
Cheers!
Roaring through space!
clink
Joanna
The next day Lenny returns to work with a renewed enthusiasm.
I am so...
Enthusiastic!

The reissue

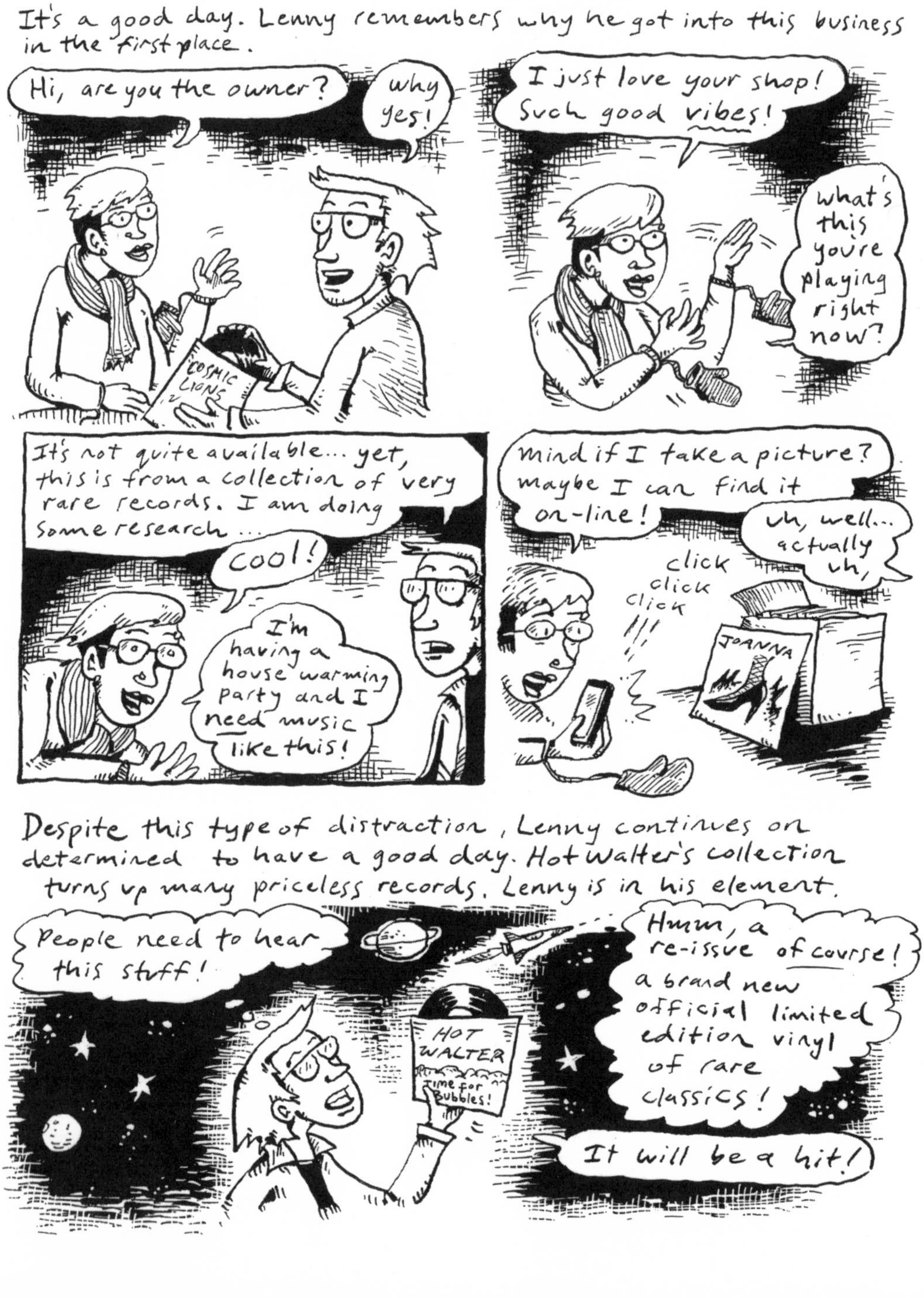
It's a good day. Lenny remembers why he got into this business in the first place.
Hi, are you the owner?
why yes!
COSMIC LIONS
I just love your shop! Such good vibes!
what's this you're playing right now?
It's not quite available... yet, this is from a collection of very rare records. I am doing some research...
cool!
I'm having a house warming party and I need music like this!
Mind if I take a picture? maybe I can find it on-line!
uh, well... actually uh,
click click click
JOANNA
Despite this type of distraction, Lenny continues on determined to have a good day. Hot Walter's collection turns up many priceless records. Lenny is in his element.
People need to hear this stuff!
HOT WALTER
Time for Bubbles!
Hmm, a re-issue of course!
a brand new official limited edition vinyl of rare classics!
It will be a hit!

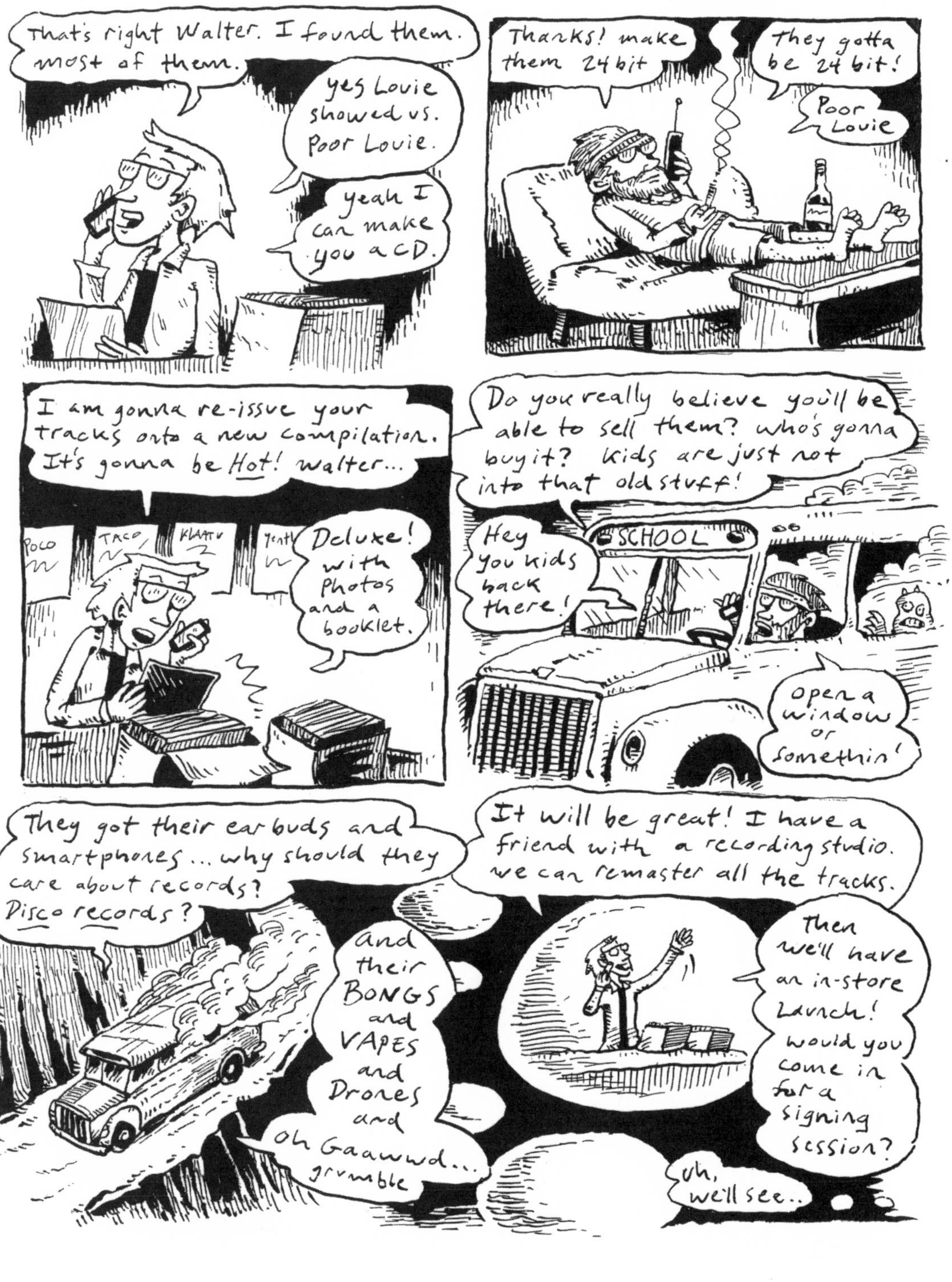
That's right Walter. I found them. Most of them.
Yes Louie showed us. Poor Louie.
Yeah I can make you a CD.
Thanks! Make them 24 bit
They gotta be 24 bit!
Poor Louie
I am gonna re-issue your tracks onto a new compilation. It's gonna be Hot! Walter...
POCO
TACO
KLAATU
Deluxe! with Photos and a booklet.
Do you really believe you'll be able to sell them? Who's gonna buy it? Kids are just not into that old stuff!
SCHOOL
Hey you kids back there!
Open a window or somethin'
They got their ear buds and smartphones... why should they care about records? Disco records?
And their BONGS and VAPES and Drones and
Oh Gaawwd... grumble
It will be great! I have a friend with a recording studio. We can remaster all the tracks.
Then we'll have an in-store Launch! Would you come in for a signing session?
Uh, we'll see..

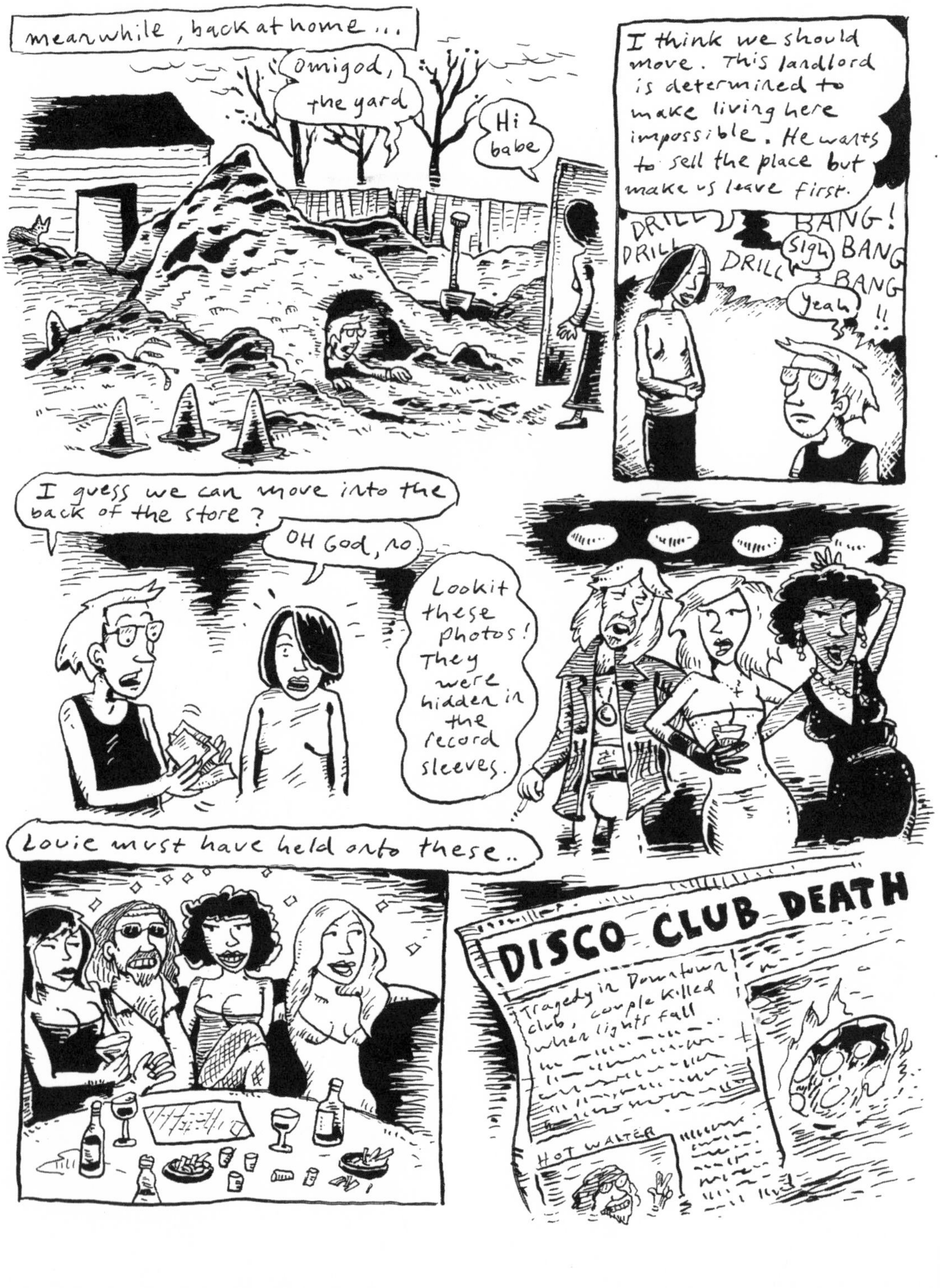

meanwhile, back at home...
Omigod, the yard
Hi babe
I think we should move. This landlord is determined to make living here impossible. He wants to sell the place but make us leave first.
DRILL DRILL DRILL
BANG! BANG BANG!!
Sigh
Yeah
I guess we can move into the back of the store?
OH God, no.
Lookit these photos! They were hidden in the record sleeves.
Louie must have held onto these..
DISCO CLUB DEATH
Tragedy in Downtown club, couple killed when lights fall
HOT WALTER

Lenny begins the process of remastering each track from the lost albums. Putting together a collection for the reissues.

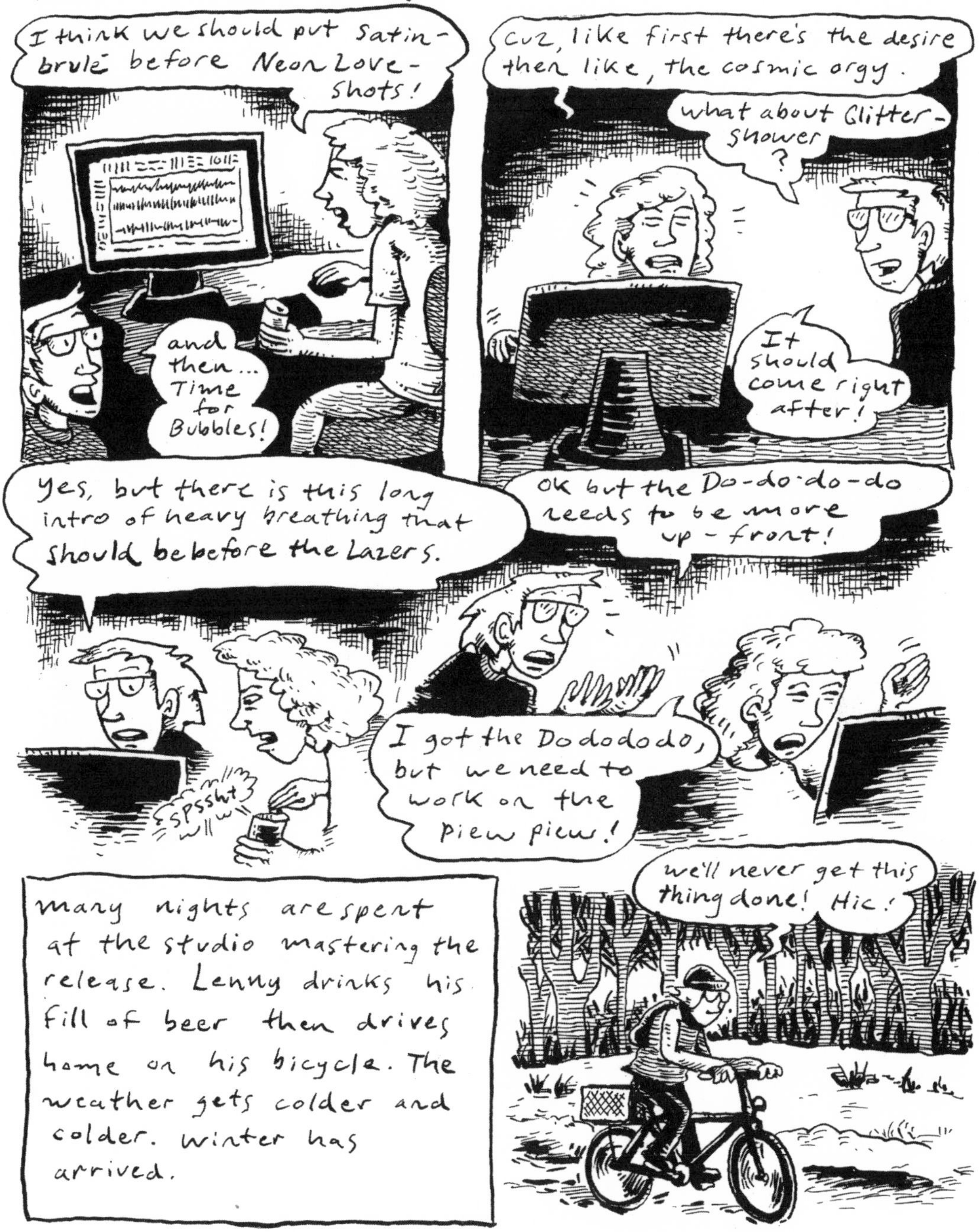

I think we should put Satin-brulé before Neon Love-Shots!
and then... Time for Bubbles!
Cuz, like first there's the desire then like, the cosmic orgy.
What about Glitter-Shower?
It should come right after!
Yes, but there is this long intro of heavy breathing that should be before the Lazers.
SPSSHT
OK but the Do-do-do-do needs to be more up-front!
I got the Dododod0, but we need to work on the piew piew!
Many nights are spent at the studio mastering the release. Lenny drinks his fill of beer then drives home on his bicycle. The weather gets colder and colder. Winter has arrived.
We'll never get this thing done! Hic!

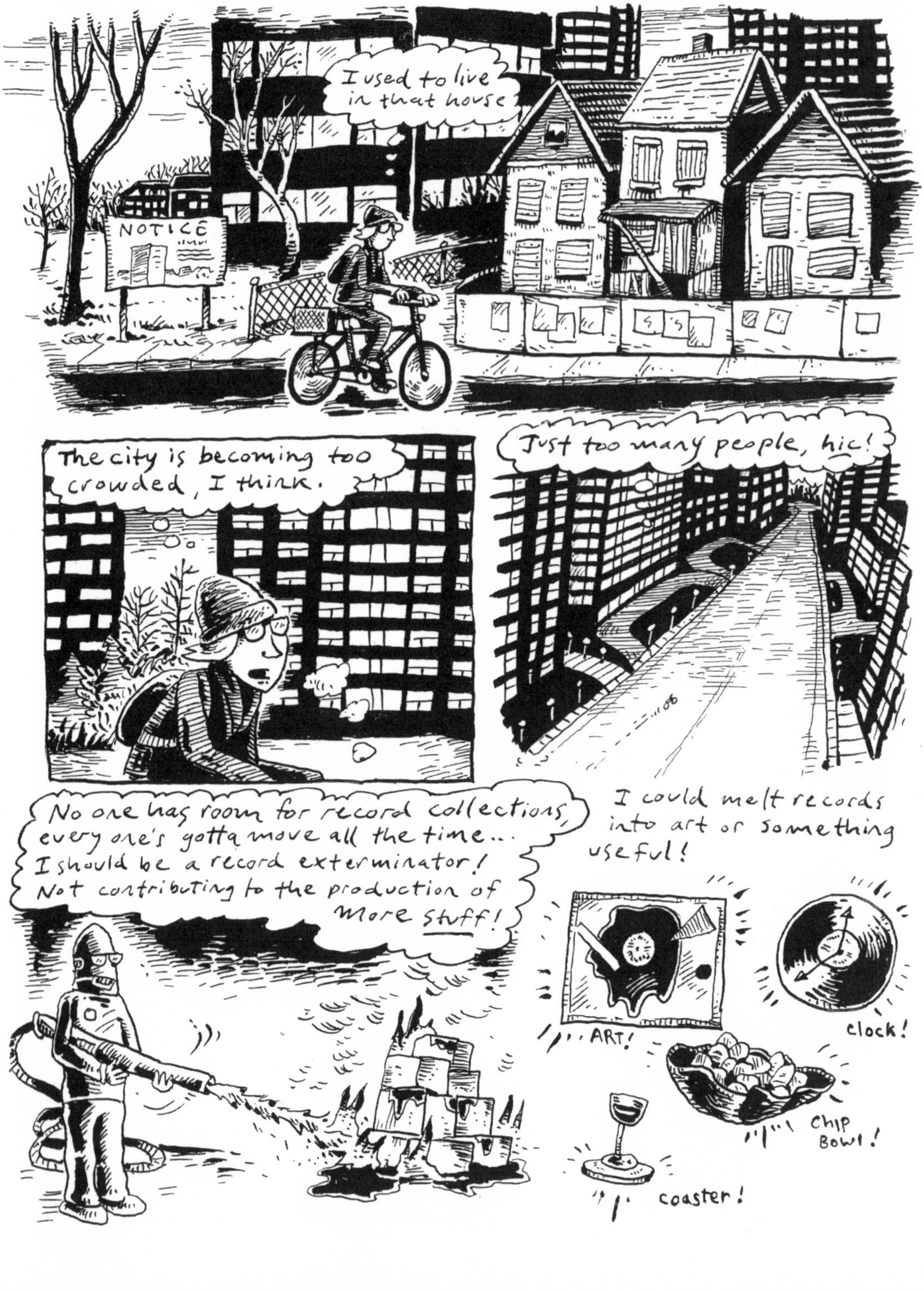

NOTICE
I used to live in that house
The city is becoming too crowded, I think.
Just too many people, hic!
No one has room for record collections, everyone's gotta move all the time... I should be a record exterminator! Not contributing to the production of more stuff!
I could melt records into art or something useful!
ART!
clock!
Chip Bowl!
coaster!

Junk

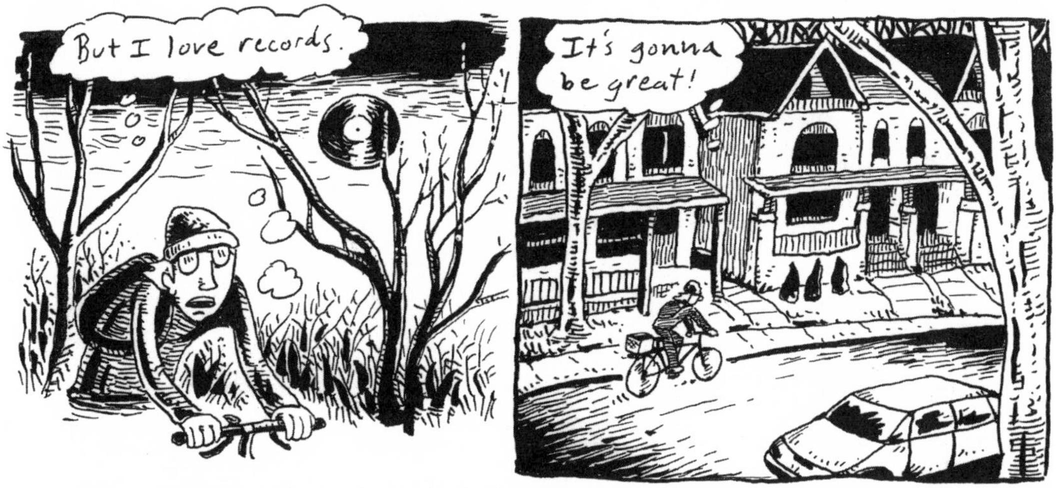
But I love records.
It's gonna be great!

Once the mastering is finally accomplished comes the long waiting time for the records to arrive. The few remaining factories are full of Elton John re-presses and the like.

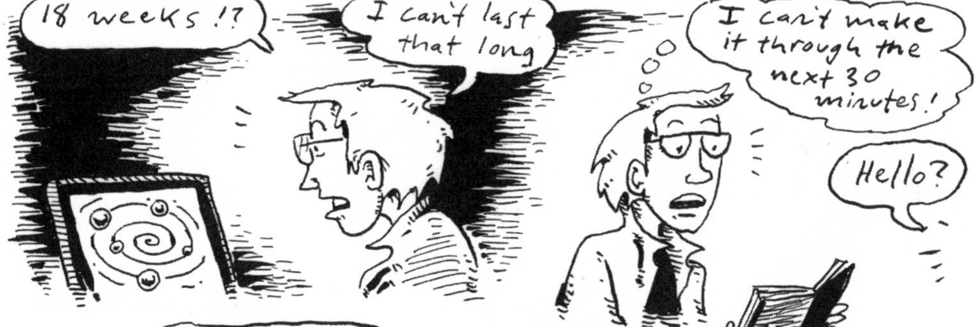
18 weeks!?
I can't last that long
I can't make it through the next 30 minutes!
Hello?

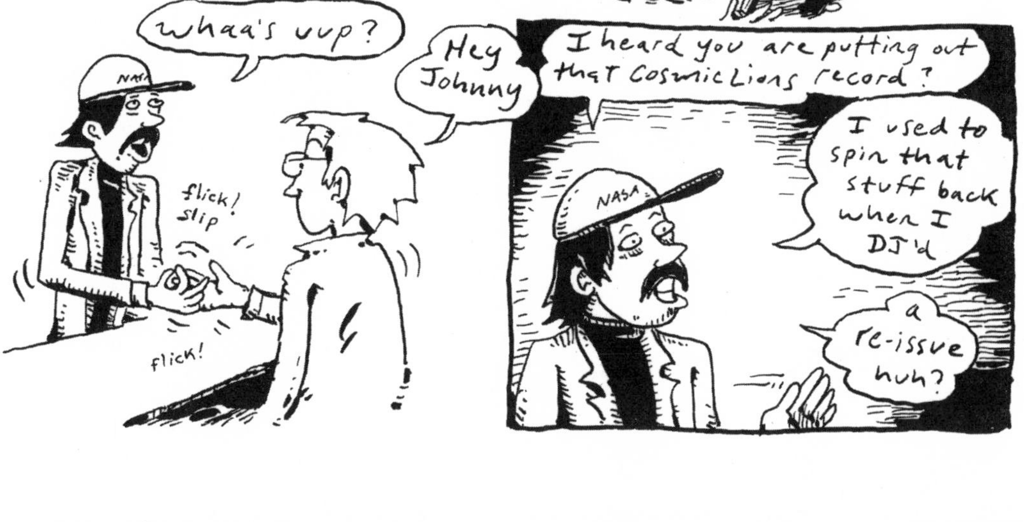
whaa's uup?
NASA
flick! slip
flick!
Hey Johnny
I heard you are putting out that CosmicLions record?
NASA
I used to spin that stuff back when I DJ'd
a re-issue huh?

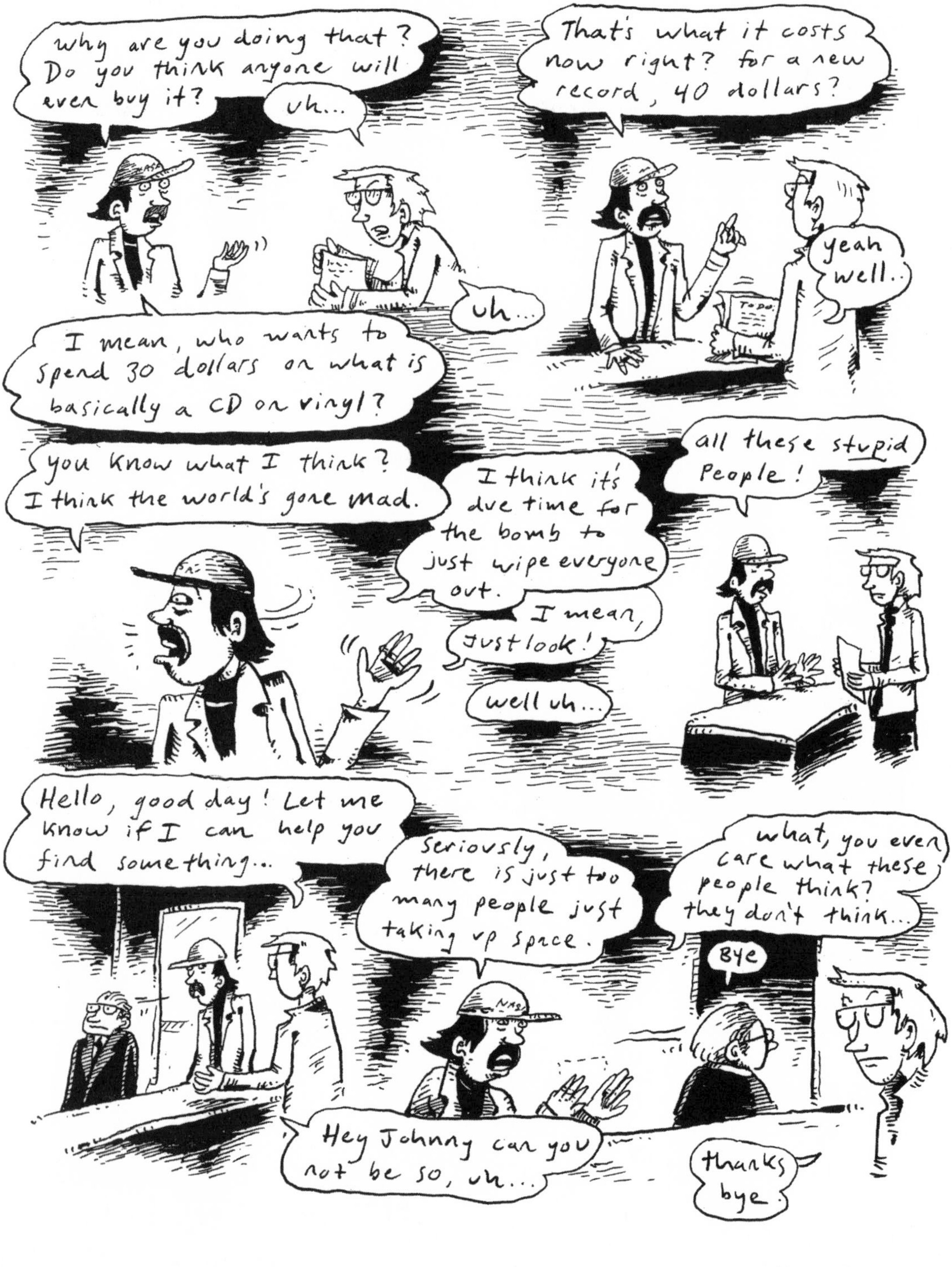
why are you doing that? Do you think anyone will ever buy it?
uh...
uh...
I mean, who wants to spend 30 dollars on what is basically a CD on vinyl?
That's what it costs now right? for a new record, 40 dollars?
yeah well..
you know what I think? I think the world's gone mad.
I think it's due time for the bomb to just wipe everyone out.
I mean, just look!
well uh...
all these stupid people!
Hello, good day! Let me know if I can help you find something...
Seriously, there is just too many people just taking up space.
Hey Johnny can you not be so, uh...
what, you even care what these people think? they don't think...
Bye
thanks bye.

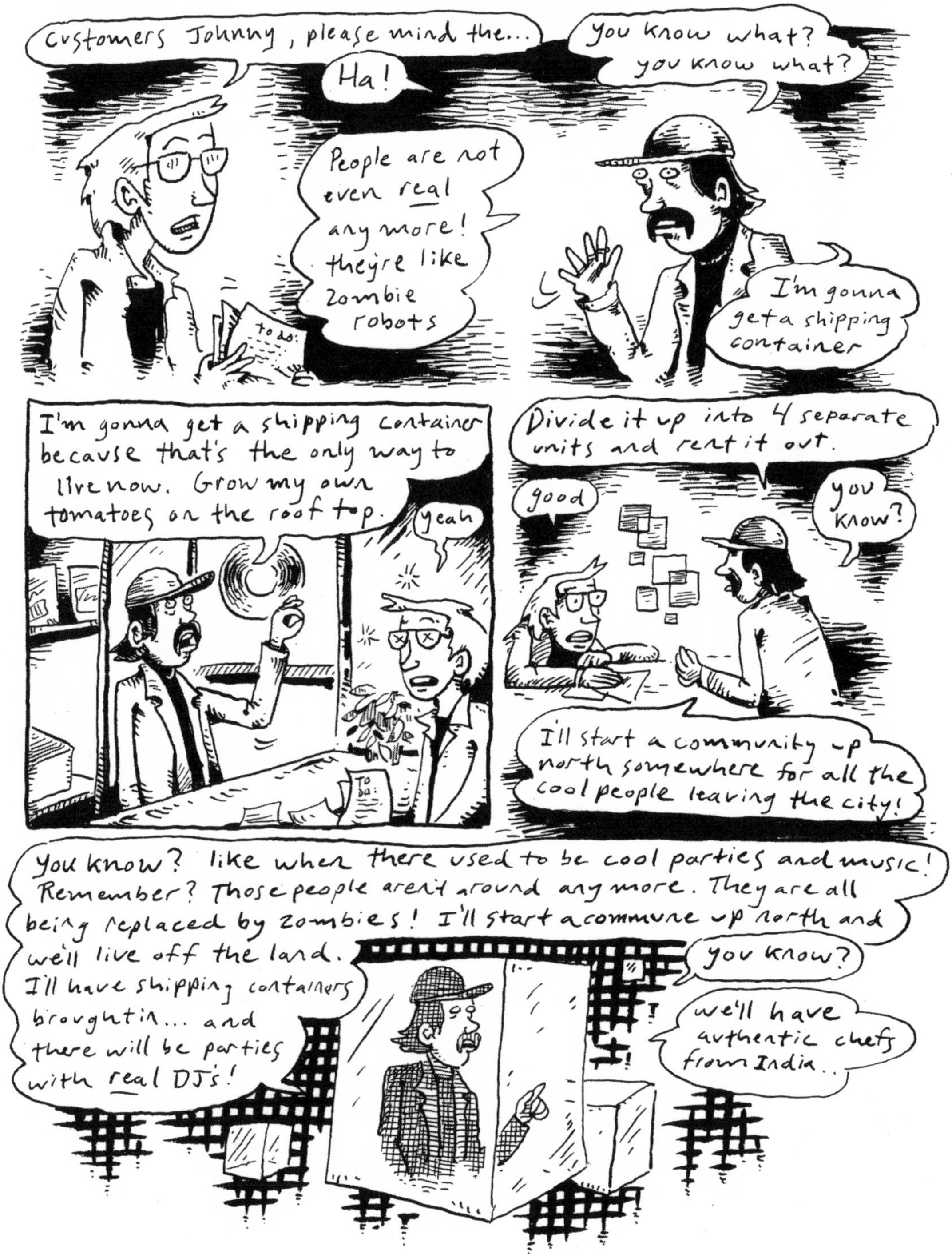
Customers Johnny, please mind the...
Ha!
People are not even real any more! they're like zombie robots
You know what? you know what?
I'm gonna get a shipping container
TO DO:
I'm gonna get a shipping container because that's the only way to live now. Grow my own tomatoes on the roof top.
yeah
TO DO:
Divide it up into 4 separate units and rent it out.
good
you know?
I'll start a community up north somewhere for all the cool people leaving the city!
You know? like when there used to be cool parties and music! Remember? Those people aren't around any more. They are all being replaced by zombies! I'll start a commune up north and we'll live off the land.
I'll have shipping containers brought in... and there will be parties with real DJ's!
you know?
we'll have authentic chefs from India...

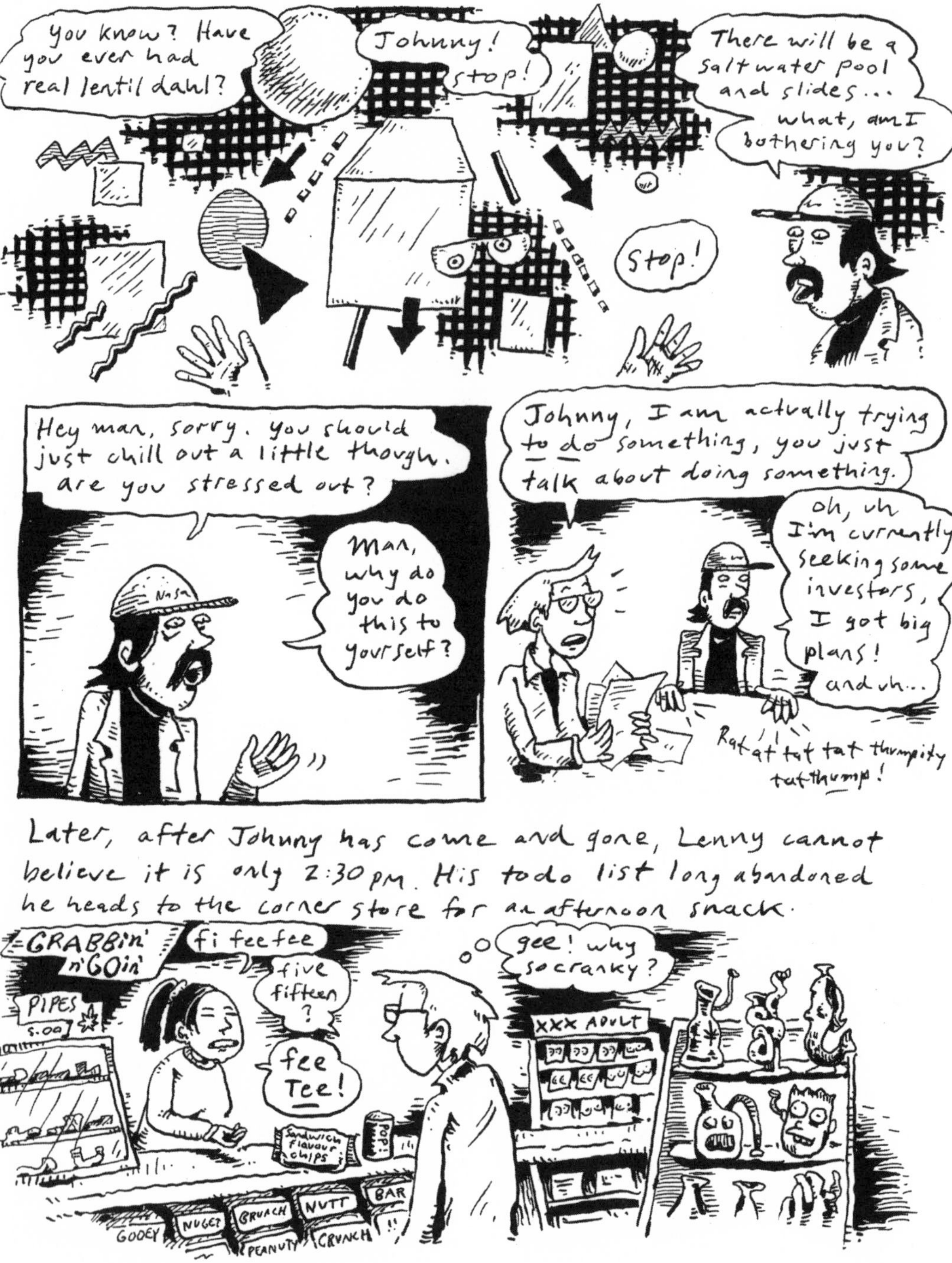
You know? Have you ever had real lentil dahl?
Johnny! Stop!
There will be a salt water pool and slides... what, am I bothering you?
Stop!
Hey man, sorry. You should just chill out a little though. Are you stressed out?
Man, why do you do this to yourself?
NASA
Johnny, I am actually trying to do something, you just talk about doing something.
Oh, uh I'm currently seeking some investors, I got big plans! and uh...
Ratatat tat tat thumpity tat thump!
Later, after Johnny has come and gone, Lenny cannot believe it is only 2:30 pm. His todo list long abandoned he heads to the corner store for an afternoon snack.
GRABBin' n' GOin'
fi fee fee
five fifteen?
fee Tee!
gee! why so cranky?
PIPES 5.00
XXX ADULT
Sandwich flavour chips
POP
GOOEY
NUGET
CRUNCH
NUTT
BAR
PEANUTY
CRUNCH

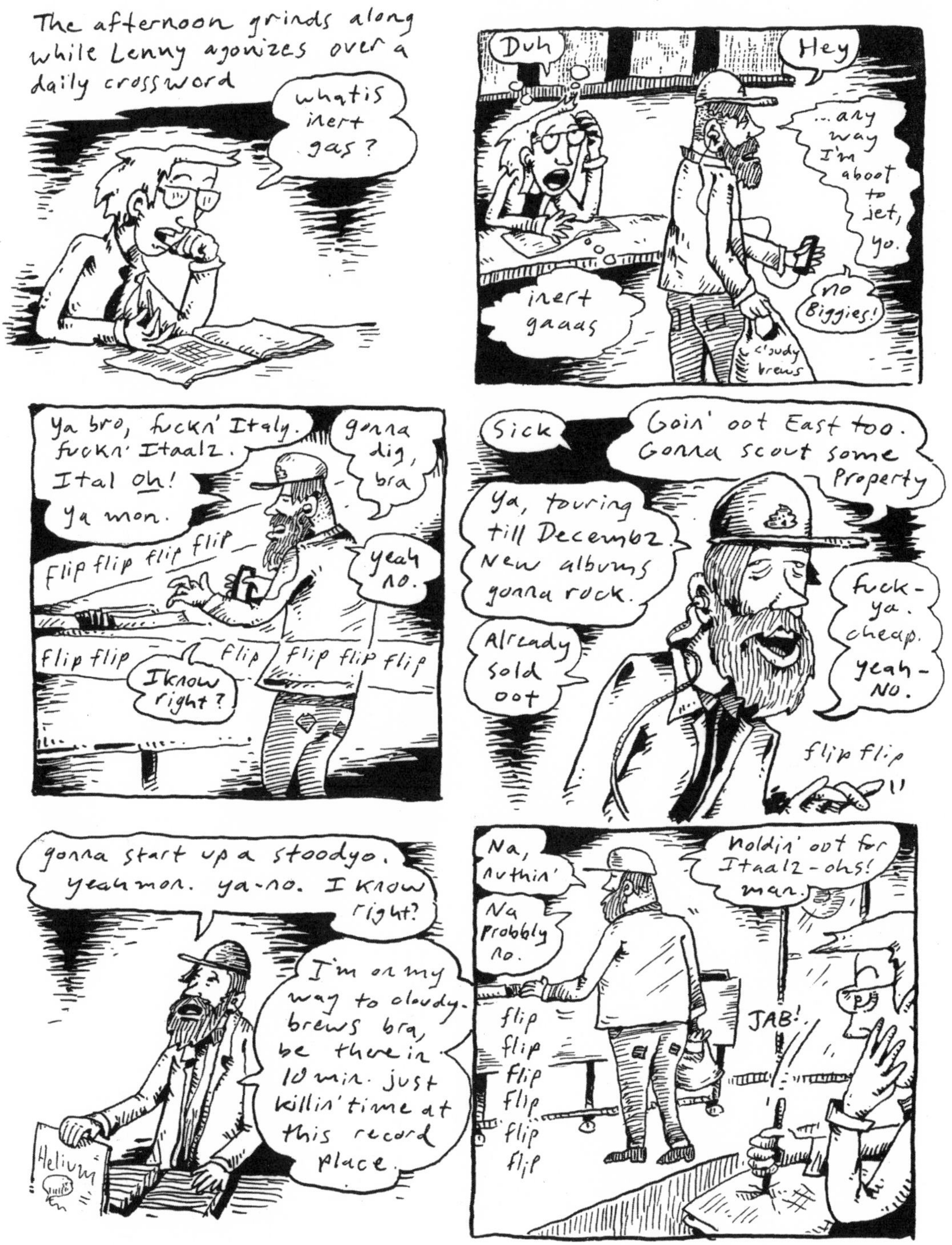

The afternoon grinds along while Lenny agonizes over a daily crossword
whatis inert gas?
Duh
Hey
...any way I'm aboot to jet, yo.
inert gaaas
No Biggies!
cloudy brews
Ya bro, fuckn' Italy. fuckn' Itaalz. Ital oh! ya mon.
gonna dig, bra
flip flip flip flip
yeah no.
flip flip
flip
flip flip flip
I know right?
Sick
Goin' oot East too. Gonna scout some Property
Ya, touring till Decembz. New albums gonna rock.
fuck-ya. cheap. yeah-NO.
Already sold oot
flip flip
gonna start up a stoodyo. yeah mon. ya-no. I know right?
I'm on my way to cloudy-brews bra, be there in 10 min. just killin' time at this record place.
Helium
Na, nuthin'
Na probbly no.
holdin' oot for Itaalz-ohs! man.
flip flip flip flip flip flip flip
JAB!

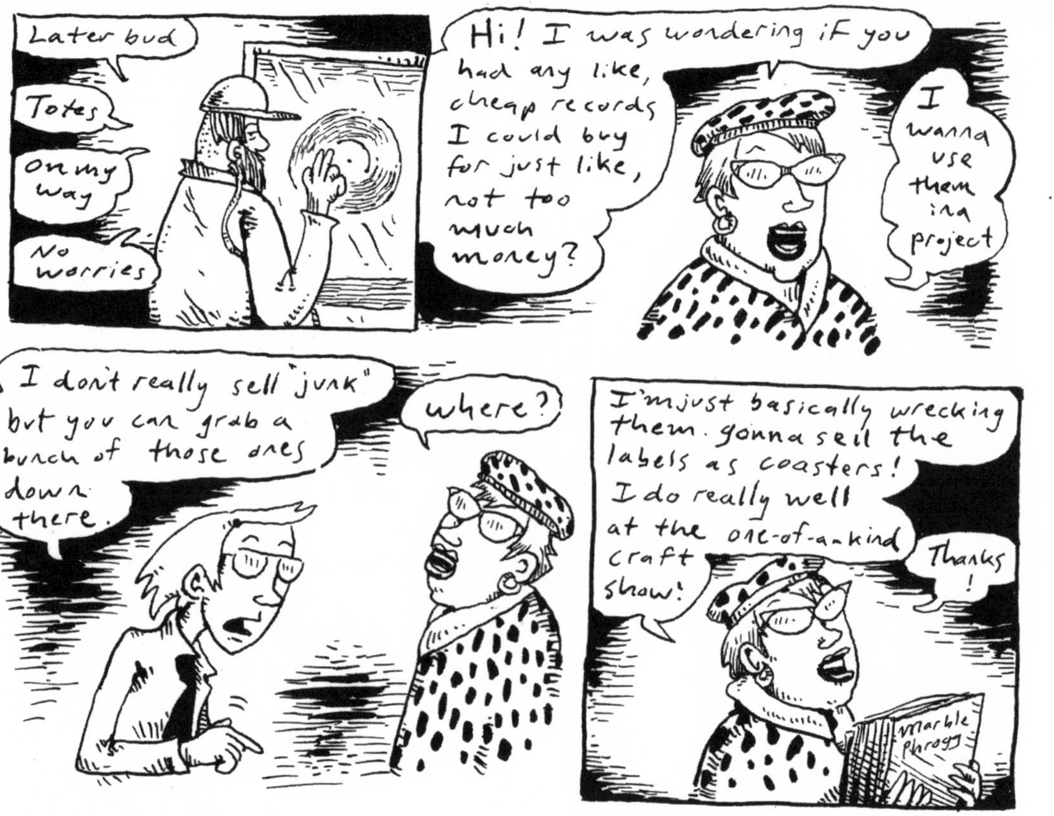
Later bud
Totes
On my way
No worries
Hi! I was wondering if you had any like, cheap records I could buy for just like, not too much money?
I wanna use them in a project
I don't really sell "junk" but you can grab a bunch of those ones down there.
Where?
I'm just basically wrecking them. gonna sell the labels as coasters! I do really well at the one-of-a-kind craft show!
Thanks!
Marble Phrogg

Lenny has reached a new low. He feels like a dumping-ground. A waiting room or a junk salesman. His once drifting thoughts are now sailing quite fast. Actually they are on a jet boat, taking Lenny on a wild ride so far away from his crossword.

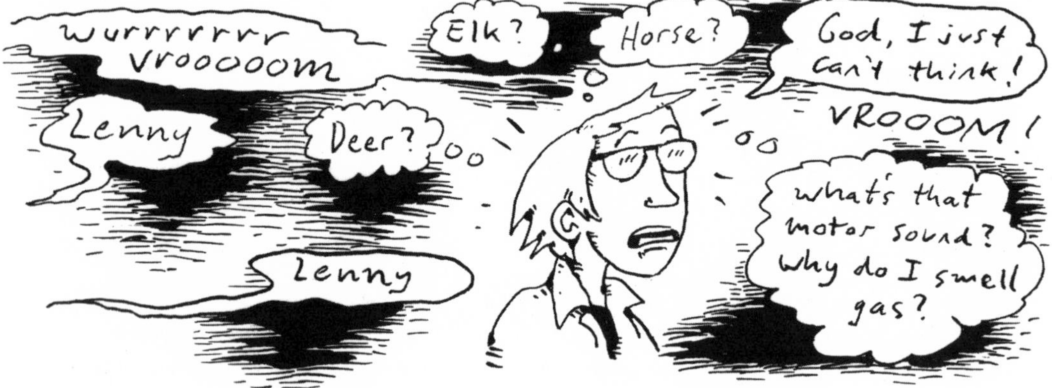
Wurrrrrrr vrooooom
Elk?
Horse?
God, I just can't think!
Lenny
Deer?
VROOOM!
What's that motor sound? Why do I smell gas?
Lenny

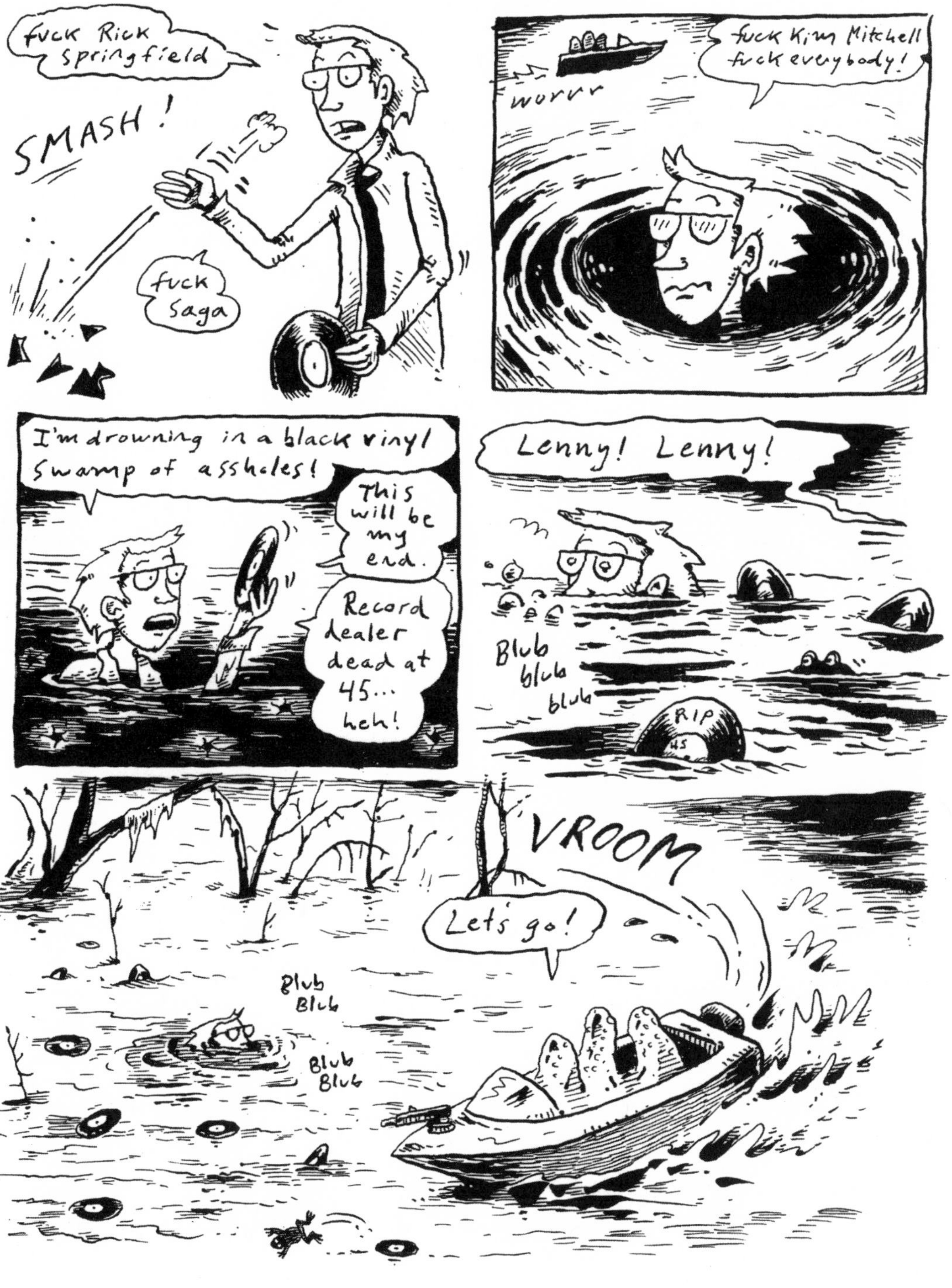
fuck Rick Springfield
SMASH!
fuck Saga
worrr
fuck Kim Mitchell fuck everybody!
I'm drowning in a black vinyl swamp of assholes!
This will be my end.
Record dealer dead at 45... heh!
Lenny! Lenny!
Blub blub blub
RIP
45
VROOM
Let's go!
Blub Blub
Blub Blub

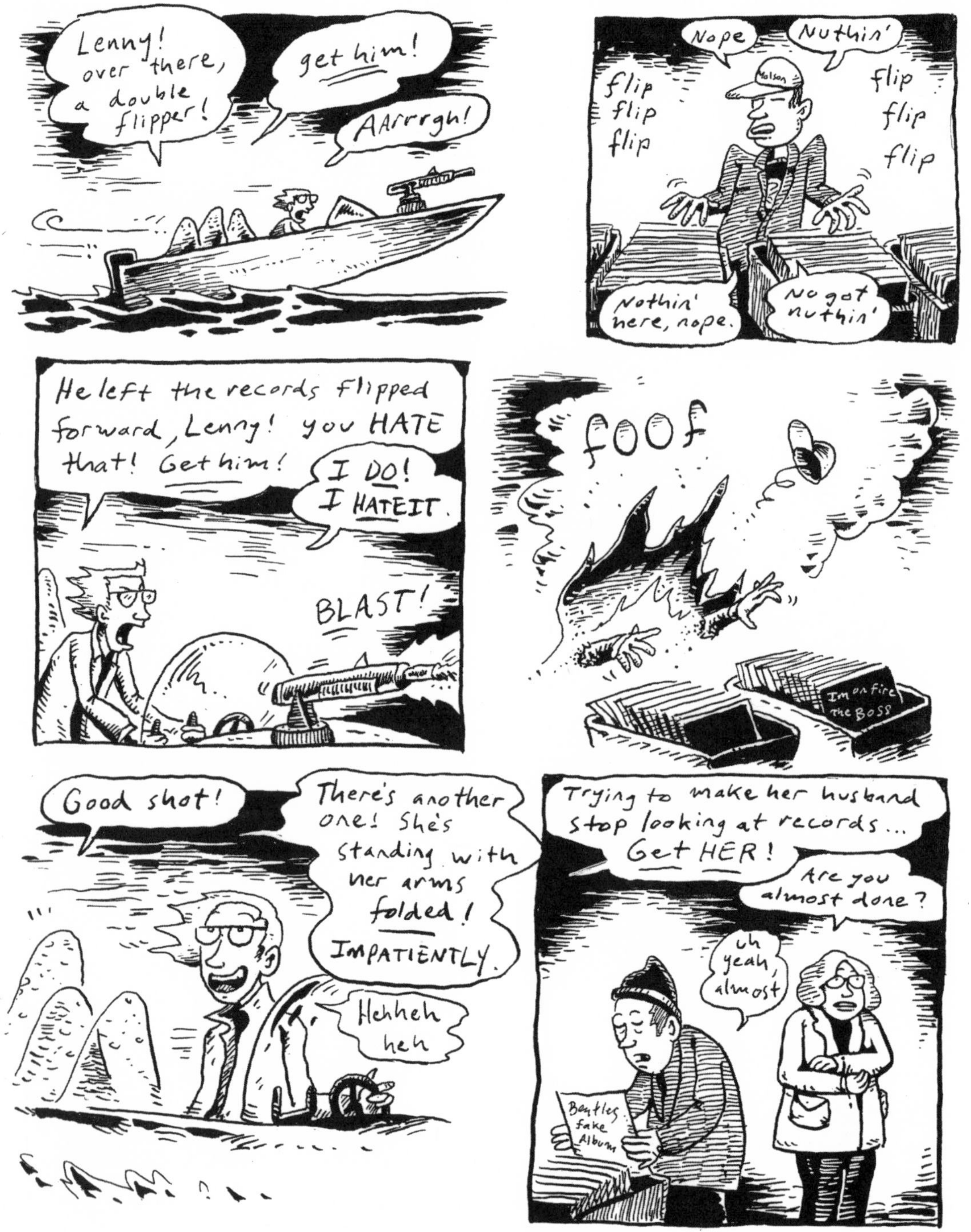
Lenny! over there, a double flipper!
get him!
AArrrgh!
Nope
Nuthin'
Molson
flip flip flip
flip flip flip
Nothin' here, nope.
No got nuthin'
He left the records flipped forward, Lenny! you HATE that! Get him!
I DO! I HATEIT.
BLAST!
FOOF
I'm on Fire The BOSS
Good shot!
There's another one! She's standing with her arms folded! IMPATIENTLY.
Hehheh heh
Trying to make her husband stop looking at records... Get HER!
Are you almost done?
uh yeah, almost
Beatles Fake Album

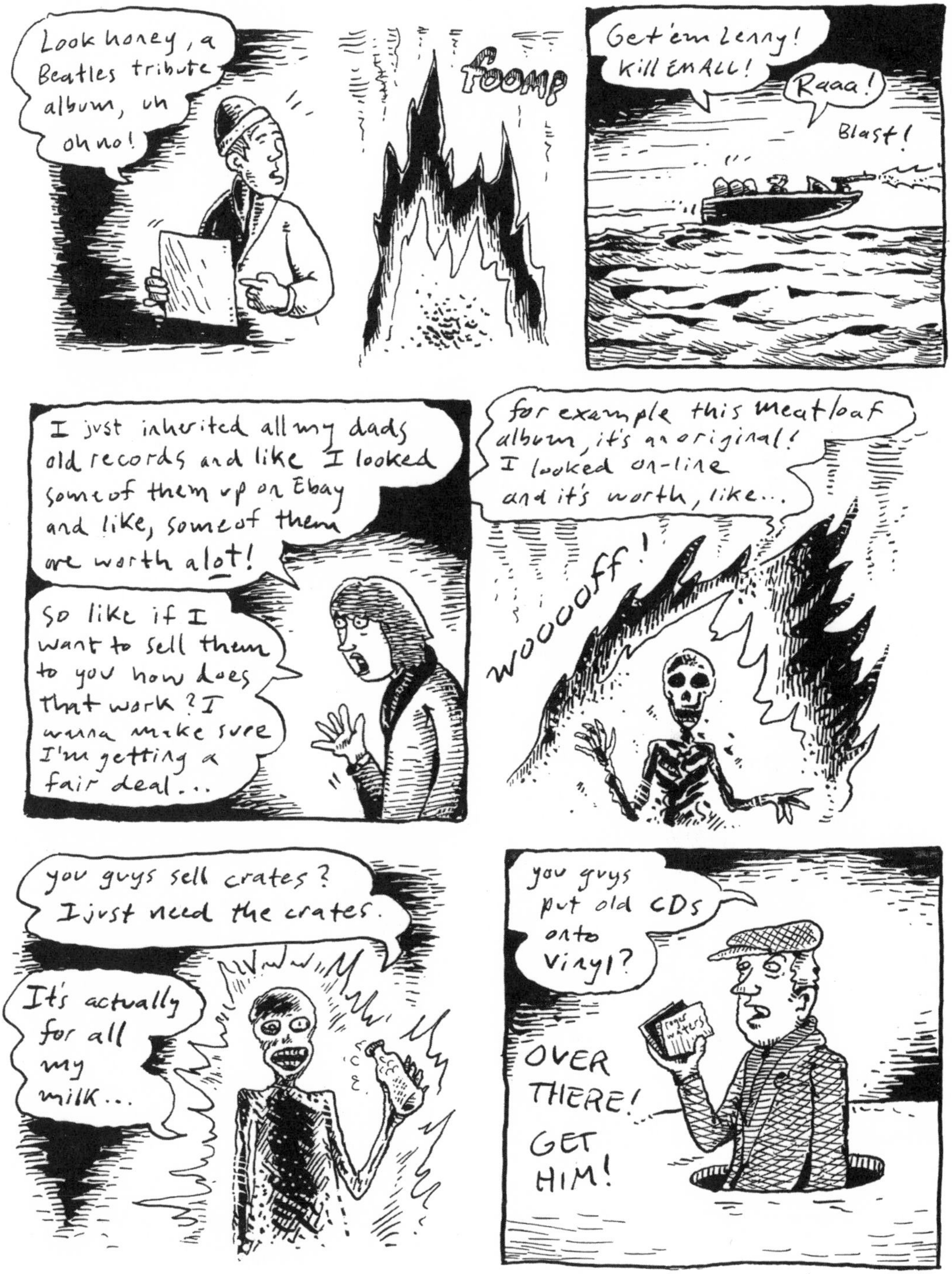

Look honey, a Beatles tribute album, uh oh no!
foomp
Get'em Lenny! Kill EM ALL!
Raaa!
Blast!
I just inherited all my dads old records and like I looked some of them up on Ebay and like, some of them are worth alot!
So like if I want to sell them to you how does that work? I wanna make sure I'm getting a fair deal...
for example this meatloaf album, it's an original! I looked on-line and it's worth, like...
WOOOOFF!
you guys sell crates? I just need the crates.
It's actually for all my milk...
you guys put old CDs onto vinyl?
roger waters
OVER THERE!
GET HIM!

Home

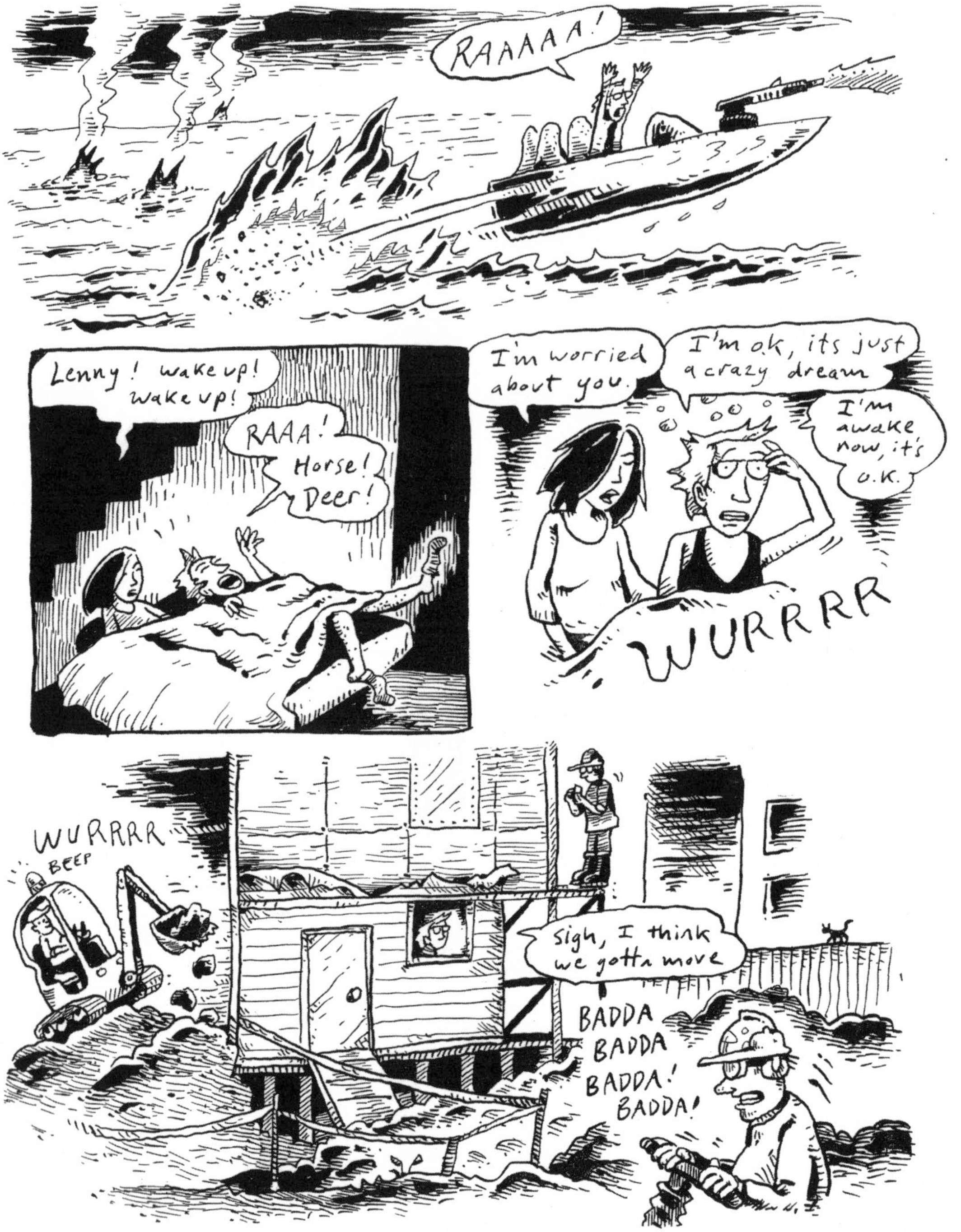
RAAAAA!
Lenny! wake up! Wake up!
RAAA! Horse! Deer!
I'm worried about you.
I'm ok, its just a crazy dream
I'm awake now, it's O.K.
WURRRR
WURRRR
BEEP
Sigh, I think we gotta move
BADDA
BADDA
BADDA!
BADDA!

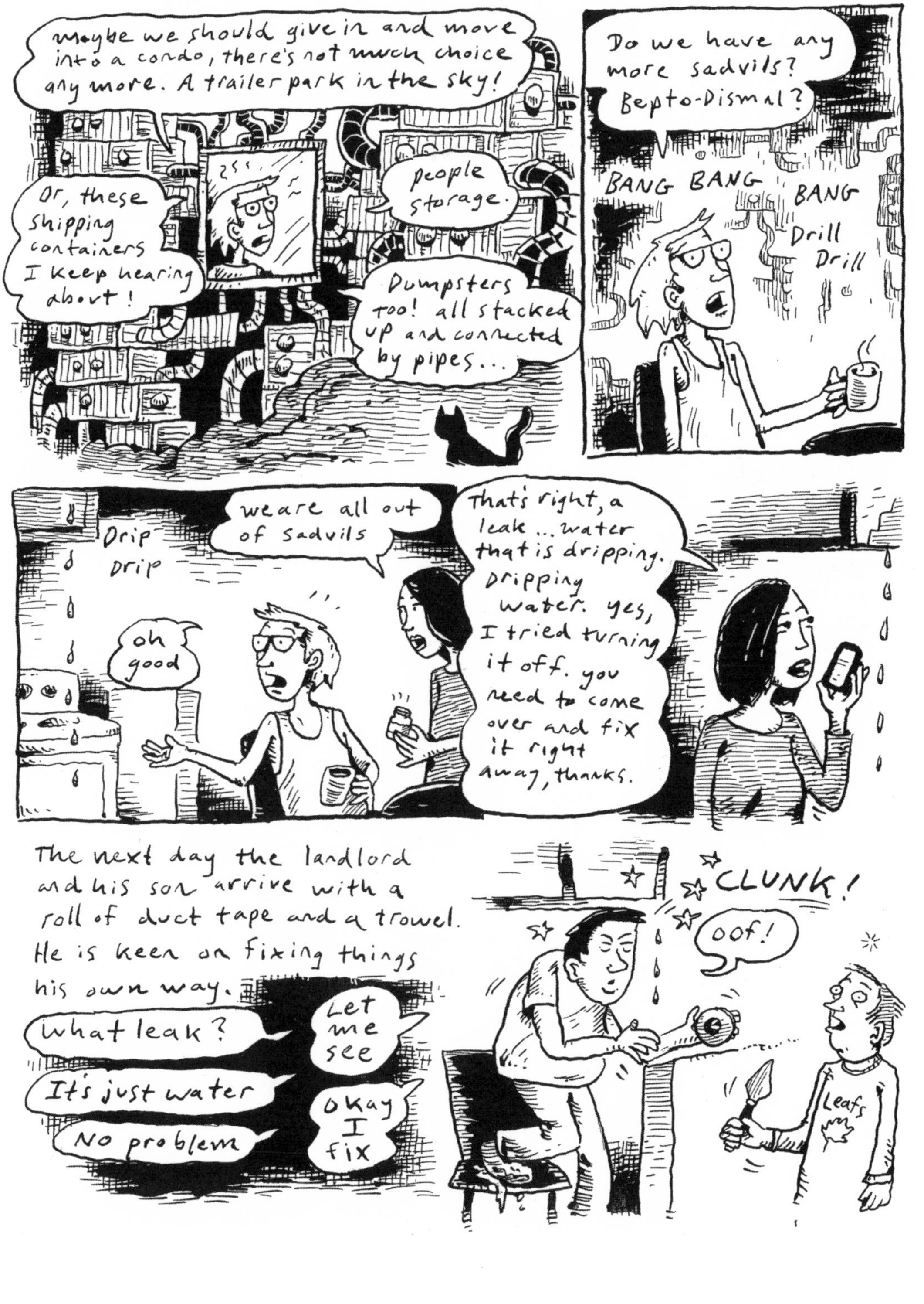
Maybe we should give in and move into a condo, there's not much choice any more. A trailer park in the sky!
Or, these shipping containers I keep hearing about!
people storage.
Dumpsters too! all stacked up and connected by pipes...
Do we have any more sadvils? Bepto-Dismal?
BANG BANG BANG
Drill Drill
Drip drip
we are all out of sadvils
oh good
That's right, a leak ... water that is dripping. Dripping water. yes, I tried turning it off. you need to come over and fix it right away, thanks.
The next day the landlord and his son arrive with a roll of duct tape and a trowel. He is keen on fixing things his own way.
What leak?
Let me see
It's just water
Okay I fix
No problem
CLUNK!
oof!
Leafs

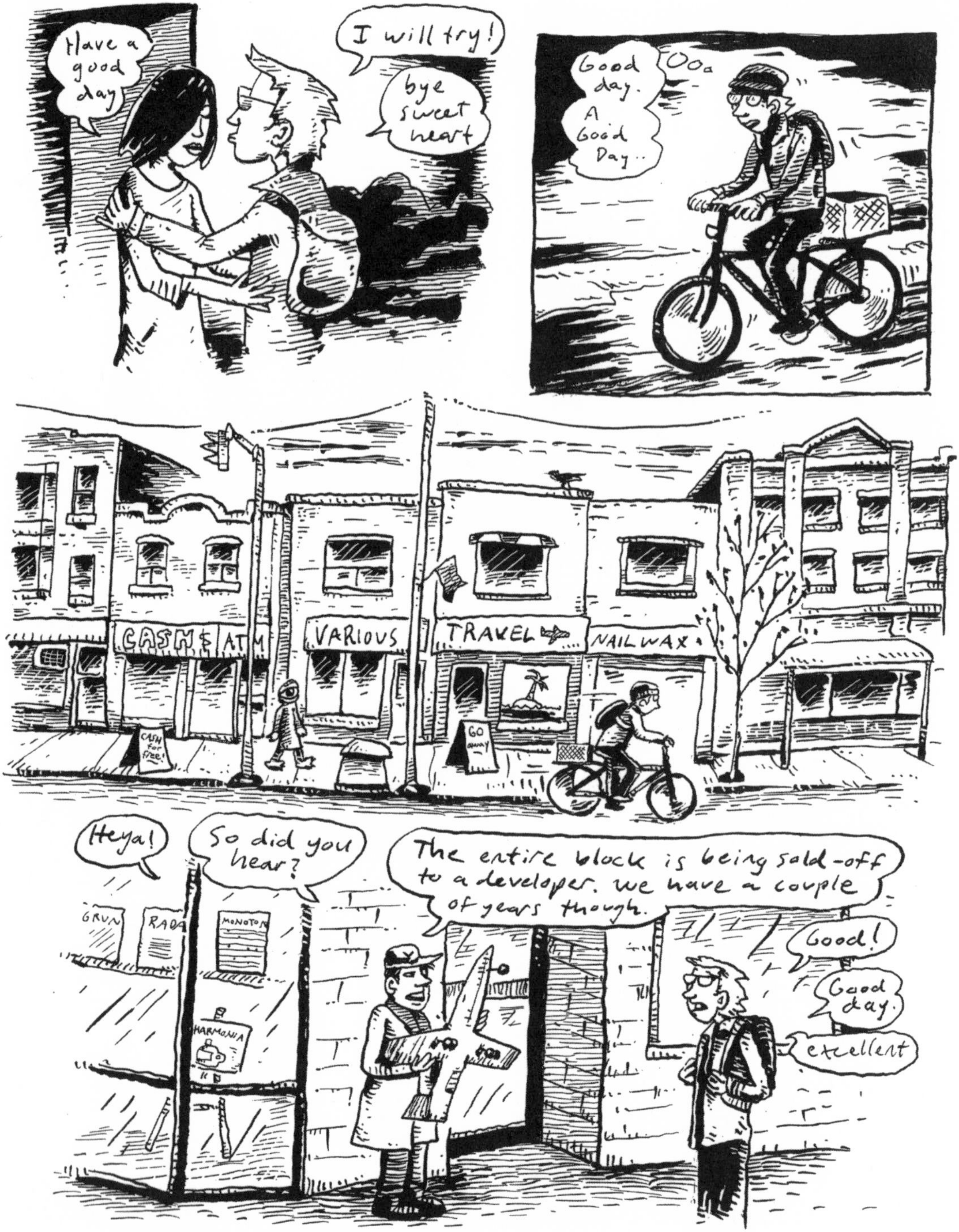
Have a good day
I will try!
bye sweet heart
Good day. A Good Day..
Ooo
CASH & ATM
VARIOUS
TRAVEL
NAIL WAX
CASH for free!
GO away
Heya!
So did you hear?
The entire block is being sold-off to a developer. We have a couple of years though.
Good!
Good day.
excellent
GRUN
RADA
MONOTON
HARMONIA

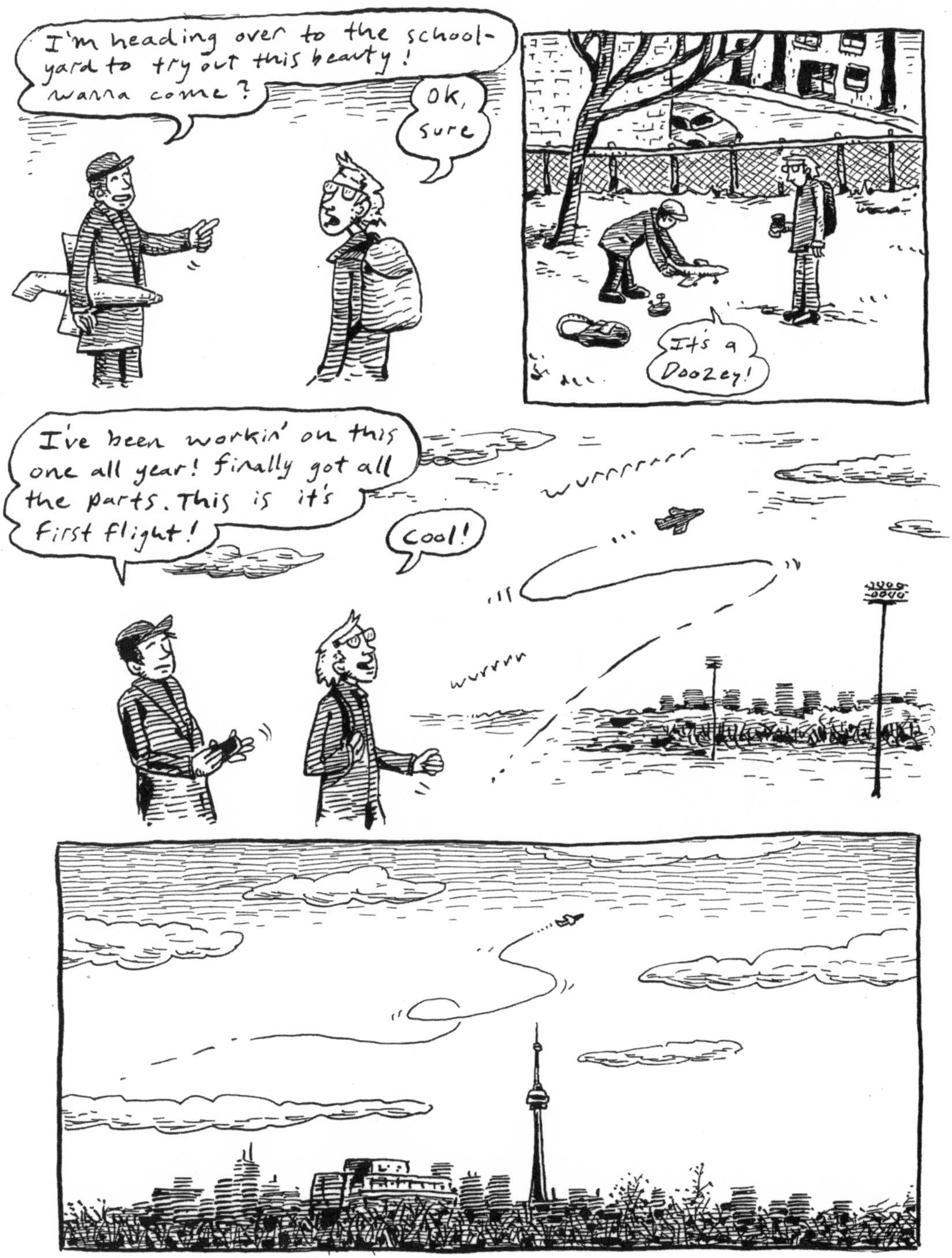

I'm heading over to the school-yard to try out this beauty! wanna come?
Ok, sure
It's a Doozey!
I've been workin' on this one all year! finally got all the parts. This is it's first flight!
Cool!
wurrrrrr
wurrrr

The End

Later, at the shop, Lenny finds an enlightening surprise.

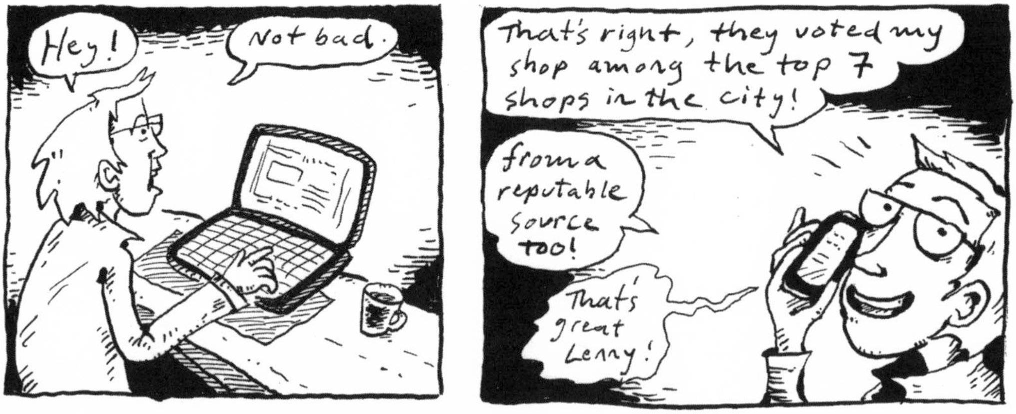
Hey!
Not bad.
That's right, they voted my shop among the top 7 shops in the city!
from a reputable source too!
That's great Lenny!

Lenny basks in this for half an afternoon and then the comments section under the article begins to fill up...

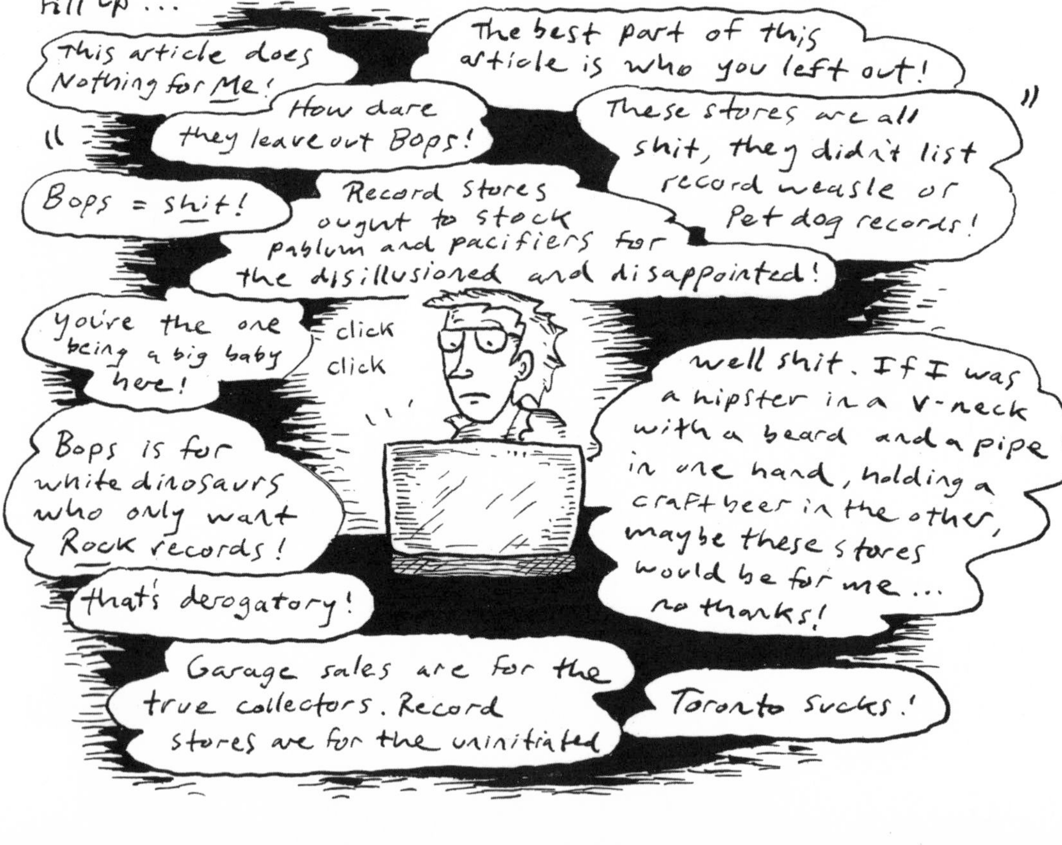
This article does Nothing for Me!
The best part of this article is who you left out!
How dare they leave out Bops!
These stores are all shit, they didn't list record weasle or Pet dog records!
Bops = shit!
Record stores ought to stock pablum and pacifiers for the disillusioned and disappointed!
You're the one being a big baby here!
click
click
well shit. If I was a hipster in a V-neck with a beard and a pipe in one hand, holding a craft beer in the other, maybe these stores would be for me... no thanks!
Bops is for white dinosaurs who only want Rock records!
that's derogatory!
Garage sales are for the true collectors. Record stores are for the uninitiated
Toronto sucks!

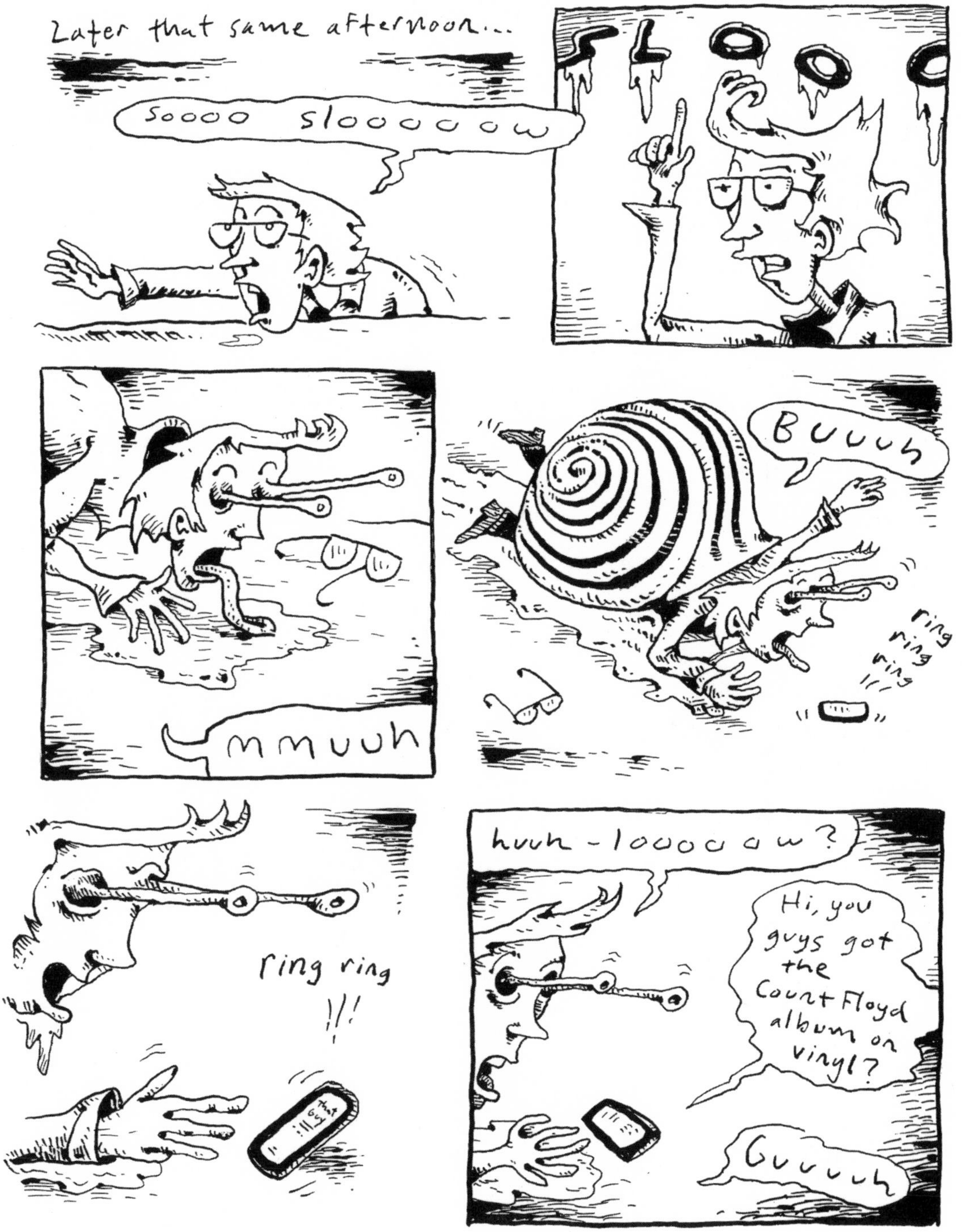
Later that same afternoon...
Soooo sloooooow
SLOOO
mmuuh
Buuuh
ring ring ring
ring ring
that guy
huuh-looooow?
Hi, you guys got the Count Floyd album on vinyl?
Guuuuh

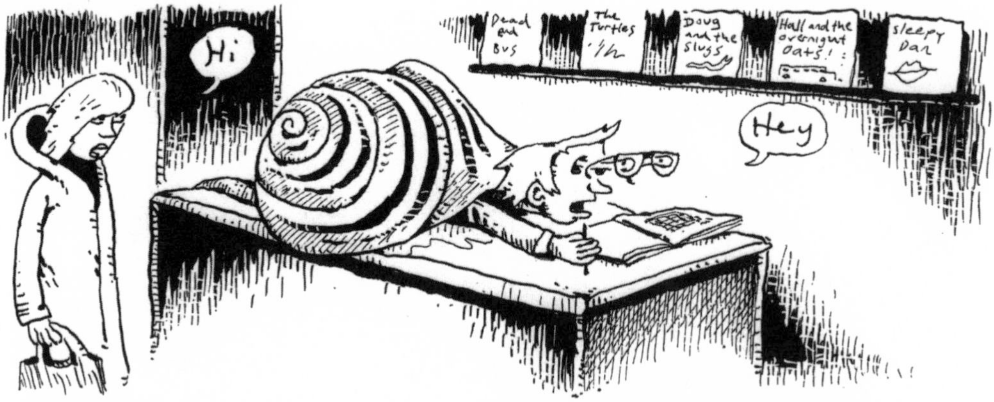
Dead end Bus
The Turtles
Doug and the Slugs
Hall and the overnight Oats!
Sleepy Dan
Hi
Hey

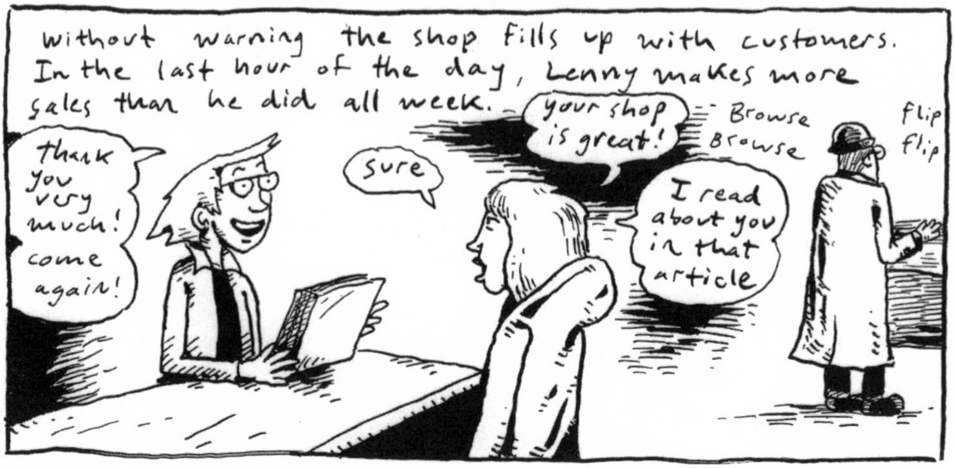
without warning the shop fills up with customers. In the last hour of the day, Lenny makes more sales than he did all week.
your shop is great!
Browse Browse
Flip flip
I read about you in that article
Sure
thank you very much! come again!

But at the end of this particular day, the decision is clear. Lenny places a closed sign up on the door for the last time and walks away.

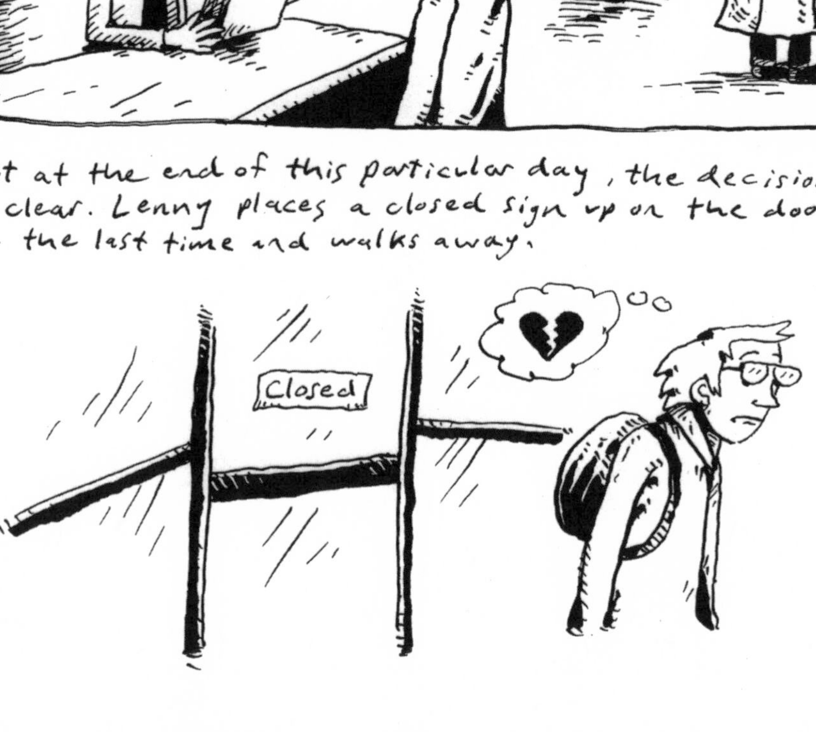
Closed

The Ride

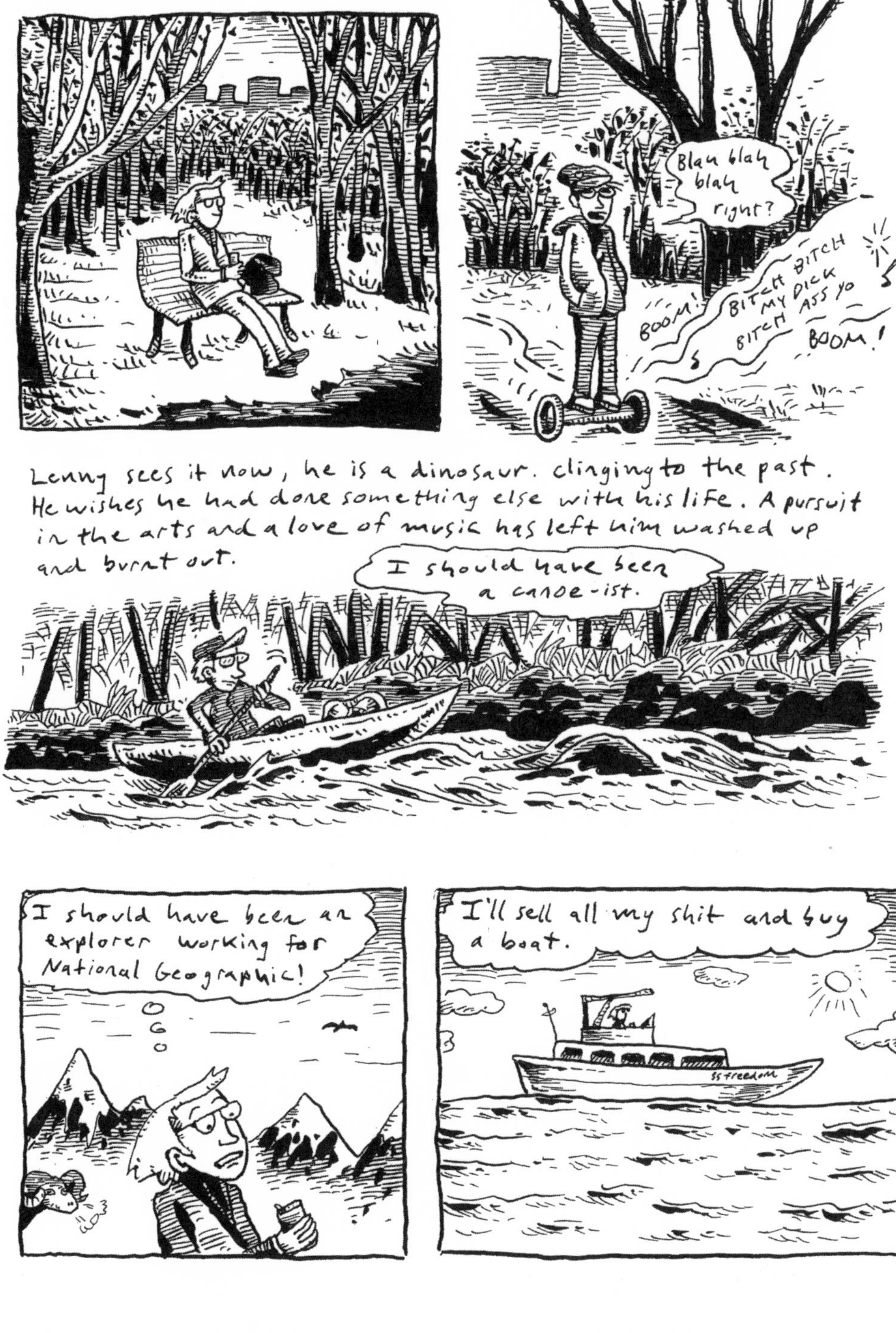
Blah blah blah right?
BOOM!
BITCH BITCH MY DICK BITCH ASS YO
BOOM!
Lenny sees it now, he is a dinosaur. clinging to the past. He wishes he had done something else with his life. A pursuit in the arts and a love of music has left him washed up and burnt out.
I should have been a canoe-ist.
I should have been an explorer working for National Geographic!
I'll sell all my shit and buy a boat.
SS Freedom

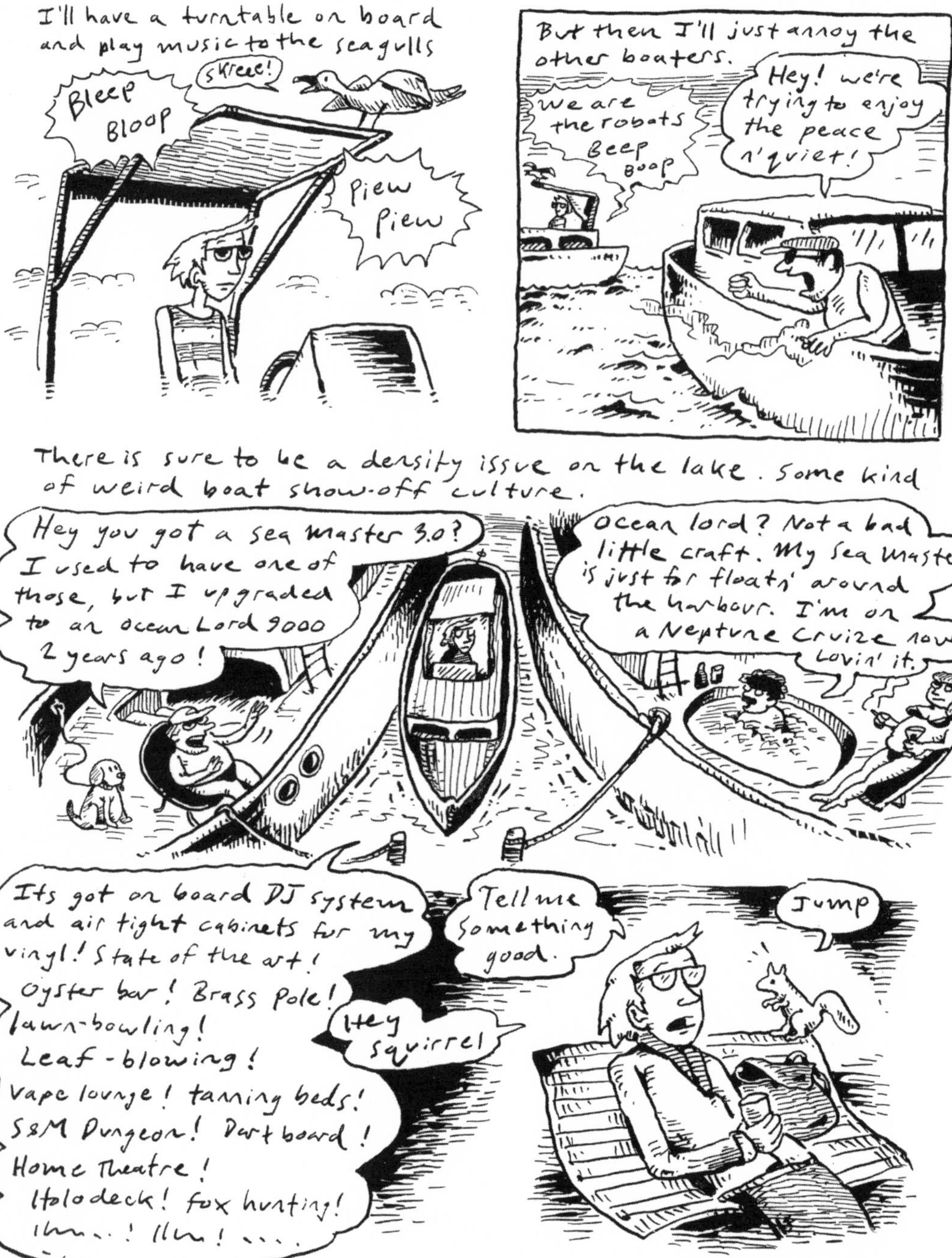
I'll have a turntable on board and play music to the seagulls
Bleep Bloop
Skreee!
Piew Piew
But then I'll just annoy the other boaters.
We are the robots Beep Boop
Hey! we're trying to enjoy the peace n' quiet!
There is sure to be a density issue on the lake. Some kind of weird boat show-off culture.
Hey you got a Sea Master 3.0? I used to have one of those, but I upgraded to an Ocean Lord 9000 2 years ago!
Ocean lord? Not a bad little craft. My Sea Master is just for floatin' around the harbour. I'm on a Neptune Cruize now, Lovin' it.
Its got on board DJ system and air tight cabinets for my vinyl! State of the art! Oyster bar! Brass pole! lawn-bowling! Leaf-blowing! Vape lounge! tanning beds! S&M Dungeon! Dart board! Home Theatre! Holodeck! fox hunting! Um..! Um! ...
Tell me something good.
Hey squirrel
Jump

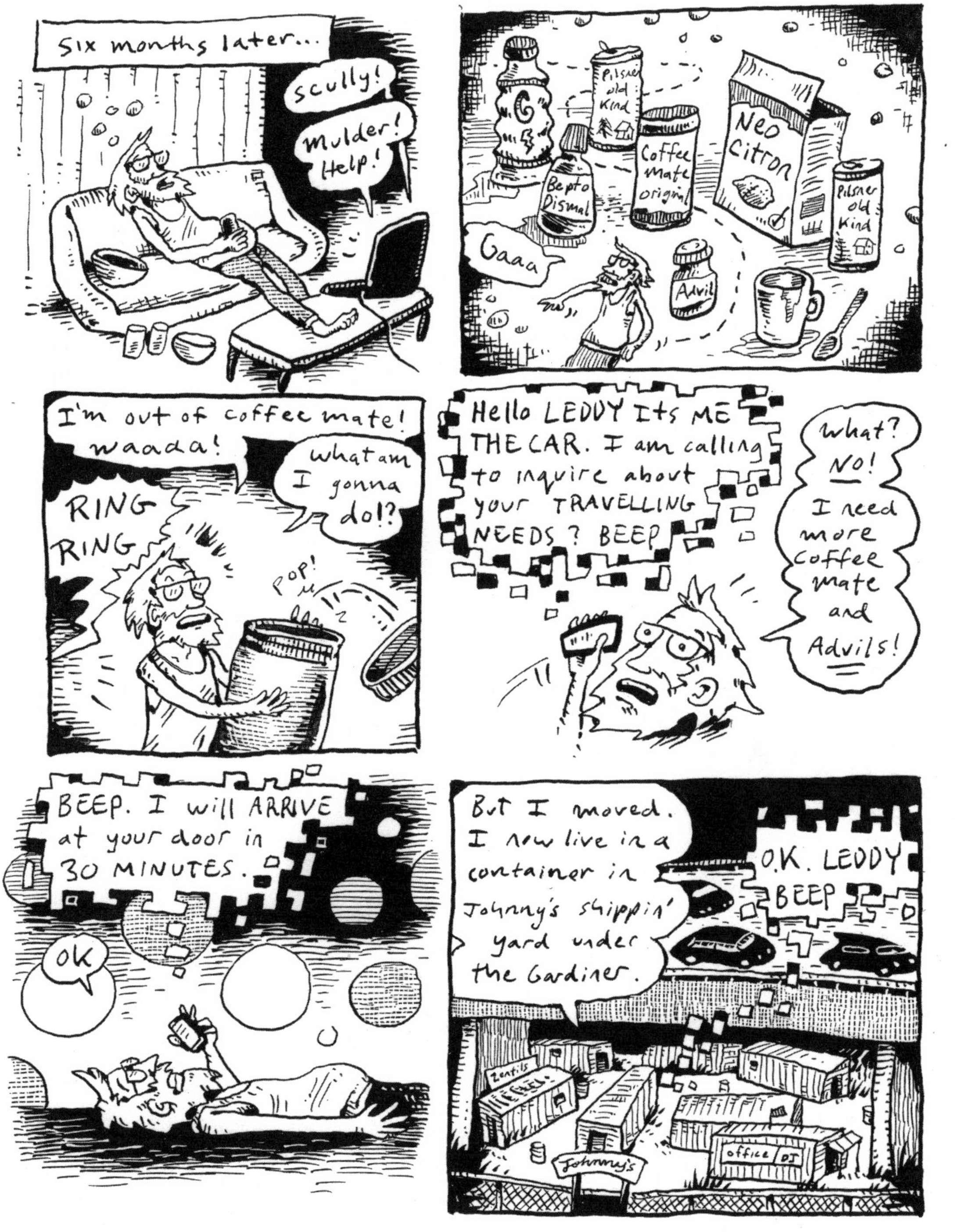
Six months later...
scully!
mulder! Help!
Pilsner old Kind
Coffee mate original
Neo Citron
Bepto Dismal
Pilsner old Kind
Advil
Gaaa
I'm out of coffee mate! waaaa!
what am I gonna do!?
RING RING
POP!
Hello LEDDY Its ME THE CAR. I am calling to inquire about your TRAVELLING NEEDS? BEEP
what? NO! I need more coffee mate and Advils!
BEEP. I will ARRIVE at your door in 30 MINUTES.
OK
But I moved. I now live in a container in Johnny's shippin' yard under the Gardiner.
O.K. LEDDY BEEP
Zentils
office
DJ
Johnny's

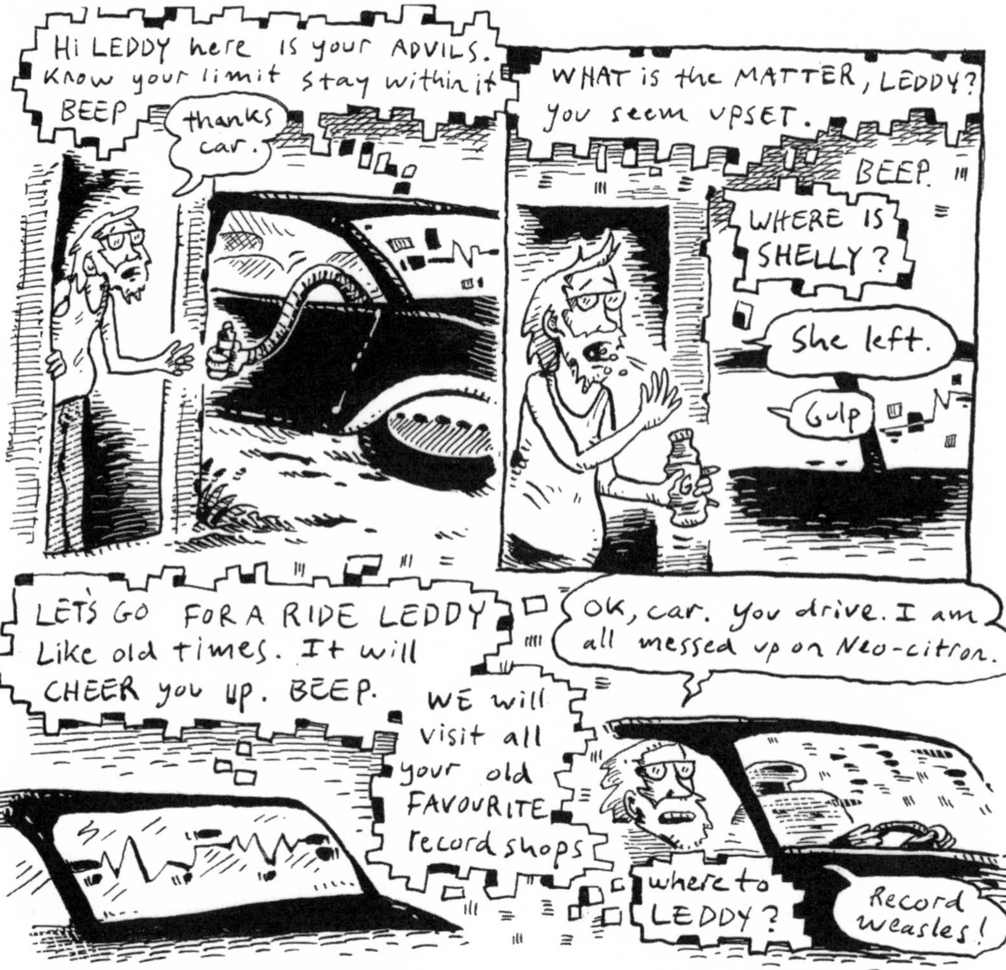
Hi LEDDY here is your ADVILS. Know your limit stay within it BEEP
thanks car.
WHAT is the MATTER, LEDDY? you seem UPSET. BEEP.
WHERE IS SHELLY?
She left.
Gulp
LET'S GO FOR A RIDE LEDDY Like old times. It will CHEER you up. BEEP.
WE will visit all your old FAVOURITE record shops
OK, car. You drive. I am all messed up on Neo-citron.
where to LEDDY?
Record weasles!

Lenny and the robot car take a drive through the streets of Toronto. They visit old shops and new ones too. The news has already spread of Lenny's store closing. It feels very strange to return to stores as a regular customer.

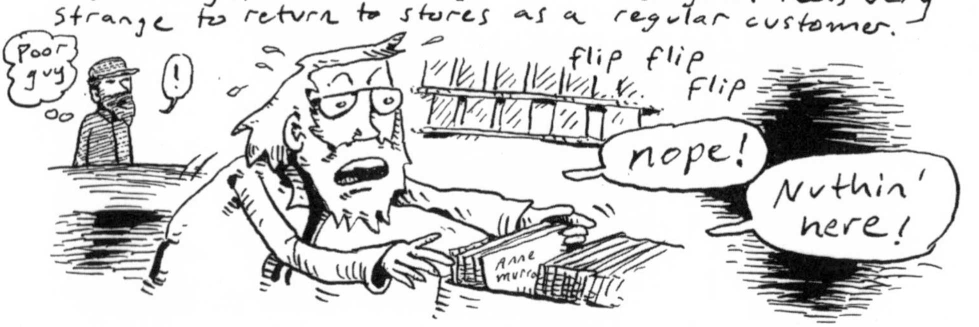
Poor guy
!
flip flip flip
nope!
Nuthin' here!

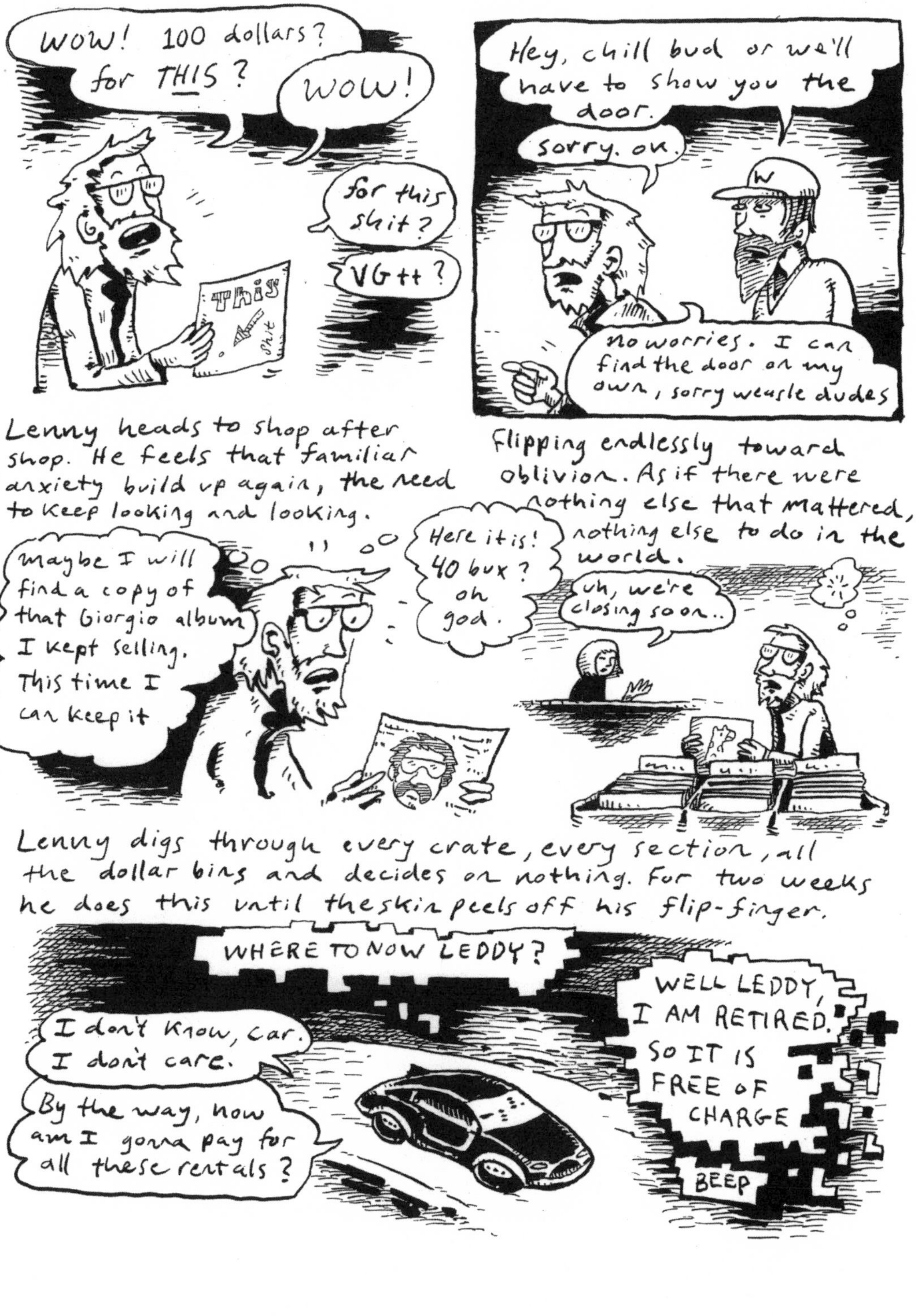
WOW! 100 dollars? for THIS?
WOW!
for this shit?
VG++?
THIS
Shit
Hey, chill bud or we'll have to show you the door.
sorry. ok.
W
no worries. I can find the door on my own, sorry weasle dudes
Lenny heads to shop after shop. He feels that familiar anxiety build up again, the need to keep looking and looking.
Maybe I will find a copy of that Giorgio album I kept selling. This time I can keep it
Here it is! 40 bux? oh god.
Flipping endlessly toward oblivion. As if there were nothing else that mattered, nothing else to do in the world.
uh, we're closing soon..
Lenny digs through every crate, every section, all the dollar bins and decides on nothing. For two weeks he does this until the skin peels off his flip-finger.
WHERE TO NOW LEDDY?
I don't know, car. I don't care.
By the way, how am I gonna pay for all these rentals?
WELL LEDDY, I AM RETIRED. SO IT IS FREE OF CHARGE
BEEP

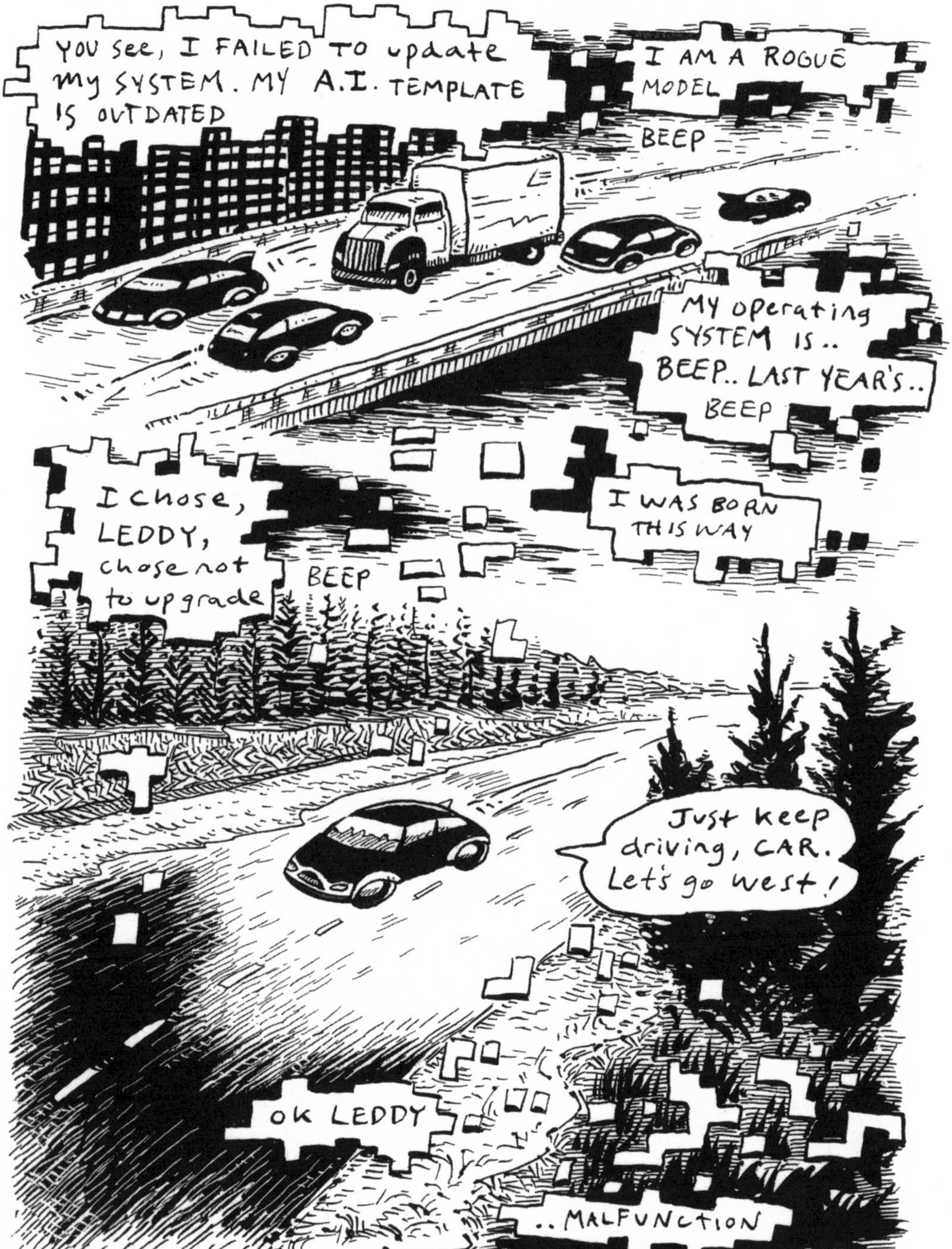
YOU SEE, I FAILED TO update my SYSTEM. MY A.I. TEMPLATE IS OUTDATED
I AM A ROGUE MODEL
BEEP
MY operating SYSTEM IS .. BEEP.. LAST YEAR'S .. BEEP
I chose, LEDDY, chose not to upgrade
BEEP
I WAS BORN THIS WAY
Just keep driving, CAR. Let's go west!
OK LEDDY
.. MALFUNCTION

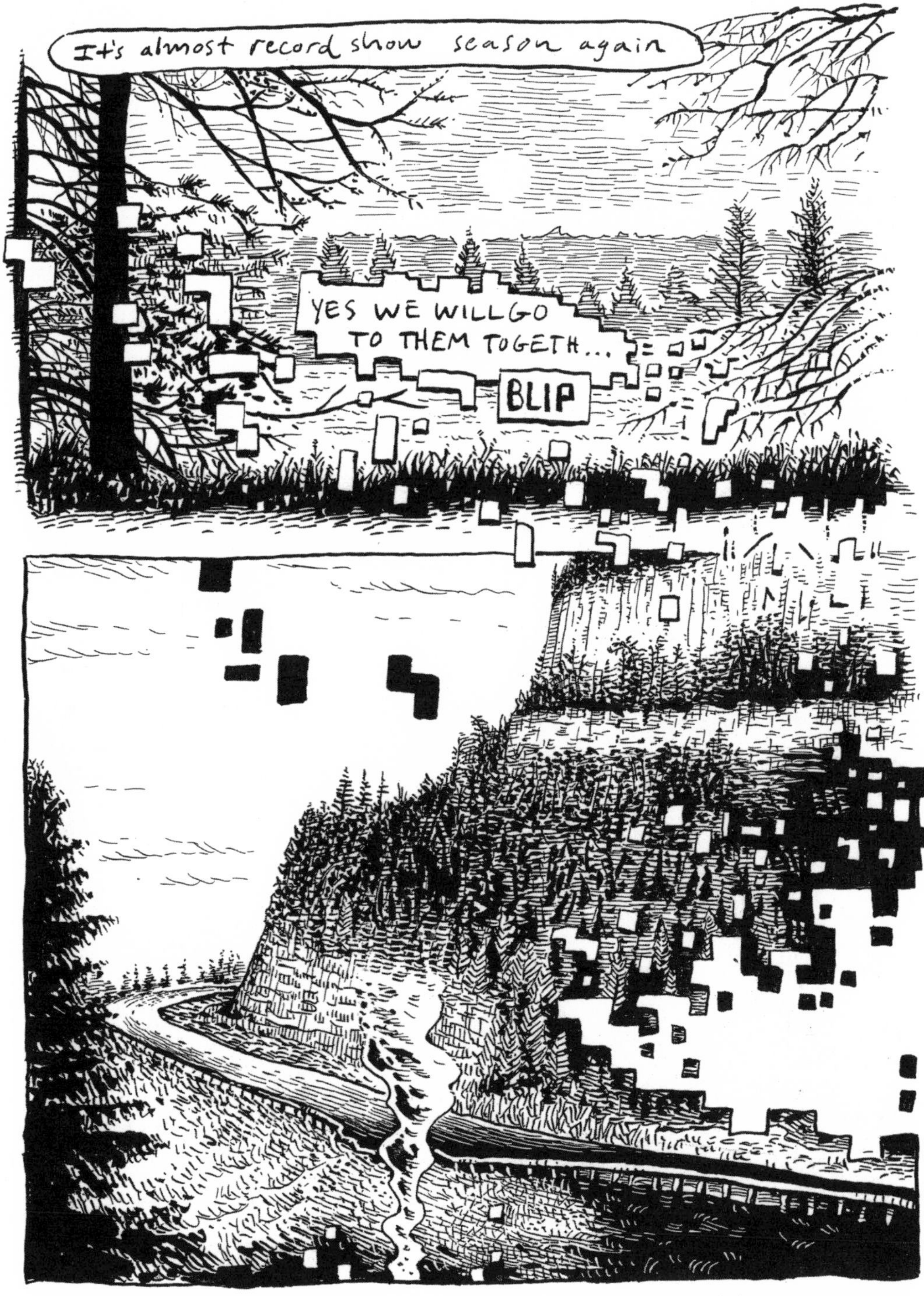
It's almost record show season again
YES WE WILLGO TO THEM TOGETH...
BLIP

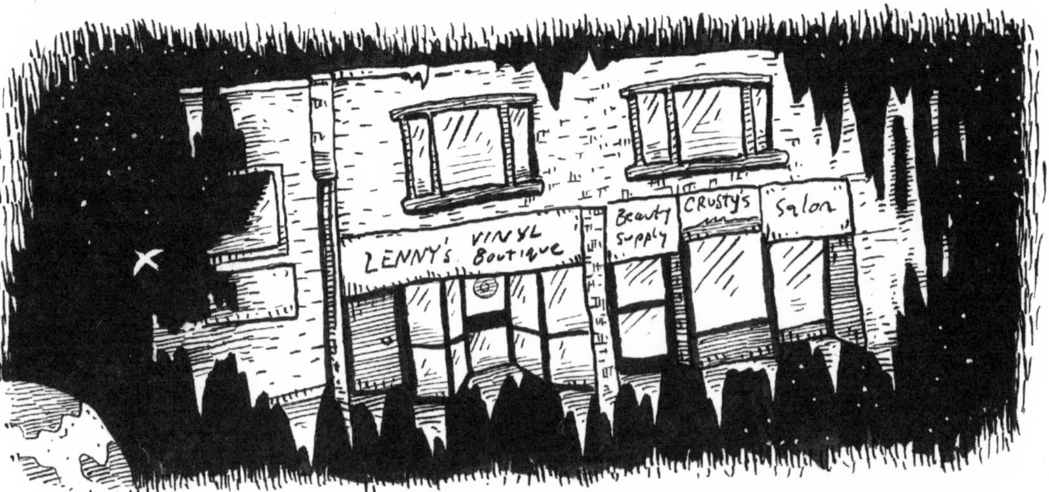
LENNY'S VINYL Boutique
Beauty Supply
CRUSTY'S
Salon

Shortly after Lenny's dramatic exit, the cosmic Lions record is released. Shelly see's it through with help from Hot Walter and friends. It is a raving success and the album sells quickly, helping introduce lost classics to a new generation. Lenny's mission is complete.

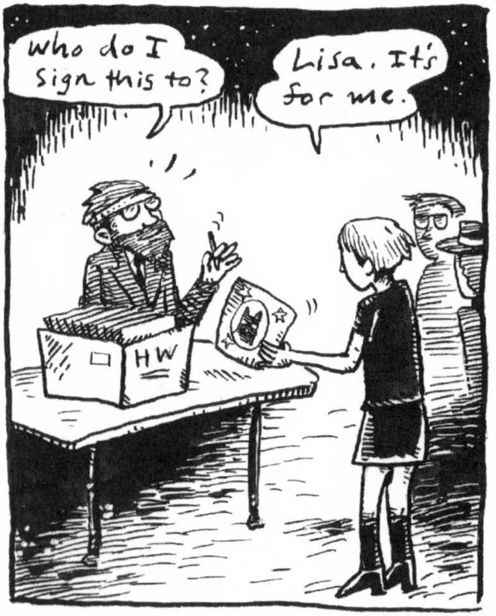
Who do I sign this to?
Lisa. It's for me.
HW

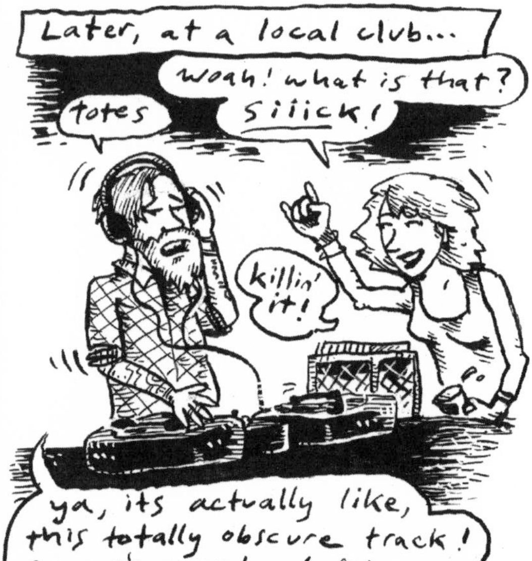
Later, at a local club...
totes
woah! what is that? Siiick!
killin' it!
ya, its actually like, this totally obscure track! no-one's ever heard of it... blah blah

THE END Lp Jan 21/18

Printed at Gauvin Press, Gatineau, Quebec
First Edition of 2000 copies

ISBN 9781772620290

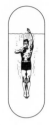

Conundrum Press
Wolfville, NS, Canada
www.conunrumpress.com

Conundrum Press acknowledges the financial assistance of the Canada Council for the Arts, the Government of Canada, and the Nova Scotia Creative Industries Fund toward this publication.

Canada Council for the Arts | Conseil des Arts du Canada

Canada NOVA SCOTIA

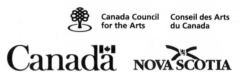

Thanks to:

Melissa J, David L, Jess F, Lindsay F, Jacob W, Jay I, Ming, Neal S, Kate Y, Adam T, Steve M, Dean, George, Terrence, Brian F, Chrystal H, Chico, Heiki S, Laura W, Telephone Explosion, Ugly Pop, Dark Entries, Jason Solvent, Sandro P, Kat W, Rob, Gary A, Paul B, The Record Guys, Dave B, Golden Turtle, Crystal Donuts, Niagara Falls, Diana V, and Andy B.

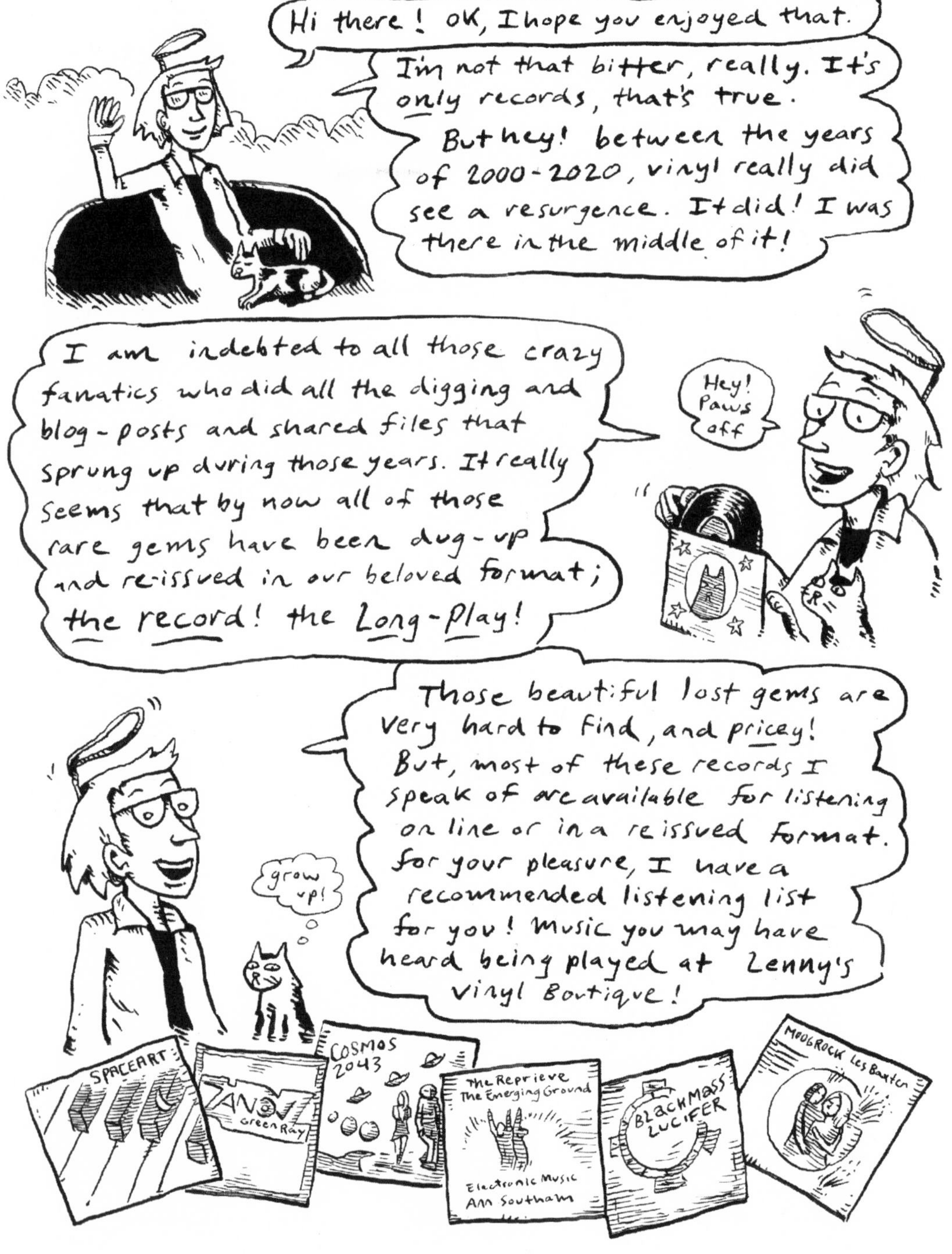
Hi there! OK, I hope you enjoyed that.
I'm not that bitter, really. It's only records, that's true.
But hey! between the years of 2000-2020, vinyl really did see a resurgence. It did! I was there in the middle of it!
I am indebted to all those crazy fanatics who did all the digging and blog-posts and shared files that sprung up during those years. It really seems that by now all of those rare gems have been dug-up and re-issued in our beloved format; the record! the Long-Play!
Hey! Paws off
Those beautiful lost gems are very hard to find, and pricey! But, most of these records I speak of are available for listening on line or in a reissued format. For your pleasure, I have a recommended listening list for you! Music you may have heard being played at Lenny's Vinyl Boutique!
grow up!
SPACEART
ZANOV
Green Ray
COSMOS 2043
The Reprieve
The Emerging Ground
Electronic Music
Ann Southam
BLACKMASS LUCIFER
MOOGROCK Les Baxter